Zen:
The Authentic Gate

Zen
The Authentic Gate

禅

Kōun Yamada

Wisdom

Wisdom Publications
199 Elm Street
Somerville, MA 02144 USA
www.wisdompubs.org

Library of Congress Cataloging-in-Publication Data
Yamada, Kōun, 1907–1989.
  [Zen no seimon. English]
  Zen : the authentic gate / Kōun Yamada.
      pages cm
  Includes bibliographical references and index.
  ISBN 1-61429-250-7 (pbk. : alk. paper)
  1. Meditation—Zen Buddhism. I. Yamada, Kōun, 1907–1989. Zen no seimon.
Translation of: II. Title.
  BQ9288.Y3513 2015
  294.3'927—dc23

                              2014047478

ISBN 978-1-61429-250-0   ebook ISBN 978-1-61429-265-4

19 18 17 16 15
5   4   3   2   1

Cover calligraphy by Kōun Yamada. Cover and interior design by Gopa&Ted2, Inc. Set in Sabon LT Pro 10/14.

Wisdom Publications' books are printed on acid-free paper and meet the guidelines for permanence and durability of the Production Guidelines for Book Longevity of the Council on Library Resources.

This book was produced with environmental mindfulness. We have elected to print this title on 30% PCW recycled paper. As a result, we have saved the following resources: 10 trees, 4 million BTUs of energy, 847 lbs. of greenhouse gases, 4,593 gallons of water, and 307 lbs. of solid waste. For more information, please visit our website, www.wisdompubs.org.

Printed in the United States of America.

Please visit www.fscus.org.

Contents

Foreword by David R. Loy   vii

Preface to the English Edition
Joan Rieck and Henry Shukman   xi

Second Preface to the English Edition
Ryōun-ken Masamichi Yamada   xiii

Author's Preface to the Japanese Edition
Kōun Yamada   xv

ZEN: THE AUTHENTIC GATE

1. Suffering and Modern-Day Humanity   3

2. The Zen View   11

3. The Principle of Salvation in Zen Buddhism   19

4. The Three Great Aims of Zen   39

5. Types of Zen Practice   59

6. Koan Practice and Just Sitting   67

7. Finding an Authentic Teacher   91

8. Depth of Enlightenment   97

9. Cause and Effect as One   119

10. Deceptive Phenomena   125

11. Belief, Understanding, Practice, Realization,
    and Personalization   133

12. Eight Great Tenets of Mahayana Buddhism   143

13. On Private Interview   163

14. Three Necessary Conditions for Zen Practice   169

15. Zen Practice for People of Other Religions   173

16. The Actual Practice of Zazen   177

17. Practical Matters   187

Translator's Afterword   201

Table of Japanese Names   207

Notes   209

Index   213

About the Author   227

Foreword

I hope that readers will forgive some self-reference, because meeting Yamada Kōun Roshi literally changed my life.

In 1972 I was living in Honolulu, reading books about Buddhism and wondering about the experience called enlightenment. A friend learned that there was a small Zen center near the university, so one evening we went to check it out. During tea after *zazen* we were told that a Japanese Zen master was arriving the following weekend to lead a seven-day meditation retreat. We looked at each other. Cool! Could we come? "Well, I think there are still a few places available . . ."

Unfortunately—or was it fortunately?—neither of us knew what a *sesshin* was. Some *zazen*, presumably, but also enjoying tea with the master, perhaps, while discussing the nature of awakening?

It was the most difficult week of my life, yet also, in retrospect, the best. I still remember my reaction when Yamada Roshi appeared that first night, to formally open the retreat. He simply walked into the dojo and up to the altar, and I thought: if Zen practice makes someone like that, it's for me. That thought helped me survive the next seven days.

Although we didn't talk about it, others must have experienced something similar. It was easy enough for a philosophy major like myself to sit around discussing D. T. Suzuki and Alan Watts, but making the leap to serious practice—actually sitting on a cushion facing the wall for hours on end—required deeper motivation, and Yamada Roshi inspired it.

Soon after that first *sesshin* I discovered *The Three Pillars of Zen*, edited by Philip Kapleau, which offered a detailed description of the type of Zen that Yamada Roshi taught. It included introductory lectures on Zen practice by Yasutani Haku'un and transcriptions of private interviews (*dokusan*) with practitioners. It turned out that Yamada was Yasutani's successor as spiritual leader of the Sanbō Kyōdan (now Sanbō Zen).

Most interesting, however, were the "Contemporary Enlightenment Experiences" toward the back of the book. The first account was by "Mr. K. Y., a Japanese businessman." He was reading on a train when he came across something Dōgen wrote after his own awakening (quoting an early Chinese text): "I came to realize clearly that mind is nothing other than rivers and mountains and the great wide earth, the sun and the moon and the stars." Sleeping later that night, Mr. K. Y. suddenly awoke and that quotation flashed into his mind:

> Then all at once I was struck as though by lightning, and the next instant heaven and earth crumbled and disappeared. Instantaneously, like surging waves, a tremendous delight welled up in me, a veritable hurricane of delight, as I laughed loudly and wildly: "Ha, ha, ha, ha, ha, ha! There's no reasoning here, no reasoning at all! Ha, ha, ha!" The empty sky split into two, then opened its enormous mouth and began to laugh uproariously: "Ha, ha, ha!"

Mr. K. Y. was Mr. Kyōzō Yamada: Yamada Roshi.

In retrospect I appreciate how this celebrated example of a profound *satori* can also be problematic: such a dramatic story can encourage "gaining ideas" and expectations that complicate one's Zen path. Nevertheless, it remains an invaluable reminder that enlightenment is not some antiquated metaphor but a genuine possibility for us today. We are encouraged not to set our sights too low.

Eventually I left Hawaii but kept in contact with Yamada Roshi. After I had made some visits to his San'un Zendo in Japan he invited me to move to Kamakura and devote myself more single-mindedly to Zen practice, including *koan* study. Observing him at home, I was even more impressed. He was neither a monastic nor a temple priest but a layman with a family and a demanding job administering a private hospital (his wife Kazue was the head doctor).

They were a formidable team. They had torn down their home to make room for a zendo that could accommodate the increasing numbers of students who came to practice with him, many from overseas; later they added a second floor, again at their own expense. And he never asked for a penny from any of us: all he expected was serious commitment to Zen practice.

Even at an advanced age he maintained a punishing schedule: commuting all the way to Tokyo almost every day, and then usually offering *dokusan* to students after he returned in the evening. The only thing that ever slowed him down was his accident—a bad fall—during a trip to Kyoto, which left him bedridden until he died a year later.

Yamada Roshi remains for me the best example of a true bodhisattva, and I continue to be inspired by him as a model of how to live compassionately and selflessly. I am eternally grateful to him, and to the Sanbō Zen tradition that continues his work. I am grateful too for this opportunity to add my appreciation for the very special teachings contained in *Zen: The Authentic Gate.* Nowhere else have I encountered such a clear and comprehensive account of the Zen path. It is wonderful that this treasure-chest is now available in English, to motivate and guide future generations of Zen students around the world.

David R. Loy
Niwot, Colorado

Publisher's Acknowledgment

T HE PUBLISHER gratefully acknowledges the generous contribution of the Hershey Family Foundation toward the publication of this book.

Preface to the English Edition

During the 1970s and '80s a small but steady flow of non-Japanese seekers arrived at San'un Zendo in Kamakura, Japan, to train in Zen under Kōun Yamada Roshi. He and his wife, Dr. Kazue Yamada, warmly welcomed them as family into the Japanese sangha, tending not only to their spiritual needs but, not infrequently, to their material ones as well. A number of these seekers were Christians or Jews who the roshi left free to continue the practice of their own religion, with no pressure to become Buddhists. One day Kōun Roshi was asked how someone could bring the practice of Zen meditation together with a Christian background. He replied, "Put your questions on the shelf and practice zazen; you'll get your own answers." And with time, for many this proved to be true. Indeed, it was the "proof" of his own experience that allowed the roshi to accept everyone who came to him for guidance and to be absolutely confident that Zen practice could help them.

Kōun Roshi's deep enlightenment shone through him. He was a powerful and compassionate presence, a person who naturally evoked feelings of respect and affection in those who knew him. His main wish was to help all people find peace by looking into themselves and realizing who they are. In this book he explains how the intrinsic nature of every human being is the "common ground" where people of all races, nationalities, and beliefs are one reality. He teaches that by practicing Zen and coming to the same experience as Shakyamuni Buddha—the realization of the empty-oneness of all beings—we can transcend the divisions that separate us and find true peace in our hearts and in this world.

Much of the Zen practiced in the West today derives from two sources: the Sōtō Zen of Shunryu Suzuki and the San Francisco Zen Center; and the Sanbō Zen of Harada Dai'un and Yasutani Haku'un, which blends their Sōtō Zen background with Rinzai training in a broad koan curriculum. The teaching lines of Robert Aitken and Philip Kapleau, and in part Taizan Maezumi, for example, derive from Sanbō Zen, and in the

West the successors of these teachers number well over a hundred. As the chief successor of Yasutani, Kōun Yamada was the abbot of Sanbō Zen from 1970 to 1989, and his influence on Western Zen has therefore been considerable.

These two streams of Zen each had a flagship book—*The Three Pillars of Zen* (1965) and Suzuki's *Zen Mind, Beginner's Mind* (1970)—and that fact may account in part for the prominence of these lineages in a culture where books are an important means of disseminating ideas. *Zen Mind, Beginner's Mind* is a collection of luminous talks given by Suzuki; *The Three Pillars of Zen* is a compilation of Zen texts, both old and recent, pertinent to the training methods of Sanbō Zen. But beyond *The Three Pillars of Zen*, comparatively little of Sanbō Zen's written teachings is widely available in English, nor are many teachers in America today directly connected with the lineage, in spite of its far-reaching influence. *Zen: The Authentic Gate*, Kōun Yamada's own introduction to Zen practice, not only in some measure redresses these deficits but also offers a chance for those whose Zen is connected with Kōun Roshi's, however distantly, to taste the water at the source. And for all readers, we hope these teachings by a great twentieth century master may be inspiring and encouraging.

We are happy to assist in bringing Paul Shepherd's translation of *Zen: The Authentic Gate* to English readers and trust it will help us all to discover and know more deeply the common ground of our true nature, the common ground that unites every being and is the central message of Zen—something of precious importance in today's divided and wounded world.

Joan Rieck and Henry Shukman
New Mexico, USA

Second Preface to the English Edition

It is my great pleasure to see this book, *Zen no Shōmon* (*The Authentic Gate of Zen*), written by my father Yamada Kōun Roshi, now being published in English under the title *Zen: The Authentic Gate*. It is a unique book, in that it was written by a person whose Zen enlightenment experience was, I believe, unusually profound in the modern history of Zen. I happened to be with Kōun Roshi myself at the actual moment of his deep awakening. I was a ten-year-old boy at the time, and was suddenly woken up by the great laughing voice of my father coming from the room next door. Frightened by his loud and continuous laughter, I opened the door and saw my mother trying in vain to cover his mouth with her hands to stop the sound. I was shocked and scared, and wondered if he had gone insane. But that was the occasion of his coming to full enlightenment, and I myself would go on to be nourished by the wisdom flowing from it during twenty-five years of Zen practice under his guidance, eventually succeeding to his Dharma.

What is Zen? Simply put, Zen is a practice of discovering one's true self by direct experience, and personalizing that discovery in day-to-day life. The discovery occurs in what we call an enlightenment experience. Buddhism and Zen began with the enlightenment experience of self-discovery by Shakyamuni Buddha some 2500 years ago in India. Shakyamuni did not leave anything written down, but his discovery has been conveyed over generations by disciples of his teaching who shared the same experience. Buddhist sutras are the explanation and description of Shakyamuni's enlightenment, which were memorized by his earliest disciples and later written down. Today in the West there is increasing interest in Zen and Buddhism, and many books have appeared in English by contemporary authors. The particular value of this one, I believe, derives from its author's having been a person of unusually profound experience. I am sure it will serve as an authentic pilot and guide for those searching for the truth about Zen, and will make a lasting contribution to the body of Zen literature. I feel proud that my father wrote this book, which I hope will someday qualify as a classic of Zen literature.

This English version is the result of great effort on the part of four people: Paul Shepherd, Joan Rieck, Henry Shukman, and Migaku Sato. Paul did the first draft of the overall translation. Joan and Henry edited and streamlined the draft, making it more focused on the essence of the Zen Way, which is so badly needed in our contemporary world. In this process, they condensed the manuscript and, in some cases, cut parts of the original Japanese text not directly related to the fundamentals of Zen. As a result, the English version is more concise, focused, and easier to read than the original. Finally, Migaku Sato checked the English translation line by line against the Japanese to confirm that it conforms to the message Kōun Roshi wanted to convey. I would also like to note that these four are all Zen masters of the Sanbō Zen Organization, who have been practicing Zen for more than twenty years, and in some cases more than twice that duration. In this place, let me express my deepest gratitude to them for their effort and compassion in making this important book available to English-speaking readers.

Ryōun-ken Masamichi Yamada

Author's Preface to the Japanese Edition

Over a period of several years, I wrote a series of articles under the title "An Introduction to Zen for Laypeople," which appeared in Sanbō Zen's bi-monthly magazine, *Awakening Gong* (*Kyōshō*). Soon after I completed the series, Mr. Ryūichi Kanda of Shunjusha Publishers asked permission to release the articles in book form. I was most happy to comply, and the book *The Authentic Gate of Zen* (Zen no Shōmon) appeared in May 1980.

Subsequently the book was translated into English by Paul Shepherd and edited by Dr. Roselyn Stone, both longtime students of mine living in Japan at the time. Certain passages, especially those relating to current events in Japan in the 1970s, have been omitted in the English translation, and others have been added in response to the questions of non-Japanese readers—the relationship of Zen to non-Buddhist religions, for example. In addition I have included some further thoughts on matters addressed in my original lectures.

It is my hope that this book will be a true aid to people around the world who are earnestly seeking a way to spiritual peace, and that it will inspire many to set out on the path of Zen practice. It is my particular wish that the book will provide sound information on matters concerning Zen and Buddhism that heretofore may have been given incomplete treatment in other books.

My sincere thanks go out to many people: to Paul Shepherd and Dr. Roselyn Stone for their unstinting work in translating and editing *The Authentic Gate of Zen*, to my foreign students, who were the first to suggest an English translation, to Robert and Margaret Tsuda, who gave a careful reading to the original manuscript, and to all those who have offered to help bring the translation to the public. I reserve my special thanks for my wife, Kazue, who has always been my pillar of support and strength.

Kōun Yamada
Kamakura, Japan
1983

Zen:
The Authentic Gate

Suffering and Modern-Day Humanity 1

Human Suffering

When pondering the suffering of humanity in the modern world, it may be helpful to remember that it was in a quest for deliverance from what he called "the four sufferings"—birth, death, sickness, and aging—that Shakyamuni Buddha left home to seek the Way more than two thousand years ago. Suffering was not unique to his time. Humans have always lived out their lives in suffering. Buddhist terminology refers to this world as *saha*, a Sanskrit expression, which could be translated as "the world of enduring" or "the land of bearing indignities." This world of ours could be seen as a process of enduring hardship. From the time we are born and become aware, right up until we enter the grave, our lives confront an unending stream of difficulties. We suffer internally from myriad passions and externally from things such as cold, heat, war, and famine. An ancient verse runs:

> The troubles of life,
> The troubles of life,
> Look out for yourself!

Today we live in an environment far more complex than that of Buddha's time. We worry about getting into the right school, applying for a decent job, and earning a living. Add to these challenges traffic jams, noise pollution, and the degradation of air and water, all of which contribute to high blood pressure, the horror of cancer, and war. We hardly have time to catch our breath between one calamity and the next. In the midst of an ever more intense struggle for existence, we have to come to grips with cultural expectations that demand we suppress and deny ourselves. We live out our lives assailed by fears, anxious in the face of threats to our very existence as a species.

In addition we suffer because of our material conditions. Even though poverty is less severe than it once was in modern industrial nations, nevertheless, the anxieties of life have failed to diminish. Working people are overwhelmed by the demands of each successive day pressing in on them. In spite of the advances of science and technology, and a corresponding economic progress, anxiety concerning material life still makes up, as in the past, the greater share of modern humanity's unease. No matter what our material condition may be, an abyss of spiritual suffering remains. Before committing suicide, the famous writer Akutagawa Ryūnosuke left a farewell note in which he wrote, "I am beset with a vague, undefined anxiety." Akutagawa was certainly not alone in feeling this "vague, undefined anxiety." This kind of spiritual angst, which has always existed in all ages and all civilizations, could well be called the fate of humankind.

The *Gateless Gate*, a well-known Zen text, presents the koan "Bodhidharma Puts the Mind to Rest":

> Bodhidharma sat facing the wall. The Second Ancestor, standing in the snow, cut off his arm and said, "Your disciple's mind is not yet at peace. I beg you, Master, give it rest."
>
> Bodhidharma said, "Bring me your mind and I will put it to rest."
>
> The Ancestor replied, "I have searched for my mind but have never been able to find it."
>
> Bodhidharma said, "I have finished putting it to rest for you."

Here we have the fundamental key to freeing ourselves from suffering. If we were to listen to a Zen master's teaching, or *teisho*, on this koan with a mind free from preconceptions and concepts, we would become enlightened on the spot. I wish to approach this topic gradually, however, and will not delve further into it at present, except to emphasize that anxiety has always been with us. In the koan just cited, the Second Zen Ancestor, Eka Daishi, beset by this same anxiety, cut off the root of that distress when he heard Bodhidharma's words and attained liberation. But his anxiety was certainly not his private store. It has existed throughout human history.

Life could be called a display of all the different forms of suffering and anxiety. Yet most of us make no serious attempt to confront our anxiety head on; instead we attempt to escape it, seeking momentary distraction in the outside world through liquor, gaming, betting at the track, sexual misadventures, the glare of neon, and the blare of loud music in the streets.

Momentary intoxication of the senses, however, will never solve the problem of spiritual anxiety; this anxiety is limitless, a bottomless pit. When we awaken from our inebriation we still suffer from that same desolate, dreary emptiness, and can find nothing to fill it up. The famous Chinese poet Li Po left the following lines:

> I cut the water with my sword and watch it flow anew.
> I raise my cup to drown my pain but it, too, flows anew.

In similar fashion, as we seek ever-stronger stimuli, the initial feeling of emptiness may turn into an attitude of nihilism and the sense that our existence is meaningless.

IGNORING MORTALITY

Denial of death is a sickness of the modern age. Aside from those faced with the immediate prospect of death—someone with incurable cancer, for example—most of us ignore death as a definite and pressing reality. Perhaps throughout history we have tended to avoid the fact of our mortality. Yet in our fast-paced world, we are so involved in our daily routines, we barely have time to think of our mortality. We are aware somewhere in the back of our minds that we all have to die, but are unable to imagine with any real force the moment when we will disappear from the face of the earth without a trace.

> Dying was always something other people did;
> What a surprise to find I'm like them!

Sorori Shinzaemon, a court favorite of Hideyoshi, wrote this comic verse, which aptly satirizes our lack of awareness of death. All of us go through the motions of daily life with some purpose behind our actions.

But isn't our impulsive, blind pursuit of immediate goals in one sense merely a stand-off with death?

People in leadership roles, in government and finance particularly, who find themselves taxed by exhausting schedules, have little time to reflect on their lives and to confront their own deaths, which nevertheless approach with unrelenting inevitability as each second ticks away. They may be aware that their workdays are a one-way ferry, but they think of life and death as somebody else's affair. Yet no matter how gorgeous and splendid their funerals may turn out to be, what meaning will it have when they finally die?

In five thousand years of recorded human history, with its rising and falling of empires, the heroes of each age have left their mark in different ways. Yet in less than a thousand years their achievements all but disappear. Alexander the Great, Caesar, Toyotomi Hideyoshi—their stories are all the same: when looked at from the perspective of eternity, the accomplishments of humankind amount to so little. Where does the true meaning behind our efforts lie? The *Diamond Sutra* tells us:

> All things are as if a dream, a phantom, a bubble,
>   a shadow;
> they are like dew, like the flicker of lightning.
> See everything like this.

We must certainly appreciate those who hold to a purpose in life, and work tirelessly day and night toward its realization. Their efforts may help their own family or even an entire nation. Yet no matter how lofty their works, no matter how much effort goes into them, we cannot determine their true value until we examine them in the light of the reality of death.

MODERN MORALITY

Another ill besetting modern humanity is the loss of morality. I will never forget a lecture by the late Koizumi Shinzō, the celebrated educator and president of economics at Keio University. His talk was titled "The Problem of Morality in Modern Times," and I will do my best to reproduce part of it here:

If I were given the chance to chaperone a group of students during a sports training camp or the like, living together with them for several days, there are a number of things I would like to leave with them. For example: "Never tell a lie; always be truthful. Be unsparing and searching with yourself."

However, if a student were to tell me that he had no intention of following my advice or paying heed to my words, I could not insist that he must do so on the grounds that these things are good or correct or necessary. I could not tell him that he should do so because it would fulfill his duties toward his family, or that by doing so he would preserve the fabric of society, or that he should do so because these things are in themselves good. If we were to search the philosophies of different ages and civilizations, we would be unable to come up with any firm grounds for saying so.

Upon hearing his words, I was unable to suppress a surprised gasp. "Is this indeed Koizumi Shinzō," I said to myself, "teacher of the Imperial Family, and honored figure in educational circles?" His words sounded to me like little more than skeptical relativism. Not long after, however, I learned that shortly before this speech, Professor Koizumi had been baptized into Christianity. Upon reflection I could imagine that although he had refrained from saying so in public, the professor may have had in mind the idea that the root of virtue can't be found by relying on philosophy alone.

> Never tell a lie; always be truthful.
> Be unsparing and searching with yourself.
> Do not take the life of living things.
> Honor your parents.

These are all fine sentiments. But it is necessary to bring back the moral basis whereby we can teach such things.

The decline of morality in the modern world is not limited to Japan but is a concern in many parts of the world, in particular North America and Europe. In Japan the Confucian ideals, which served as the pillars of virtue during the days of the samurai, continued to have an influence up until the defeat of Japan in World War II. But during the postwar period, this ethical basis lost influence, and nothing arose to replace it. Japanese parents today lack a moral standpoint from which to raise their children; teachers also lack a guidepost in teaching their students. Yet peace and order established on true morality are basic to our existence. Without them, humankind will never achieve true happiness.

Japan's postwar constitution cites the rights and dignity of the individual as basic principles. Neither constitutional nor legal scholars have much to say, however, on the basic question of *why* a human being possesses such dignity. This is held to be a self-evident truth. According to the constitution, the fundamental human right is freedom: freedom from bondage, freedom of speech, freedom of belief, and freedom to change one's place of residence. In contrast to this considerable emphasis on rights, the former Meiji Constitution posited duties as its basic framework. The shift in focus on rights has given rise to the illusion that basic rights come without corresponding duties.

Recognition of the dignity of the individual also became the foundation for the principle of the equality of individuals. Equality means equality before the law: all individuals are treated as equals under the law and discriminatory treatment is prohibited.

In the past, order in relations was derived not from the law but from traditional morality.

The legal equality of individuals proclaimed by the constitution has, as a result, encroached upon the territory of morality. Children believe they have the right to refuse to follow the counsel of their elders. We proclaim that students and teachers are equal; students then feel free to insult their teachers, and even hold "kangaroo courts" where they upbraid them.

But the sacredness and equality of the individual are in fact two aspects of one and the same thing, divided here for the purpose of explanation. But what is their basis? What is this one thing? Just why are human beings sacred and equal before the law?

This basis obviously cannot be the constitution itself. We did not become sacred and equal simply because the constitution proclaims us to be. It follows that we need to clarify the reality of that inviolability and equality. Otherwise, the freedom and equality guaranteed in the constitution are just empty concepts, manufactured by the human intellect. In the following chapters I shall attempt to explain Zen Buddhist spirituality and show how it clarifies and establishes the basis of our sacredness and equality.

The Zen View 2

FAITH-BASED SPIRITUALITY
AND EXPERIENCE-BASED SPIRITUALITY

Japanese mothers used to try to curb their children's mischief by saying, "If you aren't good, a spook will get you," or "a child snatcher will come for you." I remember being scolded like that myself as a child. Spirituality based on faith follows a similar model of trying to guide people using certain images and ideas. On the other hand, spirituality based on experience leads people to peace by having them perceive reality clearly, thereby ridding them of fear:

> Wither'd pampas grass—
> that was all it really was,
> the ghost that I saw.[1]

Religious life can be classified into five phases: belief, understanding, practice, realization, and actualization. Following this division we may describe faith-based spirituality as grounded in belief and understanding, whereas experience-based spirituality emphasizes practice, realization, and actualization.

FAITH- AND EXPERIENCE-BASED SPIRITUALITY

belief	faith-based spirituality
understanding	
practice	experience-based spirituality
realization	
actualization	

The word "practice" here means to discipline oneself, "realization" to attain enlightenment, and "actualization" to turn realization into one's daily life. In Zen terms, it means that we personalize our enlightenment and actualize it in every moment of our ordinary lives.

Zen Buddhism is at the forefront of experience-based religions. I often say that Zen is not a religion. But if salvation is considered the task of religion, it is. However, unlike faith-based religions, Zen rejects concepts and beliefs as a means of knowing the truth. Instead it aims to help us perceive reality and to find peace of mind based on that reality. Reality is what we really are: namely, our True Self. When we discover what we are, we experience peace of mind and continue to live day by day in infinite tranquility and complete satisfaction. What more do we need?

It seems to me that there are a growing number of people in the world without a religion. Renunciation of religion is a phenomenon that occurs in the course of the transition from faith-based to experience-based religion. No longer able to believe in old concepts, people believe that the objective world alone is the real world and natural science the only means of pursuing truth. Materialism is perhaps the culmination of such thought. But materialism is a fallacy arising out of ignorance about the reality of our true human nature.

People come to believe that nothing exists beyond what the world of science is able to investigate; they don't even consider the possibility of investigating or experiencing the true essence of their own nature and finding great peace of mind through that investigation. Because Zen insists on understanding reality through experience rather than faith, and offers a means of knowing the reality of who we are, it can facilitate the full transition to experience-based spirituality. I am especially grateful for the concrete and systematic nature of Zen training. Sometimes I feel that the practice of Zen, which Japan has preserved up to now, is the sole cultural property Japan can be truly proud of in the world.

THE COMMON GROUND OF EMPTY-ONENESS

Without awakening (*satori*) there is no Zen. I am not alone in feeling this. My teacher Yasutani Haku'un Roshi also thought so, as did his teacher and my grandfather in Dharma, Harada Dai'un Roshi. In fact,

Dōgen Zenji, Hakuin Zenji, and all the Zen masters and Zen ancestors throughout the history of Buddhism have known this fact. Since this is the case, we must ask what awakening is and how people become enlightened.

To put it simply, awakening is the realization that the content of both subject and object is empty and one, and that this empty-oneness is none other than the constantly changing phenomenal world of form. That is to say, actual existence is in one aspect totally empty, and in another is the phenomenal world of form that ceaselessly appears and disappears in accordance with the law of causation.

Ordinary common sense knows only the world of things: it recognizes the phenomenal world that can be objectively assessed, measured, and studied as the only world that exists. Thus we could define the phenomenal world as that which can be the object of scientific investigation. Philosophy, however, recognizes a real "essence" that exists beyond things. In Zen, for convenience sake, we use the similar term "the essential world" to refer to the world of empty-oneness, but this is completely different than the conceptual world of essence mentioned in philosophy. Although some might be tempted to think of philosophy's "essential domain" and Zen's "essential world" as the same thing, the philosophical "essence" can be arrived at intellectually, whereas Zen's domain of emptiness can only be grasped through direct experience.

To experience Zen's essential world is like seeing your own face or, more directly, seeing your own eye with your own eye. Since your own eye itself cannot become the object of seeing, the eye cannot become the object of your investigation. The only way to grasp the essential world is to experience it internally. This is called "personal realization" and is known as "awakening" or "seeing into one's own nature."

I often use the following example to explain this realization. In my body there are left and right hands, a face, a torso, and so on, which can all be examined separately. If I take a single hair from my head and a single drop of my blood and put them side-by-side, I see a black solid and a red liquid. They appear completely different from and unrelated to each other. But my hair and blood live the same life—my life, which is naturally one. From the standpoint of the single life of my body, there is no left or right, no head or torso, no hair or blood. They all live my one life, and from the aspect of life my body is one. But life itself has no form, color, or weight. It is completely empty. Furthermore, it is always completely one with my body. Life is emptiness; life (body) is form.

Zen awakening is to realize that that same relationship applies to the entire universe. The world of our essential nature is like a great ocean: any ship, regardless of whether it is a huge battleship or a tiny skiff, can maneuver freely on its surface. Or we may say the world of our essential nature is like vast and limitless outer space: in that great expanse, the earth, mountains and rivers, the sun, the moon, the stars and the planets coexist in peace. Both birds and airplanes, regardless of size, can fly freely through the vast reaches of the sky.

In the world today we can identify many forms of dualistic opposition: conflicts of interest among nations, economic conflicts, intellectual and emotional confrontations, racial and religious antagonism—the list is endless. As long as these oppositions exist, true peace is impossible, for it is as if we have poured water into a pot and are trying our best to cool it down as we continue at the same time to heat the bottom of the pot. True peace is only possible when we share a common ground for mutual understanding, even in the midst of dualistic opposition.

Among these different forms of opposition, those arising from religion seem to be the most deeply rooted. As long as religions fight with each other, peace will never come, no matter how much we cry out for it. The nature of the human being—the empty-oneness that is our essence—is the basic starting point for Buddhism. Understanding this can open the basic common ground that the religions of the world can share. The universe is one, with no subject or object, but this unity is only possible if both subject and object are empty. And that emptiness provides the common ground we so need in this world.

Only human beings have religion. But human beings are not Christians, Buddhists, Muslims, or Jews before being human, and we don't have to belong to one particular religion in order to know our true nature. People who come to know their own true nature, regardless of their faith, will gain better understanding of the true meaning of their religion. The Bible says that God made man in his image and likeness and was well pleased with the results. It stands to reason, then, that to know our own true nature is to better know God. Nonetheless, if the various religions attempt to find points of correspondence and deepen their understanding of each other in merely theoretical or intellectual terms, they are likely to end up with a correspondence that resembles ill-fitting cogs in a machine. Even though they may experience the same world, different religious traditions express it differently due to differences in the ways their conceptions of it are structured. So it is crucial that we transcend the level of thought and compare actual religious experience.

Coming to know your true nature is not religion. There is absolutely no need to renounce your religion or to become a Buddhist in order to practice Zen. It is the inherent right of every human being to experience his or her true nature. While most Buddhist sects can be thought of as religions, Zen is different. Although there are many Buddhist sects, they all share the experience of self-realization as their common core. Since Zen is solely focused on the experience of self-realization, we could say that Zen is the core of Buddhism. The theories and philosophies of the various other sects are the clothes, diverse in style and color, which we use to embellish the core. But experience of True Self is neither a theory nor a philosophy; it is simply a fact—a fact of experience, in the same way that the taste of tea is a fact. Tea tastes the same to everyone, Buddhist and Christian alike.

The awareness of any human being, regardless of their particular beliefs, will respond in the same way given certain conditions. This holds true for the Zen experience of awakening. We might compare it to the movement of balls on a billiard table: the movement of any billiard ball, regardless of its color, will follow exactly the same path, at the same angle when the ball is knocked with equal power in the same direction.

What are the conditions that move our consciousness to awaken? We concentrate our mind single-pointedly—whether counting the breath, following the breath, just sitting (*shikantaza*) or working on a koan—and we forget ourselves. We are unlikely to attain the experience of Zen, no matter how strongly we concentrate, if we try to concentrate our mind on an external object, like aiming at a target in archery. In Zen practice the mind is absorbed inwardly.

The experience attained through Zen practice is neither thought nor philosophy nor religion. It is merely a fact. And, strange as it may seem, the experience of that fact has the power to free us from the agonies and pains of the world. It emancipates us from the anxiety of worldly sufferings. No one knows why that experience has such wonderful power. But it does, and is simply so, without the need for any concept or faith. Should such a fact be called religion? I don't think so. This fact is called "awakening," "self-realization," or "enlightenment," and is accompanied by great peace of mind.

And so our common ground, the world of emptiness, is a most solemn reality rather than a product of intellectual thought. It is my deepest wish to share this world with people in positions of leadership or power—politicians, the wealthy, financiers, managers, labor leaders, scholars, artists, religious leaders, and even gangland bosses—and hope that they develop an experiential rather than an intellectual understanding of it. This would be the quickest way to transcend "me-you" dualistic opposition in all its forms, and would bring true peace to the world.

THE PROBLEM OF LIFE AND DEATH

The principal aim of Buddhism is to solve the problem of life and death—that is, to answer the question, "Where do we come from and where do we go?" If Buddhism were not able to fundamentally and thoroughly solve this problem, without leaving a trace of doubt, we might say it had no spiritual efficacy, no *raison d'être* at all. Dōgen Zenji said, "The clarification of life and death—this is Buddhism's most important concern." "Clarification" differs from belief. It refers to seeing things clearly for what they are.

If that is the case, the next question follows: What form does life and death reveal to us when we see them clearly in enlightenment? What is their true form? The answer is that the content of life and death is totally empty; their true form is no form. To put it more concretely, our minds and bodies are totally empty.

Bassui Tokushō Zenji said:

> If you would free yourself from the sufferings of birth-and-death, you must learn the direct way to become a Buddha. This way is none other than the realization of our own minds. Now, what is this mind? It is the true nature of all sentient beings, that which existed before our parents were born, hence before our own birth, and which presently exists,

unchangeable and eternal. So it is called "one's face before one's parents were born." This mind is intrinsically pure. It is not newly created when we are born, and it does not perish when we die. It is without distinction of male and female, nor has it any coloration of good or bad. It cannot be compared with anything, and so it is called "buddha nature."

"Buddha nature" is nothing but a name given to the empty nature of the mind, which is "not newly created when we are born, and does not perish when we die." In short, we must once see into our own nature directly. When we see thoroughly that our nature is intrinsically empty, the problem of life and death will vanish like mist. Know that there will come a time when you will stamp your feet with great joy, shouting, "The buddhas and Zen ancestors have never deceived me!"

Do you understand me? No? Well then, I will have to say with Yōka Daishi:

If you still don't understand, I will settle it for you now.

The Principle of Salvation 3
in Zen Buddhism

Is Zen a Religion?

For Buddhists, the realization experience of Shakyamuni Buddha is the wellspring from which the river of Buddhist teaching pours forth. Within the great flow of Buddhist tradition, the enlightenment experience is acknowledged from generation to generation, between teacher and student. When the Buddha transmitted the Dharma to the first Zen ancestor, Mahakashyapa, he confirmed his student's realization experience. In the same way this realization experience was later transmitted from Zen ancestor to Zen ancestor in direct succession.

Because the mutually acknowledged experience of enlightenment, known as "direct transmission outside the teaching," comprises the great source of Buddhism, the Zen way of Buddhadharma was given the name "teaching of the source," or *shūkyō* in Japanese. The Chinese character *shū* means "source" or "fundamental root," and the character *kyō* means "teaching." This word *shūkyō* is often translated as "religion," but it literally means "teaching the source."

Several Zen koans use the word "religion" in this distinct sense of "teaching the source." Take, for example, the instruction to Case 5 of the *Blue Cliff Record*, "Seppō's Grain of Rice": "Whoever would uphold the school's religion must be a brave-hearted person." Or Engo's commentary on this case: "Therefore, when it came to supporting the school's religion and continuing the life of the buddhas, they would spit out a word or half a phrase which would spontaneously cut off the tongues of everyone on earth." Again, the commentary on Case 10 of the same text, "Bokushū's Thieving Fool," contains the following passage: "Whoever would uphold and establish the school's religion must possess the eye and function of a true master of our school." However, the "religion" mentioned in these passages refers not to religion in general, but solely to the Zen way of Buddhadharma—the teaching that clarifies the essence realized in Zen meditation (zazen): teaching the source.

Although the term *shūkyō* had a strictly Buddhist origin, over time we Japanese began to use the term in a broader sense to refer to religion in general. This conflation of the distinct sense of *shūkyō* with the generic idea of "religion" began in the middle of the nineteenth century, with the Meiji Restoration and the ensuing rush to absorb Western thought and culture into Japan. Translators at the time inadvertently adopted the word *shūkyō* to translate the English word "religion" into Japanese. This error succeeded in confusing matters, such that *shūkyō*, which formerly referred strictly to the Zen path of realization, now came to refer to the whole panoply of faiths covered by the English word "religion." Thus, if we were to ask if Zen is a religion in the general sense of the term, we would have to say, "No."

What Is Salvation?

Although the Zen path may have been lumped together with others as a "religion," Zen differs markedly from other religions from the point of view of human salvation. The principle of salvation in Christianity, for example, is God's love. God—the all-knowing, all-powerful creator of the universe—transcends his creatures but cares about them unconditionally and offers them the hand of absolute love. Those who believe in him and take that hand are saved. This brief summation of Christian teaching ignores a number of complicated theological views about God and salvation; nevertheless, I think I am correct in understanding that it is God's absolute love that saves. If we but believe in God's unconditional salvation and take his hand, we will be saved from all suffering and calamity.

In order to understand the principle of salvation in Zen Buddhism, however, we must turn not to the transcendent power of God, but to the basic question of our own identity. What is humanity? What is this entity we call a "human being"? In Western thought these age-old questions have elicited a range of answers: Human beings are created from the dust of the earth and defiled by sin; a person is a creature composed of body and soul; or as Descartes answered, "I think, therefore I am." Zen

Buddhism provides a different answer by declaring unequivocally that we ourselves are nothing but perfect, complete, infinite, and absolute existence. And Zen aims to realize this condition not through the intellect but in living experience. All the anxieties and suffering of humanity stem from the paradox that while we are by nature perfect, we appear in the phenomenal world as imperfection itself—limited, relative, mortal, and all too fallible—unaware of our true nature. The totality of our suffering is nothing but the labor pain of our perfect and infinite nature as it strives to negate the imperfect, limited self and to manifest itself in the phenomenal world. The efforts, struggles, and advances of humanity are the activity of this essential nature revealing itself.

When we who think of ourselves as imperfect, limited, and relative beings awaken to our True Self in the experience of seeing into our own nature and accept this reality clearly, beyond any doubt, our anxiety and suffering vanish like clouds. The joy of this moment is beyond description. At the same time, we must understand one essential point: we can never realize our True Self simply by comprehending an intellectual explanation of the principle behind it. We must encounter that True Self in actual experience to the point where we can embody it as truth. Otherwise it will never have the power to bring us to a state of true peace.

Accounts of enlightenment experiences, Buddhist doctrine, and philosophy are merely explanations of the content of that experience—conceptual clothing draped on the reality of true experience. If we were to compare the experience of awakening to medicine, then accounts of such experiences would be like testaments to the efficacy of a medicine. Needless to say, the medicine and the testaments to their efficacy are two different things. Explanation comes from experience, but experience never results from explanation. No matter how many times we read statements lauding the virtues of a medicine, it won't do us a bit of good until we actually take it. Likewise, the quickest and most direct route to an experience of realization is the practice of zazen. We should all keep this clearly in mind.

Bassui Zenji, a great Japanese master and founder of Kōgoku temple in Koshu, used the following comparison to explain the principle of Buddhist salvation:

Imagine a child sleeping next to its parents, dreaming that it's being beaten. The parents cannot help the child no matter how much it suffers, for no one can enter the dreaming mind of another. If the child could awaken, it would be freed of this suffering automatically. In the same way, one who realizes that his own mind is buddha frees himself instantly from the suffering that arises from the ceaseless round of birth-and-death.[2]

The famous story of the poor son of a rich man from the Lotus Sutra uses an allegory to make the same point. I quote here from Harada Roshi's discourse on Hakuin Zenji's *Song in Praise of Zazen*:

There was a rich man (the Buddha) who had an only son (the Buddha's only child is sentient beings). The rich man spared no pains in bringing up his son in a loving atmosphere (the teachings of the Buddha). But the son, completely disregarding his father's love, ran away from home (the first step toward delusion). The father was beside himself with grief and used every means at his disposal to find his son again (skillful teaching in Buddhism). The son wandered from country to country and eventually forgot even that he was the son of a rich man.

One day he stopped at his own house, without recognizing it, to beg for some scraps from the table. The father, seeing his son, was filled with joy and sent servants to bring the boy to him (preaching the tenets of Mahayana Buddhism). The son had no way of knowing what was happening and, mistakenly concluding that he had been singled out as a thief (as we ourselves continue to cling to shallow teachings even after we have heard the truth of Buddhism), ran away in fright. When the father saw this, he realized that his son was not yet prepared to accept the truth (that we are all intrinsically awake). He therefore sent his chief servant to offer the boy a position as cleaning help at the house. The boy consented to stay on for a while as a servant, after which he quickly rose in rank, assuming jobs with more and more responsibility until he became the head servant (finally believing the principle of salvation in Mahayana Buddhism and coming to realization). He then went on to succeed his father as heir to the estate (receiving the seal of transmission and inheriting the Dharma).

In other words, although each one of us is actually the richest person in the world, we continue to see ourselves as hapless beggars, full of pain and suffering. In truth we are all intrinsically endowed with buddha nature, perfect and lacking nothing. We are, in fact, Buddha. It is only delusion that prevents our buddhahood from shining forth in its brilliance. What a pitiful state of affairs! But by awakening to our self-nature, we automatically come to peace and all suffering disappears of itself. This is true Buddhist salvation.

DUAL AND NONDUAL PERSPECTIVES

We can all recognize basic areas of divergence between Western and Eastern thought. These differences manifest themselves not only in the arts but in all sectors of culture, including the natural sciences and religion. The Western spirit, briefly put, tends to be objectively oriented, confronting the external world as an object of pursuit and investigation. This pursuit of objective goals reaches its most extreme form in the investigation of the material world, which has resulted in the development of modern science with all its achievements. In contrast, the Eastern approach focuses the light of contemplation inward, toward the heart and mind (*kokoro*) itself—the very seat of the cognitive and emotional aspects of humanity.

Western psychology takes the phenomenal products of mind as its object of scrutiny and examines mental phenomena using the same assumptions and methods as natural science. The basic mindset in the West presupposes the existence of a dualistic opposition between subject and object. In contrast, the Eastern contemplative approach culminates in a direct experience of subject apprehending subject—impossible within a logical framework built on the duality of subject and object.

This contemplative approach, which relies on direct experience without recourse to thought, is expressed in the phrase, "Transcend and directly penetrate the ground of the Tathāgata." It is the method of Zen and is why Zen is known as the way of the absolute. It is the way of subject confirming subject, mind confirming mind, and self confirming self.

Dōgen Zenji describes this path:

> To study the Buddha Way is to study the self. To study the self is to forget the self. To forget the self is to be awakened by all things. When awakened by all things, the body and mind of self and other fall away. No trace of realization remains and this traceless realization continues endlessly.[3]

Buddhism does nothing other than clarify who we are. As long as there is a self in opposition to an outside world, we cannot meet our True Self. When body and mind of both self and other fall away, then for the first time we see the true nature of self and other. Rinzai Zenji calls this "both self and other stolen away." Yōka Daishi says:

> When we verify reality,
> there is neither mind nor thing,
> and the path to hell instantly vanishes.

To the common-sense mind of many Westerners, which takes the difference between subject and object as a fundamental construct, the world is unknowable as "one thing." Even when speaking of a single and absolute God, it is always God as one in relation to His creatures. The difference between creator and created is not transcended. In Asia, by contrast, even outside strictly Buddhist circles, sayings expressing the unity of life are common: "If one leaf falls, autumn is here," "All things return to one," "One is all, all is one," and "Heaven, earth, and I are of the same root; the myriad things and I are of one body."

Edmund Husserl (1859—1938), founder of phenomenology, posited two aspects of human consciousness. The first, *noema*, is the aspect of the objective world that can become the object of intellection. The second, *noesis*, is the subjective aspect that addresses itself to the objective world—in other words, intelligence itself taken as a function. As a logical construct, noesis is always the subject and can never be the predicate. Conversely, noema is forever the predicate and never the subject.

Human consciousness can be objectified without end. For example, in the sentence "This flower is red," "this flower" is an object existing outside the subject. The subject is what determines that the flower "is red." But the judgment that "this flower is red" can itself be objectified by saying, "The statement 'this flower is red' is in error," which produces a second level of judgment. By so doing, "this flower is red" becomes subject in itself while "is in error" is the new predicate. In this way consciousness can be endlessly objectified, but at the end of the process an element remains that hasn't been objectified. This residual element is always the subject and can never be the object. It is the "eternal subject" never to become an object.

For Husserl, both noema and noesis are products of the intellect taken to be aspects of human consciousness. Surveying these ideas from the viewpoint of Zen, which apprehends a world where "the myriad objects and mind are one" and where "mind and things are nondual," noema and noesis can be seen as two aspects of the same oneness. In reality, noema is noesis, noesis is noema. The Eastern view is that this unity can be apprehended only in direct experience. So long as we try to understand this oneness through the intellect, we will never apprehend the true actuality of noesis; it will forever remain an intellectual picture with no real content. Nevertheless, it is clear that the principle of human salvation lies not in noema, the objective world, but in noesis, subjective experience.

No matter how far natural science develops in the area of the objective world, allowing us to travel even to other galaxies, these achievements, wonderful as they may be, can never serve as the means to human salvation. Even if advances in medicine and science wipe out the scourge of cancer, they still won't be able to answer the fundamental question of life and death. If we can't find basic salvation on this earth, what good will it do us to travel to distant galaxies?

A Zen koan reads: "There is not a hairsbreadth difference between oneself and others in the limitless universe." The verse points to the fundamental emptiness of space. As a koan it can trigger a direct experience of this reality. Space and time are only concepts; neither actually exists. If you can't gain salvation on this very spot, then it will be beyond your reach no matter where you go. When we awaken to the absolute, we awaken to our own nature. This is the revelation of our true face and is the ultimate aim of Zen. But a very important question remains: why does this experience save us? In order to answer this question, we turn to the question of what enlightenment is and how it is realized.

ZEN ENLIGHTENMENT

In the preceding section I explained how we humans, who think of ourselves as imperfect, limited, and mortal, can awaken to our true nature, which is complete and perfect, infinite and absolute. When we clearly realize who we are, our fears and suffering vanish like insubstantial clouds. No matter how steeped in Buddhist learning someone is, so long as they lack this basic awakening experience, that person will be an outsider to the world of Zen. Individuals differ in the depth and force of their awakening, but without some experience of realization a person will be unable to truly understand even a word of Zen.

When I say we are complete and perfect, infinite and absolute, what do I actually mean? In other words, what is the content of Zen enlightenment? In brief, Zen enlightenment is to awaken to the emptiness of the self (*ninkū*) and to the emptiness of all things (*hokkū*). These words refer to the emptiness (*kū*) of both subject and object. But what does "empty" mean in this context? The opening lines of the *Heart Sutra*, a distillation of the six hundred chapters of the *Great Perfection of Wisdom Sutra*, describe this emptiness:

> Avalokitesvara Bodhisattva, practicing the profound perfection of wisdom, clearly saw that all five aggregates are empty, transforming all suffering and distress.

Avalokitesvara, known in Japanese as Kannon, is the bodhisattva of compassion who strives to save humanity from suffering. The five aggregates are form, sensation, perception, mental action, and consciousness—the elements that comprise the entire phenomenal world in both its material and spiritual aspects. The "perfection of wisdom" refers to the most profoundly true wisdom that penetrates the depths of existence. The basis of Kannon's ability to alleviate humanity's suffering is the realization that the whole phenomenal world is empty. Seeing this clearly is the practice of the perfection of wisdom. The *Heart Sutra* continues:

> Form is none other than emptiness, emptiness none other
>   than form.
> Form is exactly emptiness, emptiness exactly form.

Emptiness can be identified as the key point that distinguishes Buddhism from other religions. But again, emptiness must be directly experienced. All the intellectual explanations in the world can never begin to convey the world of emptiness—we must experience it for ourselves. Here I will give you only the briefest summary of this emptiness.

EMPTINESS

Although the Sino-Japanese character *kū* means "empty" or "void," emptiness in Zen is neither nihilistic nor a vacuum; it doesn't mean that there is nothing at all. Even expressions such as "All things are impermanent and empty" or "From the beginning there is not one thing" do not mean that things are completely empty. If I were pressed to say something about emptiness, I would say that it doesn't depend on our five senses, it transcends them. If this weren't so, the words "Form is none other than emptiness" couldn't be reversed to read, "Emptiness is none other than form."

We usually think of ourselves as separate from the external world. We believe in the existence of an "I" that looks out on the world and sees people and nature as relative to each other. In other words, we hold as self-evident the existence of a subject that observes and an object that is observed. In the same way we believe in a subject that hears, smells, and touches, and in objects that can be heard, smelled, and touched. When we define the subject as that which observes, however, we have already conceptualized and objectified the subject, so it is no longer a true subject. It has become, using Husserl's terminology, noema and no longer noesis. The true subject is "I myself," which could further be defined as pure or absolute subject. Nevertheless, the instant we add such names, the "I" again becomes the object of the sentence and ceases to be the subject.

Emptiness of the self

Zen turns the light of introspection inward and pursues the question, "What am I?" The essence of Zen lies in the search for the infinite and absolute subject, the True Self. I can see my hands and feet. I can see my face and head in a mirror or feel them with my hands. In fact, one or more of the five senses can apprehend anything I can call *my*. But what about that *my*, or more specifically the *I* referred to by the possessive *my*? Where is this *I*? If I asked you to show me the *I*, what could you do?

The famous koan "Tosotsu's Three Barriers," Case 47 of the *Gateless Gate*, takes up this question. During the Sung Dynasty a Zen temple called Tosotsu-in, located in modern Kianghsi Province in China, housed a highly respected monk named Jūetsu Zenji. This monk routinely used the same three questions to test his students' depth of understanding:

> The purpose of making one's way through sweeping grasses and inquiring as to the subtle truth is only to realize one's own nature. Now, you venerable monks, where is your own nature at this very moment?
>
> When you have attained your own nature, you can free yourself from life-and-death. How will you free yourself from life-and-death when the light of your eyes is falling to the ground?
>
> When you have freed yourself from life-and-death, you know where to go. After your four elements have decomposed, where will you go?

These three questions require the student to grapple with life's greatest matter, the problem of life-and-death. All earnest Zen students must summon up their resources to pass through these barriers.

Putting aside discussion of the last two barriers for now, let us concentrate on the first, for it gets to the heart of our own very real problem. We can view the expression "sweeping grasses" in two ways. Grasses can be seen as the concepts and delusive thoughts sprouting profusely in our minds. We sweep them away. We can also take "sweeping grasses" to be the process of making our way along overgrown mountain trails in search of a true teacher residing in the hills. The "subtle truth" refers to the subtle Dharma of Buddhism, or more directly, to the True Self. We could take "inquiring as to the subtle truth" to refer to Zen practice itself. Indeed in the practice of Zen we eradicate thoughts and come face to face with the true fact.

Whichever interpretation we use, "sweeping grasses and inquiring as to the subtle truth" mean going on pilgrimage and practicing Zen. In their pursuit of the Way, practitioners of old all endured hardships in order to attain realization or "seeing nature." The "nature" in "seeing nature" is our own true nature. So Jūetsu Zenji seems to be pressing the student hard: "Seeing nature, seeing nature! You keep going on about seeing nature. But just tell me, where is your True Self right here and now? If it exists, then show it to me!" Where is the True Self? Where is the self that is not *my* self? Where is "Mu," or "The Sound of One Hand," "The Flowering Hedge," "Three Pounds of Flax," or "Your Face Before Your Parents Were Born"? Where is that True Self and what does it look like?

But even if you answer, "Here it is!" and slap yourself, aren't you just slapping your body, rather than the True Self? Does that mean, then, that there is no True Self? No. Because the one who is thinking now is none other than the True Self. As proof of this, can't you hear right now? Can't you see right now? Am I not sitting here writing this? And aren't you at this very moment reading these very words? It is an experiential fact beyond any doubt that the self is at this moment present, right here. Someone may answer, "It is the mind!"—in other words, "I myself am the mind. It is mind that sees, hears, reads, and moves the hand to write the page." But having determined this, we still haven't solved the problem. We have simply replaced the word "I" with the word "mind," and if asked now to show that mind, we would be as powerless as before.

Let's check this for ourselves. Does mind have form? No, it has no form. Does mind have color, weight, or odor? No, it's without color, weight, or odor. Are we able to give mind a location and say mind is here or mind is there? We can do no such thing. Does this mean then that the mind from the beginning doesn't exist? I have already explained why this can't be so. Then, where indeed is the mind? Or as Tosotsu asks, "Now, you venerable monks, where is your own nature at this very moment?"

In the koan "Bodhidharma Puts the Mind to Rest," Case 41 of

the *Gateless Gate*, the second Zen ancestor Eka Daishi says, "I have searched for the mind but have never been able to find it." Bassui Zenji comments:

> What kind of master is it who at this very moment sees colors with the eyes and hears voices with the ears, who raises a hand and moves a foot? We know these are functions of our own mind, but no one knows exactly how they are performed. It might be said that behind these actions there is no entity, and that they are being performed spontaneously. Conversely, it could be maintained that these are the acts of some entity; yet the entity is invisible. If one sees this question as unfathomable, all attempts to reason out an answer will cease, and one will be at a loss to know what to do. This is a most propitious state.

A verse by Ikkyū reads:

What is mind?
The sound of the wind in
the pine tree in the brush painting.

The India ink painting mentioned in the verse depicts a pine tree in which the wind makes a sound as it moves through its branches. The wind—which stands for the mind—is definitely blowing, but it has no form and casts no shadow. The ancients were able to hit the mark. Please savor this verse.

The questions "What is mind?" or "Who is it that hears?" hold the key to our problems. A number of scientists are convinced that mind is contained in the brain, that by studying the brain we can know the mind. But you could examine the brain all day long and never find the mind. The brain is a physical structure, which the mind uses as a tool, but it is not the mind itself, nor does it contain the mind.

We can compare the relationship between the mind and brain to the relationship between a person and the telephone. When I'm on the phone listening to someone, it's not the telephone that hears, and there is no mind listening inside the phone. My ear listens, but the ear itself is nothing more than a tool, and the mind is not in the ear. The ear is connected to the brain, but the brain also is simply a tool. The telephone, the ear, and the brain are a series of physical mechanisms, tools that the mind uses. They do not themselves contain the mind. It is not the brain that is thinking about the brain as I sit here thinking about the brain; it is always *I* who am thinking. When Eka Daishi said, "I have searched for the mind but have never been able to find it," Bodhidharma replied, "I have finished putting it to rest for you."

Mind is simply a name; the reality is unattainable, beyond our grasp. Mind is unfathomable and immeasurable, defying human wisdom. It is simultaneously the complete perfection of unlimited capabilities, virtue, and all the properties of life, and yet has no form or substance. This is called emptiness. In other words, the content of that which sees and hears is empty and cannot be grasped. Mind is emptiness. While possessing infinite capabilities, it is zero. This is called "emptiness of subject." If we directly penetrate this reality, through experience, then all fears and suffering will disappear just as if we had awakened from a bad dream. They will return to their original state of nothingness.

Zen Master Ikkyū writes:

> Mr. Original Face cuts a fancy figure;
> One look and it's love at first sight.

Just once, wouldn't you too like to fall in love like this?

Emptiness of all things

The Japanese word *hokkū* means "emptiness of all things." *Hō* means "law" and can generally be taken as a synonym for phenomena. Since all things are subject to the law of causation, the same word is used to designate those things themselves, the components of the so-called "objective world." The world of phenomena is the world apprehended by the senses—the worlds of color, form, weight, and smell. It is the world of common sense, the object of scrutiny for the subject, and the object of investigation in the natural sciences. No one doubts that the world of phenomena is subject to the natural law of cause and effect. But at the same time, the objective world is empty, void in content. The word "form" is used to refer to this world in the *Heart Sutra*.

We tend to think of the objective world of matter as the only world that really exists and to consider discussions of other possible realities as metaphysical speculation. The startling advances made by science during the last two centuries—increased productivity, economic expansion, and the flowering of a technological society—have given the scientific method great authority. As a result, we tend to reject as idealism anything that can't be proven scientifically. Buddhist experience, however, asserts that the world of form is a phenomenon, the content and substance of which are empty. Again, by "empty" I am not implying a total void: it is emptiness filled with infinite substance. In mathematics, infinity is indicated by the symbol ∞. We might designate emptiness, which is filled with infinite substance and potential, with a zero containing an infinity symbol: ⊝.

Emptiness may be conceptually explained as being "without qualities" or "undefined," because things in the objective world are constantly moving and changing. We could compare this constant movement of phenomena to the flow of a river. The river, as a river, seems to be a permanent, unchanging existence. But in actual fact the river's water is continually in motion, not stopping for even a moment. The water passing before us at this moment is completely different from the water which flowed by a second ago. The same could be said of our human bodies. We think of our body today as being the same as yesterday. But the cells of our bodies are ceaselessly undergoing metabolic processes. The molecules, atoms, and atomic particles of those cells appear and disappear at an amazing rate, far faster than the water in the river.

The water in a river flows on endlessly without a fixed nature of its own or properties. Does the flow itself exist then? In other words, does its emptiness of fixed nature exist or not? This may seem like so much intellectual play, but it's not. In response to this question, atomic physicists would say that, yes, the flow exists. The Zen experience of seeing one's nature, however, clearly establishes that even the flow doesn't exist. When Zen masters say, "From the beginning there is not one thing," or "Upon awakening, everything is empty and the thousand appearances do not exist," they are seeing through the intrinsic emptiness of the flow.

In this sense, modern physics' theory of the fundamental particle, which drives the persistent search for the source of matter, seems to come close to confirming the empty nature of matter. I feel sure that one day physics will clearly corroborate the emptiness of the objective world and the reality expressed in traditional phrases, such as: "Where there is not one thing, there is a limitless storehouse," "Form is emptiness, emptiness is form," "Emptiness is absolute, existence is mysterious," and "Myriad things in their true appearance."

Emptiness of subject and emptiness of object are one

For the sake of discussion I have divided emptiness into two categories: emptiness of the self and emptiness of all things. In reality, however, it is impossible for a person and a thing to be two, or for there to be two "emptinesses." Subject and object are empty, completely one, and yet are two sides of what is indivisibly one reality. This empty oneness is beyond the reach of our senses, and it contains limitless and wondrous potential. It is nothing other than our True Self, which is also the true nature of the universe. Buddhist philosophy refers to it as the Absolute Three Treasures, or the Stainless Dharma Body of Vairochana Buddha, or more simply as buddha nature or dharma nature. In the Zen sect, it is called "Mu," "The Sound of One Hand," "Three Pounds of Flax," "The Oak Tree in the Garden," or "Original Face before Your Parents Were Born." In everyday life it is called Dick, Jane, soldier, farmer.

It is no wonder, then, that we lack the power to cut through delusions and entanglements and are unable to solve the problem of life and death. We remain stuck in the realm of ordinary seeing until we take hold of empty oneness in our lived experience. When we see into our own nature, the experience of the emptiness of subject and object resolves the "fundamental matter" and is typically accompanied by a strong upwelling of joy. At times the experience gives rise to intense excitement, which overwhelms and obliterates consciousness of any individual self. Zen Master Hyakujō was supposedly deaf for three days following his realization. Dōgen Zenji's "body and mind falling away" was also an unmistakable experience of extreme joy. Imagine someone who has been living shut up in a pitch-black cave in the depths of despair, not knowing what to do, when suddenly the surrounding walls collapse, and he is hurled into the midst of a great light. It would hardly seem strange if that person were overcome with incredible joy.

Keizan Jōkin writes in the preface to his *Guidelines for Zazen:*[4]

Zazen directly opens and clarifies the mind ground and brings us to rest in the essential.

The "mind ground" is the true nature, the essence of mind. It is, so to speak, the universe seen from the inside. Our True Self is one with the essence of the universe—an essence that is empty but contains infinite potential. "Clarifies" means to directly experience this emptiness. When we experience emptiness of the self, we gain true peace and liberation for the first time. This is what Jōzai Daishi means by "brings us to rest in the essential." And it is what the *Heart Sutra* means when it says that Avalokitesvara Bodhisattva "clearly saw that all five aggregates are empty." That he "clearly saw" means that he came to an unmistakable realization of this fact. By seeing through to the reality of emptiness of subject and object, we are released from all suffering. This is how the bodhisattva Kannon (Avalokitesvara) saved herself and how she continues, at this very moment, to save all beings. This is called "practicing the profound perfection of wisdom."

Yōka Daishi's *Song of Realizing the Way* (*Shōdōka*) says:

When we witness reality,
there is neither person nor thing,
and all karma that leads to hell instantly vanishes.

. . .

All things are transient and empty;
This is the great and perfect enlightenment of the Tathāgata.

The hell referred to in the first stanza is Avici, one of the Eight Hells of Fire, also known as the Hell of Infinite Duration or Unlimited Suffering. When we realize the impermanence and emptiness of subject and object, this hell instantly disappears. Before National Teacher Bukkō, founder of Engakuji Temple in Kamakura, arrived from China, he was forced to flee to Neng Jen Temple in Wen Prefecture to escape the invading Mongols. When the Mongols eventually stormed that temple, Bukkō was sitting in meditation in the hall, calmly awaiting their arrival. A soldier spied him and brandished his sword, ready to cut off the master's head.

Perfectly composed as he faced death, Bukkō revealed his state of mind with the following words:

> No space in the universe to raise a single staff;
> What bliss to know that self and other are empty.
> The three-foot Yuan sword, so wondrous and heavy,
> cuts the spring breeze like a flash of lightning.

On seeing the master's composure in the face of death, the Mongol soldier lowered his sword and left with his companions.

Yōka Daishi says something similar:

> Even facing the sword of death, the mind is unmoved;
> Even drinking poison, it is quiet.

This is true release from the bonds of birth and death. This true release, or awakening, is at the heart of Zen and forms the nucleus of Mahayana Zen Buddhism.

The Zen sickness of the idea of emptiness

However, even after awakening, an important issue remains. This is the matter of "Zen sickness," which can sometimes occur following the experience of awakening. There are many types of Zen sickness, but here I wish to emphasize the danger of the sickness of "ideas of emptiness."

When awakening, we awaken to a reality that Yasutani Roshi referred to as "original nature." The content of this reality is empty, yet at the same time filled to perfection with mysterious and wondrous capabilities—in a word we awaken to emptiness. Emptiness is the stage on which the myriad phenomena continually appear and disappear, without a moment's deviation, at the mercy of the law of causation. Buddhism uses the word "law" to indicate both the law of causation and the phenomena that appear and disappear in accordance with that law. The phenomena of the objective world are known as the Dharma of the Absolute Three Treasures, while our essential nature is called the Buddha of the Absolute Three Treasures. This division into the Buddha and the Dharma of the Absolute Three Treasures provides a way of looking at two aspects of the same reality—a reality that from the beginning is one. This unitary reality in turn is known as the Sangha of the Absolute Three Treasures.

Various expressions are used in Buddhist doctrine to elucidate the contrast between the essential and the phenomenal:

Essential	Phenomenal
Essence	Phenomena
Buddha of the Absolute Three Treasures	Dharma of the Absolute Three Treasures
Essential Rank	Phenomenal Rank
Equality	Distinction
Emptiness	Form
True Void	Wondrous Existence
Void Nature	Cause and Effect
Reality	Arising from Causation
Not Having	Having
Gripping	Releasing
Principle	Practice
Darkness	Light
"Mu," "The Sound of One Hand," etc.	Mountains, Rivers, Grass, Trees, etc.

We must be clearly aware that emptiness, the essential, is only one aspect of our True Self, of the true fact. When a person experiences a thorough seeing of their nature, and verifies the oneness of both aspects of emptiness and form, of the essential and the phenomenal, there is no problem. Without such an experience he or she may fixate on only the single aspect of emptiness and fall into the so-called "idea of emptiness." This could lead to the rejection of the law of causation and give rise to a problematic Zen sickness. A person in such a condition is called "an elevated dead person."

Although in Zen training we must all pass through the stage where "there are no beings to save," if we remain stuck in that emptiness, enjoying solitary bliss, then the desire to save all beings will never arise. We may end up as self-authorized egotists who have cut ties with other sentient beings. Yōka Daishi warns us of this in a poem:

> The great void banishes cause and effect,
> yet this just invites dissipation and woe.
> To reject existence and cling to the void
> is like leaping into fire to avoid being drowned.

By awakening to our self-nature, by awakening to both emptiness and form, we come to peace. This is true Buddhist salvation. However, we must wipe away all traces of enlightenment as well, and then forget that we have wiped them away. And that practice continues endlessly. This is the Buddha Way.

The Three Great Aims of Zen 4

In the first chapters I discussed what Zen aims to achieve, focusing on awakening, or enlightenment as the basic principle underlying salvation in Zen. After this rather headlong rush into the subject, I will devote the following chapters to the merits of meditation and to a more careful examination of what Zen offers humankind.

Zen aims to accomplish the following three main goals:

1. Development of the power of concentration (*jōriki*)
2. The experience of the Supreme Way, or seeing into our own nature (*kenshō*)
3. Personalization of the Supreme Way, or the perfection of character (*mujōdō no taigen*)

My master, Yasutani Haku'un Roshi, made this threefold division, and I have inherited it. The original idea probably came from his master, Harada Sogaku Roshi. At any rate, these three goals are very clear and simple, and at the same time they are extremely mysterious and profound. In the second chapter I focused on the second of these aims—the realization experience. Here, however, I would like to discuss these aims in order, one by one.

DEVELOPMENT OF THE POWER OF CONCENTRATION

The word Zen has its origin in the Sanskrit word *dhyana*. The Chinese used two characters, *chan-na*, to represent the sound of the Sanskrit word, and the Japanese pronounced the first Chinese character, "chan," as "zen." Dhyana can be translated with the Japanese word *seiryo* ("quiet contemplation" or "contemplating quietly"), which designates a gathering up of the scattered elements of the spirit and bringing the mind to rest. Briefly, it means developing an immovable mind. In Japanese the power that comes from that concentration of mind is called *jōriki*, or "the power of concentration."

An ancient saying goes: "If the spirit is unified, what is there that cannot be done?" To accomplish any task, it is necessary to concentrate the mind totally on that one goal. Even a child knows how to make bits of wood or paper burst into flame by concentrating a beam of sunlight on them with a magnifying glass. No one would deny that when we act in the external world we need strong willpower and concentration to bring our ideas to fruition. Any person who accomplishes outstanding feats has doubtlessly developed great powers of concentration.

During the Warring States Period (1467–1568) and on up to the end of the Shōgunate (1868), Japanese warriors and swordsmen spared no efforts to develop their spirits through the practice of Zen, and warriors such as Uesugi Kenshin and Takeda Shingen practiced zazen. Considering they continuously stood on the threshold of life and death, with no room for error in tactics, their decision to practice meditation was only natural.

Today, if we are to live in peace with a minimum of suffering, we must establish a spiritual foundation—in both our social and domestic lives—that is not controlled by the external world. Normally, our daily activities are continually under the influence of our external environment, controlled and pulled around by it. Because of this, our minds are never at rest. We could say that suffering is the emotion that arises when we come under the control of the external world against our will. If someone doing the same job in our workplace receives a slightly higher wage, we are upset. If someone says something critical or unpleasant about us, we are disturbed. Feelings of jealousy, suspicion, hatred, and antagonism endlessly arise. In this way, our lives as ordinary people are at the mercy of our restless spirits.

As long as the mind is moving, it is unable to accurately reflect the various aspects of the external world, just as a warped mirror cannot reflect objects as they really are. Accordingly, we cannot expect clear judgment from an agitated mind.

We all know, in theory at least, that "haste makes waste"—that it is important to be calm and collected. Yet no matter how much we may be aware of this intellectually, our minds refuse to follow. No amount of reading up on self-discipline can develop the power of concentration to the point where we are no longer under the sway of external circumstances. The quickest and most effective route to this goal is through actually practicing Zen and developing the power of concentration.

The power of concentration helps us develop two important skills: the ability to actualize our ideas in the objective world, and the ability to free ourselves from being controlled by the world. We needn't necessarily practice Zen to develop the first ability; development of the ability to actualize one's goals is not uniquely Buddhist. The ability to free ourselves from being controlled by the world, however, is the very foundation of spiritual culture in the East. A number of arts in Japanese culture contain the suffix *dō*, which means "way," as part of their Japanese names: *kendō, judō, aikidō, shodō* (calligraphy), *sadō* (tea ceremony), *kadō* (flower arrangement), and so on. All of these disciplines rely on concentration of mind as their basis. It is by harnessing the power of concentration that the Japanese preserve the practice of these ways.

There is no limit to the depths to which concentration can be developed. Tempering it through practice can lead to marvelous abilities known as "divinely penetrating powers" (*jintsūriki*). However, if one fails to keep up the practice, these powers will seep out like water from a hole in a bucket, and in the end the person will revert to his or her original state. In addition, no matter how wondrous and mysterious the abilities developed through concentration may be, they will be of no use in solving the problem of life and death, much less questions on the meaning of life, or the mysteries of the universe if we do not maintain and use them correctly.

From ancient times, enlightenment has been referred to as the wisdom that appears from concentration of mind. So the development of concentration and the experience of seeing into our own nature are closely related to each other. Yet, by nature, the two contain quite separate elements. No matter how much we develop our power of concentration, it does not follow that we will automatically see into our own nature. Similarly, it does not necessarily follow that a person who achieves a deep realization has developed strong powers of concentration. This power requires a specific effort of its own.

THE EXPERIENCE OF THE SUPREME WAY

The experience of the Supreme Way forms the very heart of true Zen Buddhism. In fact, it is the experience of seeing into our own nature, also referred to as "awakening," that qualifies Zen as a form of Mahayana Buddhism. Without it Zen would descend to the level of mere intellectual musing.

In his *Recommending Zazen to All People* (*Fukan Zazengi*), Dōgen Zenji says:

> Even a hairsbreadth difference is already the difference between heaven and earth.

A "hairsbreadth difference" refers to even the tiniest remaining concept, and "the difference between heaven and earth" means that the experience has already become a counterfeit product merely resembling the real thing. Zen has always run the risk of becoming sullied with concepts. However, in recent years, the tendency to spread false ideas about Zen has become more pronounced, and people dismiss Zen as just another system of thought. Some people will do all they can to avoid the hardship of sitting down in meditation and exerting themselves ceaselessly toward what is beyond knowing. Instead, they resort to this philosophy or that psychological theory to form their own views about Zen. Theorizing is much easier than actually practicing zazen.

Of course Zen contains teachings and theories: the whole body of the sutras can be seen as theories about Zen, and Dōgen Zenji's *Shōbōgenzō* is filled with instruction and dogma on Zen. Yet neither the sutras nor *Shōbōgenzō* are, in any sense, mere philosophical speculation. Their authors have clearly seen through the essence of the universe with perfectly enlightened eyes, and they use every means at their disposal to bring an awareness of this same world to students of Zen.

In contrast, the mental suppositions drawn by those who have never seen this world are fundamentally different. Nowadays we come across people who have never actually practiced Zen and who lack even the slightest understanding of it, who nevertheless put on airs of being "Zen people" and confidently give lectures or write books on the subject. Zen lends itself to an academic examination based on the literary value of its documents, its philosophy, psychology, history, and so on. However, an academic approach amounts to nothing more than examining the framework of Zen and speculating about it. It is not living Zen. If we compare Zen to a large house, we could say that we haven't really entered that house until we have made our way into the living room and sat down on the couch. To approach Zen as an academic discipline is like circling the house, occasionally peeking through the gate, and making educated guesses as to the layout and construction of the house and its furnishings.

We must make another distinction here: between Mahayana Zen and so-called "Zen with the expectation of enlightenment" (taigo Zen). In Zen with the expectation of enlightenment, the practitioner still has thoughts of awakening, asking questions such as: "When will I get enlightened?" or "Why is it taking so long?" People sitting in this way can never become truly one with their koan practice or their practice of just sitting. One of the basic prerequisites for Zen experience is for the practice to become single-mindedly pure. Whether the practice is with koans or just sitting, as long as attention is divided between the koan and concerns about the outcome, the practice will never be truly pure. This is why the Zen ancestors criticized Zen with the expectation of enlightenment. To practice true Zen meditation means to sit without the slightest thought about awakening. We must put aside all other matters and throw our entire mind and body into our practice, whether we are working on a particular koan or just sitting.

Past Zen masters have repeatedly emphasized that the world of Zen enlightenment is absolutely unattainable through thoughts or concepts. Citing all those warnings would leave room for little else, so I will quote just one or two of them here. The first is the story of Tokusan Senkan Zenji:

> Tokusan Zenji, who was famous for his use of the stick in instruction, ranks with Rinzai as one of the most severe of the outstanding Zen teachers. It is said that no matter what question was brought to him, he responded with, "Tell me and I'll give you thirty blows; fail to tell me and I'll give you thirty blows!" He was a true master in using the stick to "kill" his students and "bring them back to life" again. Originally

Tokusan belonged to the Hossō sect of Buddhism and was a theoretician of Buddhist teachings. His family name was Shu, and he served as a preaching monk. He was unsurpassed in expounding the *Diamond Sutra*; his knowledge of that text earned him the nickname "Diamond Shu."

He is said to have declared: "Those who leave home to strive after diamond-like concentration may study the great meaning of Buddhism for a thousand eons and spend a further ten thousand eons performing detailed Buddhist practice, yet they still won't become a Buddha." In other words, Tokusan believed beyond a doubt that it would take an infinitely long period of time to achieve buddhahood.

At that time in the south of China, however, a group calling itself the Zen sect was preaching the doctrine "mind is Buddha." When he heard this, Tokusan seethed with self-righteous anger. "Who do they think they are, propagating such evil teachings? I'll go and dash their arguments to pieces with my preaching. I'll pulverize their falsehoods with one blow from my stick!"

With these words, Tokusan slung a portable bookrack containing his treatises on the *Diamond Sutra* over his shoulder and rushed through the mountains toward the south. When he came to the region of Feng Chu, he saw an old woman at the side of the road selling cakes fried in oil called *tenjin* (literally, "touch the mind"). Tokusan decided to treat himself to some *tenjin* and, putting down his bookrack, ordered a plate of them.

The old woman said, "That looks heavy. What are you carrying?"

"This? These are treatises on the *Diamond Sutra*."

"Oh, the *Diamond Sutra*? Well, then, I have a question for you. If you can answer me, I'll give you the *tenjin* for free as an offering. But if you can't answer, I won't even sell you any, and you'll have to buy them elsewhere."

Tokusan must have thought her strange. "Ask me anything you like," he said.

"Well, it says in the *Diamond Sutra*, 'Past mind is unattainable, present mind is unattainable, and future mind is unattainable.' Worthy monk, with what mind are you going to eat these *tenjin*?"

She was certainly an extraordinary woman. "Unattainable" means that we are unable to point to that mind and show it. Since the past mind is already gone, it is without doubt unattainable. Future mind has yet to come, so we cannot grasp it either. No one would deny that it, too, is unattainable. Many, however, might think it possible to grasp present mind, because it is the mind that exists here and now. But the instant we say "present" it is already in the past. If we say even "pres" or just "p," it has already become part of the past. We normally think of a second as the smallest unit of time, but that same second can be divided into hundredths, thousandths, or millionths of a second. There is no limit to the extent we can divide time into smaller and smaller units. This, too, would have to be called "unattainable."

In the koan "Bodhidharma Puts the Mind to Rest," Eka Daishi says: "I have searched for the mind but have never been able to find it." When asked with which of these unattainable minds he was planning to eat the cake, Tokusan, too, was stumped for an answer. Although he could interpret the *Diamond Sutra*, he didn't have the slightest understanding of living the *Diamond Sutra*.

No matter how painstaking and detailed an analysis we make of the mind, in the end it will be unattainable, unless we have experienced awakening. As Yōka Daishi says in *Song on Realizing the Way*: "Unable to attain it, you already have it."

Without true experience we are at a loss, so Tokusan ended up without the cake. I should add that in some versions of the story the old woman gives Tokusan the *tenjin* after all, out of admiration for his sincerity. At any rate, she had evidently seen promise in Tokusan, for she told him that a virtuous monk named Ryūtan Oshō was living nearby. Advising Tokusan to visit him, she pointed out the way.

Following the kind woman's directions, Tokusan arrived at Ryūtan's hermitage. Entering the gate, he called out: "I have heard of Ryūtan for a long time, but upon arriving I find neither a marsh (*tan*) nor a dragon (*ryū*)." Tokusan's words had a Zen ring to them, and Ryūtan no doubt realized that Tokusan had some karmic connection to Zen. He invited him to his room, where they spent half the night in conversation. There is no record of what was said, but there was doubtless much discussion of the Dharma.

It got very late. Taking his leave, Tokusan pulled aside the blind and stepped outside. It was pitch black. Turning around, he said, "It's so dark outside I can't see my own feet." Ryūtan lit a paper candle and gave it to Tokusan. Just as Tokusan was about to take it, Ryūtan blew it out. It is said that in that instant of total darkness Tokusan suddenly came to great enlightenment.

Tokusan bowed to Ryūtan, no doubt to show his gratitude. Ryūtan asked, "What have you seen that you are bowing like this to me?"

Tokusan replied, "I will never again doubt what you say, Venerable Monk."

The next day, Tokusan made a pile of the dissertations on the *Diamond Sutra* that he had held in such esteem. Lighting a pine torch, he said, "Even if we have exhausted abstruse doctrine, it is like placing a hair in vast space. Even if we have learned the vital points of all the truths in the world, it is like throwing a drop of water into a ravine." He then burned all of his manuscripts.

This is how the story is recorded in Engo's long commentary to the koan in Case 4 of the *Blue Cliff Record*. Tokusan is saying, "From now on, I will never doubt your teaching that mind is Buddha." All his intellectualizing and self-conceit were broken. Unless we come to this point we cannot arrive at the life of the buddhas and Zen ancestors. We must appreciate Ryūtan's power to save.

In the "Bendōwa" chapter of the *Shōbōgenzō*, Dōgen Zenji says:

The subtle Dharma of the Seven Buddhas is maintained with its true significance when an enlightened disciple following an enlightened master rightly transmits it. This is beyond the knowing of the priest of letters and learning. This being so, cease all your doubting and illusions and persevere in Zen practice under the guidance of a true teacher until you realize the meditative absorption (samadhi) of the myriad buddhas, which can be received and used freely.

The famous story "Kyōgen Strikes the Bamboo" presents another clear example of how Zen realization transcends thought:

Kyōgen Oshō was a Dharma successor of Isan Reiyū Zenji, cofounder of the Igyō sect. In his ardent pursuit of the Way, he became a monk and practiced Zen under Isan Zenji. A scholarly type with a keen intellect, he extensively studied the sutras and came to a deep intellectual understanding of Buddhist teachings, apparently finding a certain peace of mind. Isan Zenji was aware that Kyōgen had the qualities of a successor, and out of a compassionate wish to somehow bring the monk to true understanding, he gave him the koan, "What is your intrinsic face before you were conceived in your mother's womb?"

Kyōgen could not come up with a ready answer. Blushing with shame, he returned to his quarters where he thoroughly checked the records of the ancients as well as phrases he himself had jotted down, but he was unable to find anything to bring back to the old monk. At a loss, he went to Isan Zenji's room.

"No matter how I try, I cannot come up with anything. Please tell me the answer, Master," he begged.

Isan replied, "If I tell you, it will still be my understanding and not your own. If I go into an explanation now, you will resent me for it later. I will not tell you."

Overcome with sorrow, Kyōgen said, "A rice cake painted on a piece of paper will never fill my belly!"

He then took all his books and notes and burned them, intending to forsake any further study of the Way of the Buddha in this life. "It was foolhardy of me to believe that such an unpromising and inferior person as I could come to true realization."

Having resolved to forsake the world, he asked Isan Zenji's permission and left the monastery. Going as far as Nanyang, to a place where the famous National Teacher Echū was said to have practiced, he built a small hermitage and led a solitary life. On the surface of his mind he had abandoned all hope of solving his koan, and he contented himself with spending each day in the quiet life of a recluse. In his subconscious, however, he was undoubtedly still pursuing the question of his "intrinsic face."

One morning years later, as Kyōgen was sweeping in the garden, a pebble swept up by his broom hit a stalk of bamboo in the thicket: "Tock!" The instant he heard the sound all his thoughts and illusions were blown away. There was nothing but that "tock!" in the whole universe. For the first time, Kyōgen saw his intrinsic face, his True Self.

How happy he must have been! Only those who have experienced this same world can understand the joy of that moment. This sudden experience characteristic of Zen, also known as *kachi ichige*, is a cry of great surprise and shock at the instant when body and mind fall away. Such a quality of suddenness is an indispensible element of truly seeing our nature, and without it, an experience of awakening cannot be confirmed.

Kyōgen returned to his room where he bathed and lit incense. Then he joined his hands, turned in the direction of Isan Zenji's temple, and prostrated himself.

"My master's benevolence is even greater than that of my own parents. If he had answered my question with a logical explanation I would never have known the joy I have found today."

Kyōgen then composed a verse:

One knock!—and all knowledge is forgotten,
there is no need for further searching;
Not a trace left anywhere,
all actions now uplift the ancient road.
Never falling into despondency,

sounds and colors are beyond solemnity;
All the accomplished ones on the Way
praise me, saying, "Well done!"

We may find little to connect with our own lives when hearing about how figures from the distant past saw into their own nature. So let me give a more recent example that might seem more relevant.

A young American couple came to Japan with the objective of practicing Zen. They became members of our Kamakura Zen group and devoted themselves for three years to ardent practice. D, the husband, was tall of frame and ruddy-faced. His eyes peered out of deep sockets, surveying the room carefully in fish-like circumspection. At first glance he had the appearance of a solitary forsaken lover. (Please forgive me, D, for any indiscretion!) But upon talking to him, I found him to be high-spirited, while at the same time naive, easily hurt, and somewhat shy. He had read the works of D. T. Suzuki and many other books on Zen, and he had developed a highly speculative, almost overly logical interest in Zen. It was also D who initially wanted to come to Japan to pursue Zen practice.

His wife had yet to lose the qualities of a timid young girl and barely spoke a word. From an early age she had devoted herself to the piano, giving her first concert at the age of thirteen. Since then she had appeared frequently on the concert stage and developed into a pianist of formidable skills. Sometime after our first meeting, she told me shyly that she had graduated from a prestigious music conservatory in New York and held two degrees in music. When the famous pianist Vladimir Ashkenazy made his first concert tour of Japan, she procured tickets for my wife and me, and the three of us went together. Sitting by her side that night I had an opportunity to listen seriously to a program of piano music for the first time in a long while. During the concert she told me how she had studied under Ashkenazy's teacher, one of the outstanding Russian virtuosi, and had made preparations with his blessings to go and study in the Soviet Union. If it hadn't been for her husband's staunch determination to travel to Japan, she would have been a fellow student of Ashkenazy's.

From her student days she had devoted all her time to piano practice, closed up in her own little world with no friend to confide in. Lacking opportunities to talk with people, her English vocabulary was limited. She felt as if she were living isolated in a tower with just a single small window opened up on the outside world. When she met her husband, she said it was like discovering another person also living in a little one-window tower.

Both husband and wife devoted themselves wholeheartedly to zazen. They attended all the intensive Zen retreats (*sesshin*) and group meditation sessions (*zazenkai*) under Yasutani Roshi and even traveled to Mishima to participate in additional intensive retreats at Ryūtakuji under Nakagawa Sōen Roshi. In May of 1967 we held a retreat under the guidance of Yasutani Roshi. True to form, husband and wife participated and practiced with fervor. About a week after the retreat ended, they both appeared at my door with something to tell me. They spoke haltingly in English sprinkled with Japanese.

On the afternoon of the last day of the retreat, when the final private interview was over and everyone was practicing walking meditation just prior to the closing ceremonies, D's wife suddenly felt an instantaneous release from the "desperate" state she had been in. She was overwhelmed by an indescribable happiness and tears of joy flowed copiously. She didn't know what had happened but the experience had been very wonderful and mysterious. When she returned home, she found that the kitchen work she had always loathed was now extremely pleasant. Whatever she did, whether it was cleaning or weeding the garden, brought her intense happiness. She thought it must be a temporary aberration of the spirit and watched herself, expecting to return to normal after a while. But she remained in the same state of mind, and it seemed there was no end to this feeling of relaxed happiness. The couple had come to inquire just what this might mean.

I received her in private interview and checked her understanding of the koan Mu, which was her practice. As far as I could see, her experience was a true *kenshō*—she had truly seen her own nature. She passed with ease all the checking questions. I was convinced that she had seen into her own nature but decided to send her to Yasutani Roshi for further confirmation. He also questioned her carefully and confirmed her experience as an unqualified kenshō.

We went through several follow-up koans after this and her understanding of them was very good. The power of Zen enlightenment is a mysterious thing indeed. Once when, in the course of ensuing koan study, I presented her with a new koan she suddenly burst out laughing. When I asked her what was so funny, she said, "You keep asking me the same thing time after time. I was beginning to think you were stupid." (Uh-oh! One has to be on one's toes at a time like that.)

There is an ancient Zen saying that goes, "Pass one barrier, and you have passed myriad barriers in the same instant." If we clearly experience a single koan, the other koans will become transparent. At the same time, by passing through each koan, the world of essential reality becomes that much clearer and we gain more freedom in our everyday lives—a freedom that develops and spreads to all areas of life. Thus, although it is true that we see the same thing with each koan, it is still necessary to go through this step-by-step koan process. Unless the initial experience is fairly solid, however, the process of koan study will not go that smoothly.

"Was my wife's experience a shallow one?" D gave me a look that seemed to fear any answer to the contrary.

"No, it was by no means shallow. Her experience had a clarity not often found among my Japanese students up to now."

Upon hearing this, he shook his head in apparent disbelief.

Evidently he found it hard to accept that his wife, who had never read a page of a Zen book in her life and knew next to nothing about the subject, had experienced the same seeing into her own nature that even brave masters of old struggled to attain. Actually, it was probably precisely because she had never opened a book on Zen and knew next to nothing about it that she came to realization as she did. Also because she had devoted herself to intensive piano practice from childhood, she had developed powers of concentration far exceeding those of most people. When these same powers of concentration were channeled into koan practice, she was able to enter into a deep state of meditative absorption in a relatively short time. It was a case where the development of concentration in one kind of practice brought about results in Zen practice.

The philosopher Nishida Kitarō provides another example of the ineffectiveness of intellectual understanding to bring us peace of mind. Soon after he had retired from his post at Kyoto University and settled down in Kamakura, Nishida wrote a series of discursive essays under the title "Kamakura Jottings" for one of the monthly magazines. I remember one line from that series that went something like this: "When I read Unmon's statement that 'Every day is a good day,' I feel my doom has been sealed."

The first time I came across this phrase I was fresh out of university, a newcomer to the work world, searching for a guidepost in my life. Believing that philosophy might help in that search, I combed bookstores looking for works on the subject. Professor Nishida's words made a strong impression on me. What did it mean when Nishida Kitarō—philosophical genius with untiring speculative powers, a man who had struggled all his life in single-minded philosophical pursuit—stated that he felt his doom had been sealed when he read a single phrase of Master Unmon? Having devoted his entire life to a painful search for that ineffable "something" and having failed in the end to grasp it, he must have felt he had encountered in Unmon a man on an unapproachably different level, who had that something in the palm of his hand to use as he wished. Certainly, through philosophy we might come closer to that ineffable something. Yet no matter how close we approach, we will forever circle around it, without being able to touch it. This is philosophy's tragic fate: it lacks the power to cut off our delusions and make us free.

Some members of the Sōtō Zen sect, however, not only consider awakening unnecessary but also reject any attempt to attain realization. They support their position with the example of Dōgen Zenji whose practice was "just sitting." Since sitting itself is the activity of Buddha, they argue, if we practice carefully, we don't need to achieve awakening. A more extreme position holds that since Dōgen Zenji has already come to great enlightenment and acts in kindness to reveal the Way, we simply need to believe in his realization and carry it out in our lives; any further effort toward realization would be an act of blasphemy toward the buddhas and Zen ancestors. Similarly, some Christians say that it is enough to "simply believe" that Jesus died for our sins.

In his writings, Yasutani Haku'un Roshi has given a thorough treatment of this problem, and I need only add a few points to what he has already said. First of all, there is clearly no error in believing the teachings of the sect founder to the letter and earnestly carrying them out. But in reading Dōgen Zenji and professing to believe in every word, they ignore his most important injunction, namely: "Devote yourself solely to sitting zazen and attain the fallen-away body and mind." Here lies the crux of the problem—they fail to engage in the same life-and-death struggle as their sect founder by sitting in meditation until they achieve great enlightenment.

Second, some argue that the Supreme Way is the practice and actualization of awakening and that sitting with this conviction is in itself true Zen meditation. From the viewpoint of the essential world, there is an element of truth in this argument. But accepting this explanation at face value, we run the risk of overlooking the other side of the coin, the world of actual practice in the phenomenal world.[5] The final objective of Zen Buddhism is to realize the Supreme Way, the perfect enlightenment referred to in sutras as "unexcelled complete awakening."[6]

So long as that objective is not achieved, we cannot attain fundamental salvation. Underlying the conviction that zazen itself is both the practice and actualization of awakening is the faith that if we practice meditation with complete fervor, the Supreme Way will definitely reveal itself—that our essential nature will reveal itself in the world of phenomena. That revelation of the essential nature necessarily takes the form of clear realization at a particular point in time. As Dōgen Zenji said: "At this point my life's search has come to an end." "At this point" means "a particular instant in the flow of time." And "my life's search has come to an end" indicates the clear experience of self-realization.

PERSONALIZATION OF THE SUPREME WAY— THE PERFECTION OF CHARACTER

In the preceding section, I gave an overview of the meaning and content of the experience of seeing into one's own nature. Seeing into our own nature is an unmistakable, actual fact in our consciousness. Even though we say that in seeing into our own nature all knowledge is forgotten, we nevertheless definitely experience that world where all is forgotten. It is, however, not an ordinary experience by means of the senses. The seer suddenly sees the very nature of the seer without objectifying it, without filtering it through the medium of thought. He or she instantaneously and directly grasps it. This is characteristic of direct experience of Zen. Myriad individual differences exist in the depth and completeness of the experience, but when a qualified master confirms a person's experience of seeing into their own nature, they experience a world where self and other are the same and the world of dualistic opposition believed in until then is revealed to be a world of illusion.

Nevertheless I would be going too far if I said that from that point onward the mind would automatically act in direct response to what has been experienced, totally freed from distinctions of self and other. They may have realized that there is fundamentally no self and no other, but the emotions and delusions based on dualistic ideas are as stubbornly rooted as ever. The person realizes they are illusions but is still unable to do anything about them. Because their seeing of their nature was not thoroughgoing enough perhaps, vexations may even increase, and the intense practice that follows enlightenment begins.

To borrow a metaphor from the art of calligraphy, seeing your own nature can be likened to finally being able to distinguish between good and inferior brushwork. We may vary in our ability to judge, of course, but nonetheless we will have an eye for what is good and what isn't. Still, this doesn't mean that we are now able to write characters well. In order to become able to write calligraphy freely at will, a long period of devoted application is necessary. Nevertheless, until we can judge between good and bad brushwork in calligraphy, we lack a goal toward which we can direct our efforts. Otherwise, it would be like navigating without a compass, not knowing where we will end up. We must first, before anything else, install that compass.

One can understand therefore why Mahayana Zen Buddhism prioritizes the clear eye of seeing our own nature as an initial objective. It is very rare, while in the process of making the eye clear, to break through to complete clarity in one stroke. The opening of a thumb-size hole is above average, and generally the openings are no larger than a bean or grain of rice. Nevertheless, the fact that a hole has been made is decisive: no matter how small it may be, a hole is a hole and differs from a mere scratch on the surface. Once a person has seen into their own nature, no matter how shallow it is, seeing into one's own nature is seeing into one's own nature, and something decidedly different has appeared in that person's experience of life.

The first and clearest change is a deep sense of peace of mind. An ancient sage sang in praise of it: "To whom can I extend this fresh breeze on putting down the burden?" The subtle and wonderful feeling of release, the lightness of heart that follows seeing into one's own nature, truly defies description.

Next, the change appears in our understanding when we read Zen writings and listen to lectures on Dharma. Up to that point, we felt we partially understood the teachings, but something seemed out of focus, as if covered by a veil of cloud. Now the words are perfectly clear. In my own experience my new understanding was like a thin stream of crystal-clear water issuing into a muddy field. If these various changes fail to appear at all, it means that what was thought to be an experience of seeing into one's own nature was actually a temporary psychological aberration brought about in an excited state—in short, a type of delusion. It is the responsibility of the Zen master to distinguish between the two.

In koan practice, after we pass the first barrier of the initial koan, we are usually given further koans to work on in rapid succession as a means of gradually clarifying that new vision and widening the opening. When the inner eye opens completely and the division between the phenomenal world of everyday common sense and the essential world of enlightenment completely disappears, it is called perfect enlightenment. Actually the division between the phenomenal and the essential never existed, but as ordinary people we see the world only as the phenomenal world and are unaware of the essential.

As long as the mind doesn't act in accordance with what it has experienced in seeing into our own nature, what was seen will become mere knowledge and will fail to be integrated into our lives; it will fail to become our flesh and blood. No matter how wonderful the initial experience of seeing through the distinction of self and other, if we are still unable to live the life where self and other are one, then the awakening has not been personalized and our character will remain much as it was before the experience. If we cannot feel others' sadness as our own and rejoice in their good fortune, if we are unable to live the reality where self-gain and altruism are the same, then we have not embodied the world where self and other are one.

What is character, actually? Who do we refer to when we speak of a person of exceptional character? Until we are clear on this point, ethics, morals, and their objectives will also remain unclear. A person we feel to be of high character is not necessarily someone of high social standing, a great artist, or a wealthy person. Rather, we intuitively sense in that person an inner unity—the weaker a person's feeling of dualistic opposition, the more we feel him or her to be a person of character. We could define the word character as "the extent to which a person's essential nature is concretely realized in the phenomenal person." The essential nature is buddha nature, the Buddha's limitless, inexhaustible wisdom and virtue. The structure and appearance through which buddha nature reveals itself in the world is also limitless and inexhaustible. That which obscures the brilliance of our essential nature is called "illusion" in Buddhism, "sin" in Christianity, and "defilement" in Shintō. The distinction between self and other is the fundamental source of all three.

The world of oneness—where no distinction between self and other exists—is the true reality; it is our essential nature and we are instinctively aware of it, enlightened or not. Yet even after the experience of seeing into our own nature, illusions of dualistic opposition cling to us. How can we free ourselves of them? The best, simplest, and most direct way is to continue sitting meditation (zazen). If we go on practicing assiduously, our illusions will decrease of themselves and the marvelous virtue of buddha nature will reveal itself in us. This practice is what we call "personalization of the Supreme Way."

The above can also be applied to ethics and morality, for the final foundation and authority for both is buddha nature. Our essential nature is the ultimate authority for distinguishing between good and evil. Buddha nature is another name for the Buddhist precepts; the precepts are the mode in which buddha nature believes in, accepts, extols, and practices buddha nature itself. They are the marvelous form and function of buddha nature revealing itself on the plane of action.

The sixteen Buddhist precepts are divided into three classifications:

1. Three precepts of taking refuge in the Buddha, Dharma, and Sangha.
2. Three cumulative pure precepts (the three bodhisattva ideals): the commandment to keep the precepts, to practice good works, and to liberate all beings.
3. Ten grave precepts: against killing, stealing, misuse of sex, lying, dealing in intoxicants, speaking of another's faults, praising oneself and censuring others, begrudging the Dharma treasure, getting angry, and vilifying the Three Treasures.

The precepts manifest where belief and practice act as the norms. Their manifestation is an ascending, developmental process whereby the one buddha nature—the Buddha's wisdom and virtue—reveals itself, starting at the fundamental level of substance and ascending gradually to the more concrete levels of appearance and function. The precepts are a union of philosophy and ethics in a harmonious whole. If, for example, we think of buddha nature as the invisible life in a tree, we can see the first group of precepts as the roots, the second as the trunk, and the ten grave precepts as the leaves and branches.

We tend to think about precepts as concerned with forbidden actions or punishable practices, seeing them as something foisted upon us from outside. Actually they are the Supreme Way—a natural development of our essential nature. Looking at it in this way, we could say that "character" is the extent to which the sixteen Buddhist precepts have revealed themselves in an individual. The sum total of buddha nature is Zen; the marvelous virtues produced by our True Self are the precepts.

What I have said so far about the personalization of the Supreme Way is only half of what the topic actually encompasses. I will take up the most important aspect of personalization—namely, personalization of the Way from the viewpoint of Supreme Vehicle Zen, the highest form of Zen practice—in the ensuing chapters.

Types of Zen Practice 5

Zen practice can be divided into categories based on its purpose. During the Tang Dynasty in China the monk Keihō Shūmitsu Zenji (Ch. Kui Feng) gathered together the recorded sayings and verses of the Zen ancestors to compile the *Collected Discourses from the Wellspring of Zen* (*Zengen Shosenshū*). In his preface, he identifies five categories of Zen meditation, dividing them by aim. In this chapter we will examine three of them:

1. Ordinary Zen (*Bompu* Zen)
2. Mahayana or Great Vehicle Zen (*Daijō* Zen)
3. Supreme Vehicle Zen (*Saijōjō* Zen)

ORDINARY ZEN (*Bompu Zen*)

The Japanese word *bompu* means an ordinary person or common mortal and may at first seem disparaging. But bompu simply means someone who is neither a saint nor a great sinner, in other words, the average individual. Generally, people engaged in ordinary Zen will practice either counting or following the breath. Ordinary Zen contains no religious or philosophical elements. Shūmitsu Zenji describes it as "believing in the law of causation and practicing with joy in hardship." The person simply believes that by practicing Zen meditation some good effects or merit will accrue.

The objective of ordinary Zen is to increase happiness in the usual secular sense. The practice of meditation is beneficial for cultivating and focusing the mind. As the power of concentration develops, practitioners become increasingly free from the influences of their surroundings, and their powers of perception and decision-making become more incisive and accurate. As a result, they work more efficiently and make fewer errors in business or managerial interactions. In recent years in Japan, it has become the custom for businesses to send new employees to a Zen temple for a couple of days of practice as part of their general training.

If someone practices zazen correctly, character defects may be purified, resulting in a more balanced personality. Zazen is also good for the health. When the mind grows calmer, health improves and both body and spirit become sound; the practice may even prolong life.

We should never underestimate the value of ordinary Zen. Nevertheless, if we practice it without the goal of enlightenment, we will never solve with finality the problems of life nor accomplish our ultimate aim.

Mahayana or Great Vehicle Zen (*Daijō Zen*)

Mahayana Zen has enlightenment as its objective. Shūmitsu Zenji describes its aim: "To awaken to and practice the truth that self and things are both empty." Clear apprehension of the fact that both self and things are totally empty is the core of Mahayana Zen practice. Without it, there is no difference between Zen and philosophy.

Iida Tōin Roshi writes:

> Bodhidharma said, "Point directly to mind, see into the nature of things and achieve buddhahood." Without seeing into one's own nature there is no attainment of buddhahood and no Buddha Way. Seeing into our own nature (*kenshō*) is usually taken to mean seeing through to our buddha nature. But in actuality, "seeing (*ken*)" is "not-seeing," and "nature (*shō*)" is "no-nature." Seeing into one's own nature means to do away with all names and aspects and directly attain to body and mind falling away (*shinjin datsuraku*). Would what we call "seeing into one's own nature" today ever receive Bodhidharma's seal of approval? I have my doubts.
>
> Why do I say this? Because these experiences of seeing into one's own nature often lack the suddenness connoted by the phrase, *kachi ichige*. This phrase indicates a startled cry at something unexpected . . . It is the word used to express the instant when body and mind have fallen away and you have totally forgotten yourself. It is not merely the sound. It is the

state of one who has reached true enlightenment where neither words nor concepts are of any use in describing it. It is Shakyamuni Buddha's "In forty-nine years I have not preached a single word," uttered on his deathbed. It is a sincere student of a master with a great bodhisattva spirit practicing just sitting or a koan with pure concentration and reaching the point where, by some chance circumstance, all concepts and delusions are cut off, and mind and body fall away. In other words, it is a true moment of sudden awakening.

Tōin Roshi goes on to offer examples of such a moment:

> There was Rei'un who, after thirty years of assiduous practice, happened one day to glance at peach blossoms and cried out, "Having reached this point there is nothing left to doubt!" Isan confirmed his realization saying, "Those who begin practice due to karmic causations are slow to give up." There was also Chōkei who wore out seven cushions in continuous sitting over twenty-seven years until one day he cried out, "Wonder of wonders! If one but rolls up the blinds and sees the world laid out before him!" Or Shakyamuni himself, who after six years of practice came to enlightenment on the eighth day of the twelfth month when he happened to look up at the planet Venus. . . .
>   Or, again, recall the story of Gensha who took leave of Seppō to cross over the mountains. On the way, he happened to stub his toe on a stone. At the sight of the blood and the rush of pain, he cried out, "This body does not exist! Where does the pain come from?" Kōsankoku saw through the koan, "What do I have to hide from you?" when he smelled the fragrance of the sweet osmanthus blossoms. Batsudabara attained "meditative absorption in water" when he entered the tub to bathe. There is also the case of Hakuin Zenji who came to realization when someone hit him on the head during his begging rounds. Dregs of delusion remained, however, and it was not until one night in his forty-second year that he happened to hear the sound of a cricket. This experience

completely wiped away any remaining traces of delusion and brought him at last to perfect enlightenment. . . . Bukkō Zenji practiced with the koan Mu for six years until one night he happened to hear the sound of the *han* (the wooden board struck to summon monks to an assembly) and attained the great death. On the spot he composed the following verse:

> A single blow has pulverized the core of the spirit.
> The iron face of Nata[7] juts forth.
> My ears are as if deaf, my mouth dumb.
> Touch it and sparks will fly. . . .

These are all examples of the instant of great enlightenment. *If the thousand buddhas and ten-thousand Zen ancestors had not encountered this moment, no one would have attained buddhahood or become a true founding ancestor.* [Emphasis mine.]

To deny the experience of seeing into one's own nature or to say that the experience of sudden enlightenment is unnecessary is like a person who has never tasted sugar denying that sugar is sweet.

Supreme Vehicle Zen (*Saijōjō Zen*)

Shūmitsu Zenji describes Supreme Vehicle Zen as follows: "If we suddenly realize that self-nature is from the beginning pure and without stain, that delusive passions do not exist, that we have always been endowed with the fullness of wisdom, that this mind is Buddha and that after all we are not different from this, and we practice accordingly, this is Supreme Vehicle Zen."

In his instruction, "suddenly realize" comes prior to practice, but the correct order should be believe, understand, practice, realize, and "enter" or personalize our realization. We believe and understand intellectually that self-nature is pure and without stain, that delusive passions do not exist, that we are endowed with the fullness of wisdom, and that this mind is Buddha. Actually practicing meditation, with this belief and understanding as its basis, we verify that understanding through experience and continue practicing to personalize it; this is Supreme Vehicle Zen.

Mahayana Zen teaches that even delusions are nothing other than the wisdom of awakening, life and death are nirvana, and the delusive world itself is the Lotus Land. First, having recognized delusion, life-and-death, and the phenomenal world as aspects of a limited, relative universe, we clearly realize when we see into our own nature that all of these are none other than the wisdom of awakening, nirvana, and the land of quiet light. The standpoint of Mahayana Zen is that infinite, absolute reality wears the clothes of limitation and relativity. Supreme Vehicle Zen, however, simply confronts us with the essential world where "all beings are intrinsically awake" and admits no other expedients. Having arrived at this point, there is no acknowledgment of delusive passions, and thus no preaching of any need to seek the wisdom of awakening. Since there is no recognition of life and death, there are no exhortations to seek nirvana. Since there is no world of delusion, there is no urging to seek the land of quiet light. We simply believe and understand the infinite and absolute truth: that we are intrinsically awake. Then we practice this, wake up, embody the experience, and live it. From this perspective, zazen itself is both the reality and the realization of enlightenment. To believe, understand, practice, realize, and personalize this is Supreme Vehicle Zen. Dōgen Zenji brought Supreme Vehicle Zen to prominence and urged its practice.

Supreme Vehicle Zen is the highest form of Zen practice and could be defined as "meditation that transcends the world of awakening and distinctions between enlightened and unenlightened." While Mahayana Zen has self-realization as its immediate goal, Zen at this highest level is zazen such that sitting itself is the actualization and practice of enlightenment. We could define Mahayana Zen as being Rinzai in character, as opposed to the Sōtō aspect of Zen. In modern Japan, the instruction in Rinzai Zen, which holds up self-realization as the goal of meditation, is characterized by the use of koans. The Sōtō Zen sect, which emphasizes meditation as the total expression of the Buddha Way, singles out the practice of "just sitting" as the authentic way of Zen.

This division does not in any way imply that the two types of Zen are incompatible with each other. On the contrary, like the two sides of one sheet of paper, they exist in an extremely intimate, indivisible symbiosis.

When one is uppermost the other necessarily backs it, because the two remain in a relationship of mutual existence. Just as when the back of the hand is uppermost, the palm is below it, and vice versa, so when Mahayana Zen comes to the fore, Supreme Vehicle Zen is always in the background, and if Supreme Vehicle Zen is to the fore, Mahayana Zen always backs it. The more important side of the actualization of the Supreme Way is precisely the fact that the practice of just sitting that the Sōtō sect advocates is itself the actualization of the Supreme Way. As I have said before, whether enlightened or not "all beings are intrinsically Buddha." So from the essential point of view they are living exactly the same life as Shakyamuni Buddha. The only difference is that we don't recognize the essential nature in the visible world of everyday life due to the appearance of dualistic distinctions from the opposition between subject and object. Wrong views[8] are like a vapor covering the transparent surface of a crystal: they cloud our essential nature, which is completely clear from the beginning.

When we earnestly practice true zazen, however, these wrong views don't stir one bit, and the entirety of our essential nature is revealed. In this sense, just sitting is the purest form of meditation, a single great path for both beginner and perfectly enlightened alike. Although seeing into one's own nature is not stated as the immediate goal in Supreme Way Zen, when a practitioner penetrates to the heart of just sitting, it is necessarily accompanied by seeing into one's own nature.

Whether a person has been practicing zazen for thirty years or for one day, there is not the slightest distinction between him or her and Shakyamuni Buddha, Amida, Manjushri, or Bodhidharma. As Dōgen Zenji says: "A beginner's meditation is the complete expression of perfect enlightenment. This is called 'personalization of the Supreme Way.'"

The personalization of the Supreme Way discussed in the last chapter looked at practice from the perspective of the phenomenal world.[9] The personalization of the Supreme Way I discuss here is from the perspective of the essential world,[10] where no distinctions exist. In other words, when anyone, anywhere, at any time engages in just sitting, it is the complete and perfect expression of the Supreme Way. The value of Zen meditation is absolute, not relative, and that is why the above statement is true. It is for this reason that it is called Supreme Way Zen—it is the highest and most perfect Zen.

In the "Bendōwa" chapter of the Shōbōgenzō, Dōgen Zenji describes the sublime scenery of the personalization of the Supreme Way, employing language of solemn profundity to describe it. There are probably no words anywhere else that praise the merit of Zen meditation with such eloquence.

> According to the authentic doctrine of our sect, this personally and directly transmitted Buddhadharma is the highest of the high: from the very beginning when you come to see the master it is not necessary to burn incense, make prostrations, pray to the Buddha, practice penance, or study sutras; just sit and let body and mind fall away.
>
> If even for a short time one sits erect in meditative absorption and impresses the buddha seal upon the three sources of karma—physical, verbal, and mental actions—everything in the world of things will become the buddha seal and all space will become enlightenment. Consequently, all the buddhas who have thus come will experience an increase in the joy they take in the Dharma of the original ground, and the sublimity of their enlightenment to the Way will be renewed. Moreover, all beings in the worlds in all directions—in the three bad destinies and six karmic pathways—will become altogether and simultaneously clear and pure of body and mind.
>
> . . .
>
> At this very moment, the lands of the earth in all directions with their grasses and trees, as well as the walls and fences with their tiles and pebbles, are seen to be performing the Buddha's work. Those who consequently make use of storms and floods as they arise in the world are benefited by the wonderful and incomprehensible activity of the Buddha, and will manifest realization, which lies close at hand. And because those who accept and use these floods and firestorms are benefited by the saving activity of essential realization, those who live with and speak to them join them in possessing limitless buddha virtues, and work to cause the limitless, unceasing, incomprehensible, and immeasurable Buddhadharma to roll forth widely, everywhere without exception, inside and outside of the universe.
>
> . . .

You must know that even if the innumerable buddhas in all directions should try to fathom the virtue of a single person's zazen, encouraging each other and using their buddha wisdom, they would not be able to even come close.

Although Rinzai Zen makes seeing into one's own nature the immediate goal of practice, the practice of meditation does continue after seeing into one's own nature in that tradition as well. In both Rinzai and Sōtō Zen, teachers take up the practice of just sitting after great enlightenment and instruct their students to do likewise.

The teacher of Harada Sogaku Roshi, Toyoda Dokutan Roshi—who was said to have been particularly outstanding among a number of fine Rinzai masters in the Meiji Period—possessed a keen enlightened vision and a well-mellowed character. Toyoda Roshi usually urged students who had finished formal koan training to practice just sitting. Although a person may have attained great enlightenment, a clear Dharma eye alone doesn't make a person mature in character and able to act freely from the depths of enlightenment. Real practice begins after great enlightenment. Depending on one's effort, it is possible to bring the enlightened eye to perfect clarity in a single lifetime.

But to make that enlightenment one's very flesh and blood, the process of fusing with it until it becomes our daily life—the process known as "the absolute perfection of character"—is never-ending. It could hardly be accomplished in three or four lifetimes, much less in one. Shakyamuni Buddha's enlightenment came after eons of practice, and his practice is said still to be going on.

As the "Buddha of Innocent Truth," our true nature is perfectly pure and without stain; with continued polishing, it can become infinitely more beautiful. Yet looking at human nature from the phenomenal side, no matter how much we grind away at our delusions, dregs will always remain, for we are truly full of faults. Regardless of the perspective, whether polishing a single pearl or cleaning the endless dregs of delusion, just sitting is the finest, most effective, and simplest means for accomplishing the task.

Koan Practice and Just Sitting 6

In the preceding section I touched on the subject of Mahayana Zen and Supreme Vehicle Zen and mentioned how in modern Japanese Zen, the Rinzai sect emphasizes Mahayana Zen in contrast to the Sōtō sect's emphasis on Supreme Vehicle Zen. The two sects also differ when it comes to practice: the characteristic practice of Rinzai is the study of koans, while in the Sōtō sect it is just sitting. In former times, just sitting was called "silent illumination" Zen,[11] while koan practice was called Zen that "sees through words,"[12] and the two were set up as opposites. The two types of practice therefore have their own lineages and have sometimes criticized one another. But whether the practice is just sitting or working on koans, the final aim is always to reach a true Zen experience.

KOAN STUDY—ZEN THAT SEES THROUGH WORDS

Historical background

Koan study has its origin in the great realization of Shakyamuni Buddha. A number of koans in the Zen records such as the *Gateless Gate*, *Blue Cliff Record*, and the *Book of Equanimity* are based on the Buddha's enlightenment. The content of Shakyamuni Buddha's great seeing into his own nature preserved its true life through twenty-eight generations of masters in India, before Bodhidharma transmitted it to China.

It was not until the time of the Sixth Zen Ancestor in China, Enō (Hui-neng), that the Zen path truly emerged. After transmission through the two masters Nangaku Ejō and Seigen Gyōshi, the Zen tradition split into five schools and seven sects. Along with these developments, there began to be an increase both in the quantity and quality of Zen koans, and they were put in systematic order. In one sense, Zen history could be called the history of the koan, and by tracing the evolution of the koan we can see Zen's internal process of deepening.

Many people mistakenly believe that Dōgen Zenji, who advocated just sitting under all circumstances, maintained a disinterest in koans for his sect; this is wrong. Dōgen himself compiled and wrote a preface to the compendium *300 Ancient Koans* in 1235 CE, when he was thirty-six years old. In addition, he frequently cites koans throughout the ninety-five chapters of his *Shōbōgenzō*.

The significance of the koan

What is a koan? In his work "Evening Talks from a Mountain Hermitage," Chūhō Oshō from Temmoku-san monastery asks: "Why is that which the buddhas and ancestors used at the right time known as 'koan'?" To which he gives the following answer:

> A *kōan* (literally, "public record") can be compared to a public document from the central government. Whether the royal way will lead to order or strife depends on the presence of the law. "Public" (*kō*) refers to the ultimate principle whereby saints and sages make their actions one, and whereby all under heaven follow the same road. "Record" (*an*) is the official document that records how saints and sages carry out that principle. There has never yet been a country without a government. There has never yet been a central government without recorded laws. Laws are used when one desires to judge what is unjust in the country.

The original meaning of the word *kōan* was "a directive from the state." Just as the state or a public body sets up regulations and rules as standard for conduct, the Zen koan acts as the standard for judging the authenticity and depth of Zen insight.

The essence of the koan: its seeming irrationality

The expression *Zen mondo* refers to an exchange of questions and answers between two or more Zen practitioners, often taking place in the context of a Zen koan. The term was used traditionally in Japan as a synonym for something difficult to understand, where the exact meaning seems impossible to figure out. Zen uses terms like "unintelligible," "ungraspable," "no trace to be found," and "no news," all of which point to the difficulty of using common sense to understand the koan.

Attempting to understand the incomprehensible is like diving into water to grab the clouds. Yet, in spite of the koan's stubborn resistance to intellectualizing, I will nevertheless try to offer an intellectual understanding of the koan.

The term "the phenomenal" in Tōzan's (Dongshan) *Five Modes of the Essential and the Phenomenal* refers to all phenomena. Buddhist scriptures refer to this as "being," "difference," "phenomena," "things," "figures," or "karma." In other words, the phenomenal is everything we can apprehend with our senses—the realm where we experience dualistic opposition between subject and object. It is usually the only world that we know. Our common sense is common sense within this world; our logic is logic within this world.

However, phenomena are only one side of reality. The other side— that of the essential world—is called "the essential." Buddhist scriptures distinguish between the phenomenal and the essential and speak of "being" in opposition to "non-being," "difference" in opposition to "sameness," "phenomena" in opposition to "emptiness," "things" in opposition to "principles," "figures" in opposition to "substance," and "cause and effect" in opposition to "void nature." This language may imply that the phenomenal and the essential, or phenomena and emptiness, refer to two different things, but they are actually one and the same. It is simply a matter of looking at a single reality from two different perspectives, and seeing two distinct aspects of it. For convenience's sake we divide this single reality into the two aspects of the essential and the phenomenal.

The world of the essential, the essence of phenomena, is unknown to ordinary unenlightened people, who can't even imagine that another aspect of things exists. Accordingly, they cannot grasp the essential world with the logic or thought commonly used to understand the phenomenal world. The world of essence is not merely an "illusory flower,"[13] nor is it a product of the intellect; it really exists. But that world can only be apprehended in the living experience that Zen calls enlightenment.

Koans always deal with the essential world. It is the essential world that makes the koan what it is: without it the koan wouldn't exist as a koan. The essential world—represented by ⊖—is completely empty and contains limitless potential. The actual world, the world of true fact, can be expressed as a fraction. Let the numerator α be the phenomenal—that is, anything in the phenomenal world. Let the denominator be the essential ⊖—that is, the essential world. However, α and ⊖ are not two separate things but are one from the beginning. We could say that α is the other side of ⊖ and vice versa. The *Heart Sutra* expresses this when it states, "Form is none other than emptiness, emptiness none other than form. Form is exactly emptiness, emptiness exactly form."

The common sense, logic, and thought that give order to the phenomenal world are useless in the essential world. We could even say that in the world of ⊖ there is no consciousness, no theory, no logic. But the world of $\alpha/\ominus$—the world of the actual, the true fact—differs radically from the world of simply α. For example, the world of α operates according to the principles "one is not two" or "two is larger than one." But in the world of $\alpha/\ominus$, "one is everything, everything is one." Thus it is said: "In one there are many kinds; in two there are not two." Although this is incomprehensible to common sense in the world of α, once we clearly experience the world of $\alpha/\ominus$, the incomprehensible appears as fact—completely natural and not in the least mysterious.

This is what people, as they pretend to understand Zen, may call "Zen reason beyond all reasoning," "understanding beyond understanding," "inexpressible," or "not setting up words." But "inexpressible" and "not setting up words" express the unshakable fact of the world of ⊖, as well as that of $\alpha/\ominus$. It is not a verbal maneuver to do away with a reality that is inexplicable through common sense. Conversely, when we truly understand a koan, it is proof that we have grasped that essential world. It is for this reason that the koan exists as a "public record," the standard for determining the authenticity and depth of a practitioner's insight.

Once we grasp this essential world it will be "like a dragon gaining the water," or "like a tiger roaming in the mountains." We will be able to cut right through a hundred koans or a thousand koans like a master chef slicing through tofu with a razor-sharp knife. The ancients said the same: "Pass one barrier and you pass a thousand or ten thousand at the same time." This is the "authentic view" of which Rinzai Zenji spoke.

Koans in the Sōtō sect

For a true Zen experience, an experience of the essential world is key, and the essential world is itself a koan. In the Sōtō sect in particular, this is what is predominantly meant when one speaks of a koan. In his book *Essentials of Zen*, Arai Sekizen Roshi states:

> In our Sōtō sect in particular, the koan that our illustrious founder Dōgen Zenji spoke of should be taken as another name for Buddhism, or the Way of the Zen ancestors. When Shakyamuni speaks of the Great Perfection of Wisdom or the Lotus of the Wonderful Law it is precisely a koan. When he speaks of the emptiness of the five aggregates or the true aspect of all phenomena, this is also a koan. When Bodhidharma said, "vast emptiness; nothing sacred," and when Sōkei said, "not one thing from the beginning," was this any different than a koan? This is Buddhism, the Way of the Zen ancestors. All of Buddha's disciples must take this Dharma principle to heart; it is a problem which they must work on and practice.

Dōgen Zenji's *Recommending Zazen to All People (Fukan Zazengi)* has the line: "The koan manifests (*koan genjō*); it has not been caught in the net and put in the basket." The "net" and "basket" are the delusive thinking that robs us of true freedom. This passage implies that when we practice meditation correctly, there is no way that concepts and delusions can enter into consciousness.

In his "Warnings on Zen Practice," Taiso Daishi (Keizan Zenji) instructs us:

> When in the midst of not thinking you reveal the ultimate meaning, then your vision is none other than the koan itself. When in the midst of not striving you achieve realization, then the koan is none other than your own vision.

Harada Sogaku Roshi writes in his *Discourse on Recommending Zazen to All People*:

Although we speak of koans, they are none other than Buddhism itself. We also say "true aspect," "suchness," "the original face," "the true Dharma," "the Three Treasures," "the subtle law," and so forth, to refer to the same thing. In other words, the word "Buddhadharma" is a koan. In short, "the true reality of the universe," "the treasury of the true Dharma eye," "the subtle mind of nirvana": these are all koans.

I have used the fraction $\alpha/\ominus$ to symbolically illustrate the manifest koan (genjō koan). Everything in the phenomenal world is the total expression and realization of the essential world. As I have already stated, $\ominus$ is our True Self, which is empty and contains limitless capabilities; it is the essential world. When we see this clearly, then each thing is the complete and perfect expression of our True Self and of the ultimate truth of the universe. Sun, moon, stars, every tree and blade of grass, and every action, large and subtle—there isn't one of these that is not a complete revelation of the scenery of the essential world.

However, if we lack an understanding of the world of $\ominus$, and take only the aspect of the phenomenal world to be the manifest koan, thinking it to be some special form of Zen preached by Dōgen Zenji, and present this to people who become convinced of it, that would be highly misleading.

Koans in the Rinzai sect

On the subject of the koan in the Rinzai sect, Harada Roshi says that koans should be properly known as "old case" (kosoku) koans. Although there is no actual error in referring to the koans in the Gateless Gate, the Blue Cliff Record, or the 1,700 classical koans as simply "koans" (since they all show the Buddhadharma), it is more accurate to refer to them as old case koans. When we say that these koans are an expression of the Buddhadharma, it means that all of them deal with the essential world.

Koan study in modern Rinzai Zen usually begins with Jōshū's "Mu" or Hakuin's "The Sound of One Hand." These koans help the student break through the initial barrier—that is, to see into one's own nature and gain a glimpse of the essential world. After a student has seen into their own nature, the teacher assigns them a series of koans to work on in subsequent practice. The essential world grows ever clearer with the process of passing each koan, while the insight of seeing into one's own nature gradually becomes the student's flesh and blood. As insight deepens, the student develops greater alertness and is able to respond more skillfully to the problems of daily life. In order to make this subsequent practice as effective as possible, in the Rinzai sect koans have been organized into a fixed order that students are encouraged to follow. Hakuin Zenji, the ancestor who revived Japanese Rinzai Zen, originally developed this system, which has greatly influenced Zen in modern Japan.

Any koan system presupposes the existence of different types of koans. Asahina Sōgen Roshi explains this in detail in the third chapter of the third volume of his series of monographs entitled *Zen*,[14] which I will now summarize.

THE CLASSIFICATION OF KOANS

Strictly speaking, a koan doesn't lend itself to classification. Superficially, koans seem to be myriad in variety, but when deeply understood they all prove to express the same world of awakening. Nevertheless, koans have long been categorized in various ways according to their characteristics. The special character of these classifications is their division of koans according to level of practice. It might seem illogical to give a ranking order to Zen experiences, which presuppose a direct leap onto the ground of the Buddha. Actually, though, an indispensible part of practice is the necessary pulling of the student upward, step by step, and it was experience in guiding students through koan practice that led to this graduated system. The classifications of koans included both a three-way classification and a five-way classification.

Three-way classification

National Teacher Shōichi was the first teacher in Japan to make use of the following three-way classification of koans:

1. koans that teach through principle (*richi*)
2. koans that teach through devices (*kikan*)
3. koans that are directed upward (*kōjō*)

Richi means "principle." Koans that teach through principle use words and phrases that concern the principles set forth in sutras and the writings of Zen ancestors, such as "Buddha," "buddha nature," "dharma body," and "the ultimate truth of Buddhism."

The *ki* in the word *kikan* means "activity," whereas *kan* means "setting up a barrier," "closing the door," or "sliding the bolt shut." The Zen ancestors' freedom of activity arose out of the world of awakening and found expression in words and actions that went beyond the reach of common sense. Koans that teach through devices clearly illustrate the difference between the world of awakening and the world of everyday thought, and when they penetrate a student's mind they may throw him or her into the ravine of "great doubt." If the student is able to burst through those doubts, he or she will gain the enlightened eye. In this sense, we could say that koans that teach through devices are more advanced than koans that teach through principle. Most of the koans that the Zen ancestors have left to us fall within this category.

"Directed upward" refers to the process wherein the practitioner who has attained enlightenment endlessly continues to practice in order to personalize the experience and to wipe away the last dregs from it. The goal here is to become a truly free person, no longer slave to anything. Teachers gave the utterances and verses that flowed out of that state of consciousness to students as koans to be thoroughly savored. These "upward" koans also have a counterpoint in koans that are directed "downward" (*kōge*), which refer to the world of phenomena and differentiation. What is downward, the phenomenal world that appears clearly and distinctly before our eyes, is of one reality with what is upward: one but two, two but one.

The *Recorded Sayings of National Teacher Shōichi* (*Shōichi Goroku*) contains the following passage:

> The buddhas and Zen ancestors produced them: principle, devices, directed upward, and directed downward. In fact, the ultimate truth of the buddhas and ancestors transcends the barrier of subtle activity. Know that you must see through to the ultimate principle of the Buddha, and master the briars and thorns. Recognize that you must pass the barrier of subtle activity to overcome the silver mountains and iron walls. Then and only then will you have arrived at the essence.

The *Dharma Words of National Teacher Daiō* (*Daiō Kokushi Hōgo*) explains the meaning of principle, devices, and upward:

> In this sect there are three types of meaning. They are principle, devices, and directed upward. The first category, principle, includes the principles and words that represent the buddhas' preaching and the "heart nature" revealed by the ancestors. The next category, devices, is where the buddhas and ancestors, acting out of true mercy, twisted noses or blinked their eyes, uttered phrases such as "in the midst of mud, flying in the sky" or "the stone horse enters the water." The final category, directed upward, refers to the direct teachings of the buddhas and ancestors, the true aspect of the myriad things—the aspect where the sky is the sky, the earth is the earth, mountains are mountains, and rivers are rivers. The eyes are horizontal and the nose is vertical.

The following passage from National Teacher Musō Sōseki's *Dialogues in a Dream* (*Muchū Mondō*) clearly explains the relationship between teaching through principle and teaching through devices. Perhaps because *Dialogues in a Dream* was written for an audience of lay disciples, he doesn't mention the expression "directed upward." Please savor this passage:

> *Question*: What do the expressions "teaching through principle" and "teaching through devices" mean?
>
> *Answer*: If one is speaking from the standpoint of Original Nature there is nothing to refer to as "teaching through principle" or "teaching through devices." However, when utilizing expedient means to raise up the fundamental truth, the expression "teaching through principle" is applied to those methods that employ reason as a way to encourage students, while the expression "teaching through devices" is applied to those methods that do not employ reason, that is, methods such as the stick, the shout, and the koan. In either case these are no more than expedients, like calling Little Jade.
>
> An ancient master said,

Prior to Baso and Hyakujō, many teachers utilized the "teaching through principle" approach and few used the "teaching through devices" approach. Subsequent to Baso and Hyakujō, many teachers utilized the "teaching through devices" approach and few used the "teaching through principle" approach. In so doing, their policy was to "watch the wind and set the sails accordingly."

Present-day students who like teaching through principle tend to dislike teaching through devices, and those who like teaching through devices tend to dislike teaching through principle. Neither type of student understands the methods of the founding masters. If you say that teaching through devices is the superior method, would you then say that all of the masters prior to Baso and Hyakujō lacked the Zen eye? If you say that teaching through principle is superior, would you say that Rinzai and Tōzan did not know the true meaning of Zen?[15]

Five-way classification

Hakuin and his successors used the following five-way classification:

1. Dharma body koans (*hosshin*)
2. Koans that teach through devices (*kikan*)
3. Koans that clarify with words (*gonsen*)
4. Koans that are difficult to pass (*nantō*)
5. Koans of the five modes and ten grave precepts (*go-i jūjūkin*)

The five-way classification of koans broadly practiced by Hakuin's followers is the same, in respect to their goals and order of classification, as the above three-way classification, but the expansion of the original three-way classification increased its exactness. In addition, Hakuin's adoption of Tōzan Daishi's *Five Modes of the Essential and the Phenomenal* as koans, and his inclusion of the ten grave precepts from the *Brahmajala Sutra*, made his koan system even more comprehensive.

While Harada Roshi praised Hakuin Zenji's broad vision, he called his failure to include the three precepts of taking refuge, or "threefold return,"[16] and the three cumulative pure precepts[17] a case of "plowing a field and forgetting the seed." Moreover, Hakuin Zenji takes up only the five modes of the essential and the phenomenal, and completely overlooks the five modes of merit and honor, which are front-to-back with the former. Shouldn't this, too, be called "forgetting the seed"?

Dharma body koans

The ancients explained the "Dharma body" to be "the Dharma that forms the body." The Dharma body is also referred to as "true suchness," "as it really is," "Dharma nature," "buddha nature," "awakening," or "nirvana"; it is the true reality of the universe, one's True Self, one's own "master" who sees, hears, senses, and thinks.

Dharma body koans make this matter clear. The Dharma body is the very basis of enlightenment. By clarifying the Dharma body, the Zen student clarifies the True Self, clarifies the universe, is freed from life and death, and gains great peace. Koans that teach through principle, koans that teach through devices, koans that are directed upward, and all the other koans have no other purpose than to clarify the Dharma body, and once rooted in the Dharma body, to realize the activity of perfect freedom. All koans necessarily return to the point of origin; all koans begin in the essential world, the world of ☯, and return to it.

The following are examples of Dharma body koans:

> A monk asked Jōshū in all earnestness, "Does a dog have buddha nature or not?"
> Jōshū said, "*Mu!* (No!)"

> Hakuin said, "We know the sound of two hands clapping. What is the sound of one hand?"

> A monk asked Tōzan, in all earnestness, "What is Buddha?"
> Tōzan replied, "Three pounds of flax."

> Taibai asked Baso, in all earnestness, "What is Buddha?"
> Baso replied, "The very mind is Buddha."

> A monk asked Baso, in all earnestness, "What is Buddha?"
> Baso replied, "No mind, no Buddha."

These are all examples of fundamental koans. The first two are known respectively as "Mu" and "The Sound of One Hand." The following koans examine the world of the Dharma body in more detail:

> There is not a hairsbreadth separating the boundless universe and the ground of your own self; in the ten generations from then until now, from beginning to end, there has been no departure from this understanding.

> A monk asked Dairyū, "When the body of form disintegrates, where is the indestructible Dharma body?"
> Dairyū answered, "The mountain flowers bloom like brocade; the water wells up blue as indigo."

> On Mt. Godai a cloud is cooking rice; before an old Buddhist shrine a dog is pissing toward heaven.

Although there are endless koans of this sort, if we truly pass the koan "Mu" or "The Sound of One Hand," or any other single koan, then we should be able to understand all other koans. The koans "Mu" and "The Sound of One Hand" also include detailed checking questions[18] that are used as follow-up after an initial realization experience. These are "Dharma tools" used to bring the student to an understanding of both the dharma body's basis and its activity.

Koans that teach through devices

The explanation of koans that teach through devices is generally the same as it was in the three-way classification, where koans that teach through devices and koans that teach through principle were understood to be two aspects of the same experience. In the five-way classification, however, "koans that teach through devices" refers to koans intended to further clarify the world of the Dharma body that has already been made apparent through koans that teach through principle, and to induce the free and unhesitating activity that stems from it. Koans that teach through devices are therefore distinguished from koans that teach through principle in that they are one level more advanced. The Zen practitioner is freed from the tendency to fall into "views of equality" or to stop at a passive view of the universe by working on koans that teach through devices.

If the student's practice does not reach the stage of skillfully handling the troubles of the phenomenal world with magnanimous action, then the practice of meditation is not useful in daily life. An endless number of koans that teach through devices and the greater part of the ancestral koans fall into this category:

> In response to Rinzai's question, "What is the fundamental truth of Buddhism?" Ōbaku gave him sixty blows.

The *Record of Rinzai* (*Rinzai-roku*) is filled with koans that teach through devices such as this. The greater number of koans that appear in Zen collections like the *Gateless Gate, Blue Cliff Record,* and the *Book of Equanimity* also fall into this category. Since there are too many to list in full, I will cite just one more:

> Case 62 of *Blue Cliff Record*
> Unmon addressed the assembly, saying, "Within heaven and earth, throughout space and time, there is a jewel hidden in the mountain of form. Pick up a lamp and go into the Buddha hall, take the triple gate and put it on the lamp."

Koans that clarify with words

"To clarify with words" means to make use of words and phrases to express the fundamental truth. Some may think that Zen dislikes words, as implied by expressions like "cut off words"[19] or "do not set up letters,"[20] but many outstanding Zen adepts have expressed their state of consciousness in words and have used a single word or phrase to cut off delusions in their students. The real problem with words is the concepts and thoughts that stick to and become entangled with them.

It's said that light actually danced around Jōshū's lips when he spoke. Let's look at several cases and thereby appreciate Jōshū's "Zen of lips and tongue":

Case 7 of *Gateless Gate*
A monk asked Jōshū in all earnestness, "I have just entered this monastery. I beg you, Master, please give me instructions."
Jōshū asked, "Have you eaten your rice gruel yet?"
"Yes, I have," answered the monk.
Jōshū said, "Then wash your bowls."
The monk attained some realization.

Case 9 of *Blue Cliff Record*
A monk asked Jōshū, "What is Jōshū?"
Jōshū answered, "East gate, west gate, south gate, north gate."

Case 58 of *Blue Cliff Record*
A monk asked Jōshū, "Isn't the saying 'The Ultimate Way has no difficulties; just avoid picking and choosing' a pitfall for people of these times?"
Jōshū said, "Once someone asked me that. I am sorry that even after five years I still can't give an answer."

Next, let's look at Unmon, who stands out among the founders of the five schools of Chinese Zen due to his remarkable use of words in teaching. In *Gateway to the Essentials of Meticulous Practice in the Five Zen Schools*, the Japanese master Tōrei Zenji says of Unmon, "The Unmon sect has its principle in the selection of words and phrases to deal with the relative degree of closeness and distance, intimacy and estrangement." Here are some examples from the *Blue Cliff Record*:

Case 6 of *Blue Cliff Record*
Unmon said, "I don't ask about before the fifteenth day, try to say something about after the fifteenth day."
Unmon himself answered for everyone, "Every day is a good day."

Case 47 of *Blue Cliff Record*
A monk asked Unmon, "What is the Dharma body?"
Unmon said, "The Six cannot gather it up."

Case 60 of *Blue Cliff Record*
Unmon showed his staff to the assembly and said, "This staff has changed into a dragon and swallowed the entire universe. Mountains, rivers, the great earth: where are they to be found?"

Case 83 of *Blue Cliff Record*
Unmon, teaching the assembly, said, "The ancient Buddha and the pillar merge. What level of mental activity is this?" He himself answered on their behalf, "On South Mountain clouds gather; on North Mountain rain falls."

There are almost endless examples of such koans; every word, every phrase could be called an example of a koan that clarifies with words. It has been said since ancient times that one of Unmon's phrases contains three phrases. The chapter on Unmon's disciple Tokusan Enmitsu in *Collected Biographies of Zen Masters (Gotō-Egen)* provides an explanation of the "three phrases":

He addressed the assembled monks saying, "I have three phrases which I will reveal to all of you. One phrase is 'totally covering the universe'; another phrase is 'cutting off the myriad streams'; and the third phrase is 'wave following upon wave'."

"Totally covering the universe"[21] means that the Zen master's response to the student's question is like a box made by master craftsmen such that the box and the lid fit together so perfectly that not a drop of water can seep in: the master's reply matches the question exactly. The second phrase, "cutting off myriad streams,"[22] refers to a Zen master's utterance that severs the student's delusions. The final phrase, "wave following upon wave,"[23] refers to the master's ability to respond immediately and appropriately to a student's aspiration, using a single word or phrase to teach the Dharma, just as a large wave is always followed by a smaller one without the slightest gap.

To be able to use even one of these responses is no easy task, but a single word or saying from Unmon contained the activity of all three.

Imagine how highly Unmon's utterances have been valued. Please appreciate that any one of them contains the activity of all three phrases.

Koans that are difficult to pass

These koans are called "difficult to pass," but the difficulty of a koan actually lies with the student, not with the koan: a koan may be easy for one person and difficult for another, and vice versa. Therefore it is inappropriate to objectively decide a particular koan is difficult to pass. But the practice in the Hakuin lineage of classifying certain koans as difficult has certain merit. Once we have reached a certain level of realization, we tend to become satisfied with our attainment and lose our eagerness to persist along the path. Yet, in reality, there is no place on the path of meditation where we can say, "This is far enough." As the phrase "The blue sky, too, must be beaten" points out, the dust of delusion clings everywhere; even when we think we have cleansed ourselves of it thoroughly, we find there is still plenty left. Zen history is filled with examples of people who stopped part-way in their practice. Besides not finally tasting the Dharma peace of the great freedom, these people lack the power to save others. The koans that are difficult to pass are a warning blow, a signal that there are still mountains to climb.

At first reading, the reader will probably find these koans that are difficult to pass extremely difficult. While undoubtedly they are challenging, they serve the important function of wiping away all concepts and thoughts from the experience of awakening. As may be expected in koan work in the Rinzai sect, its standard "ancestral Zen" has been polished to perfection. These koans have the ability to bring forth the vigorous activity of the human being, pure and undefiled, totally freed of opinions about Buddha or Dharma—to say nothing of dualisms such as self and other, deluded and enlightened, ordinary and holy.

Look at this verse, for example:

> The wind blows in the azure sky,
> and the floating clouds disappear.
> The moon rises over the blue mountain,
> a single bright jewel.

Or this:

The rain lifts, the clouds converge.
The dawning is midway.
Like myriad delineated peaks
lie the emerald crags.

True appreciation of the flavor of such teaching can only come after having examined and passed these so-called koans that are difficult to pass in the private interview room.

Hakuin Zenji has eight "difficult" koans. Rinzai practitioners are already quite familiar with them, but the average layperson may not know them. They appear in a poem written by Hakuin Zenji known as "The Grinding Song of Old Lady Shushin" (Shushin Obaba Konahiki-uta):

> If, while eating the food of the Flowing Rock Zen sect, you do not go through these barriers, you cannot pass muster. 'Sozan's Tomb,' 'Goso's Cow Passing Through a Latticed Window,' 'Kenpō's Three Types,' 'The Rhinoceros Horn Fan,' 'Haku'un's Not Yet,' 'Nansen's Passing Away,' 'Seijo and Her Soul Are Separated,' and 'The Old Woman Burns Down the Hermitage': these are known as the claws and fangs of the Dharma Cave, or the holy talisman which takes away life. When you have passed through these barriers and have searched widely through the Buddhist and non-Buddhist scriptures, collecting limitless Dharma treasures, you must then rescue the three fundamental activities.[24]

In discussing koans that are difficult to pass, I must warn against getting too caught up in figuring out solutions to them and thereby straying from the true way of meditation, which is to "rest at peace in the essential." Although we call these koans "difficult," they are no more than tools to deepen the experience of awakening and eventually eliminate all trace of that experience. However, if we overlook the basic requisite of awakening and devote our time to figuring out answers to these koans, we will be scurrying here and there over the waves and eddies of the phenomenal world without taking even a step into the world of the essential. Although we may have formally passed the eight difficult koans, we are actually right where we started, not knowing the essential world even in our dreams and unable to gain true peace of mind. The cases of this happening are not as few as one might think.[25]

JUST SITTING—
THE ZEN OF "SILENT ILLUMINATION"

Dōgen Zenji clearly and forcefully distills the lifeblood of "just sitting" with his exhortation: "Just sit and attain the fallen-away body and mind."[26] "The fallen-away body and mind" is the most important point here. Without experiencing this, just sitting would be nothing more than a "Zen of little consequence" (buji zen). It is precisely with respect to this point that just sitting is most easily abused. "Body and mind fall away" are the words that triggered for Dōgen Zenji his own "breaking through the bottom of the bucket," and they are the words that he used to express his enlightenment, his experience of "the emptiness of self and things." His experience doesn't differ in the least from the experiences of Zen ancestors down through the ages. If this were not so, Dōgen Zenji couldn't have said, "Buddhadharma has been directly and rightly transmitted."

In the year 1223 at the age of twenty-four, Dōgen Zenji left with Eisai Zenji's outstanding student, Myōzen Oshō, for Sung China. At that time Myōzen was Dōgen's own master. After many travels, Dōgen eventually met Tendō Nyojō Zenji at his temple on Tendō Mountain, a meeting in which Dōgen Zenji finally found a teacher to whom he could fully entrust his own practice.

Up to that time Dōgen Zenji had practiced for nine years under Eisai Zenji and Myōzen Zenji and had mastered the teachings of the Rinzai School. An ordinary person might have been satisfied at this point, but Dōgen, with his intense spirit of self-scrutiny, was not yet convinced. He was undoubtedly aware that traces of delusion, like a fine mist, had not yet been cleared away. Later in his *Recommending Zazen to All People* he would write, "Even a hairsbreadth difference is already the difference between heaven and earth." These words certainly came from personal experience; we can imagine that Dōgen's decision to travel to Sung China was thus for the purpose of wiping away this "hairsbreadth difference." When he came upon Nyojō Zenji he recognized him as his true teacher. The meeting of the two men was undoubtedly the result of profound and subtle Dharma relations—the result of efforts on the part of the buddhas and Zen ancestors.

Dōgen Zenji studied under Nyojō Zenji for more than two years, devoting himself to selfless practice toward the final goal of all Zen students. One night, during the predawn sitting period, Nyojō Zenji came upon a monk dozing on his cushion. With an unusually stern voice he rebuked the monk, "In the practice of Zen, body and mind must fall away. What are you doing sleeping?"

When Dōgen, who was sitting in the zendo, heard the words "body and mind must fall away," he was suddenly enlightened. He forgot himself completely. He jumped up and followed Nyojō Zenji to his room, where he lit incense and prostrated himself before his master.

"Why are you lighting incense?" Nyojō Zenji asked.

Dōgen Zenji replied, "Body and mind have fallen away."

Nyojō Zenji said, "Body and mind fallen away; fallen away body and mind"—words of confirmation.

Dōgen Zenji, scrupulous to the end, said, "It is but a momentary occurrence. Please do not bestow the seal of approval upon me lightly."

"I do not confirm you without reason," Nyojō said as he reconfirmed him. Nyojō Zenji had an unerring eye.

"Why do you say that you do not confirm me without reason?" asked Dōgen.

Nyojō Zenji then gave his final seal of approval, saying, "Fallen away body and mind."

As this exchange makes clear, the statements "body and mind fallen away" and "fallen away body and mind" are both expressions of the content of great enlightenment, namely, that self and things are both totally void.

In his *Commentary on Transmission of the Lamp* (*Denkō-roku Dokugo*), Yasutani Haku'un Roshi says the following:

To bow to the Buddha and shuffle through pages of sutras is

delusion. But do not take this as an excuse for neglecting the sutras and prostrations. Dōgen himself, founder of Eihei, said that burning incense, making prostrations, atonement, and the sutras are unnecessary. But attached to this is an unconditional condition, namely, to "just sit and attain the fallen away body and mind." This "just" is absolute in authority and does away with all attending factors. It is, stated in this way, a categorically indispensable condition. He is saying that if you sit and achieve great enlightenment (the practical aspect), without ever leaving the state where body and mind have fallen away (the absolute aspect), then there is no need to burn incense or make prostrations.

In chapter 22 of the *Transmission of the Lamp*, where Vasubandhu comes to great enlightenment, Keizan Zenji instructs us:

> Thinking it necessary to become a buddha or to attain the Way, or feeling it necessary, in the course of attaining the Way, to perform penance, to sit long hours without rest, to bow to the buddhas and read sutras in an attempt to amass merit, is to throw flowers at a clear sky, to drill holes where there were none. Even should you do these things for thousands upon millions of eons it would not set you free.

These words were spoken from the standpoint of perfect enlightenment; those who have not reached that state should not take them literally. Keizan Zenji is saying that even though the injunction to "just sit" exists, true Buddhism does not consist merely of sitting on a cushion for long hours. Without once experiencing body and mind falling away, we cannot be freed, but will remain in the six worlds, unable to escape from suffering birth and death. Therefore Keizan Zenji continues:

> Even though this may be so, both those who have just begun to practice and those who have been practicing for some time must investigate this matter and arrive at a place of peace. What, then, should you do? If you do not achieve great enlightenment for yourself, you will be deceived by the words

of others; open your eyes to see and devils will make sport of you. If you still have only an intellectual understanding that there is no Dharma to realize, despite having heard what I have to say, it will not do; it is merely thinking. If someone were to come now and preach that there is a Dharma to be attained, that there is a Dharma for which you must further practice, your spirits would be mixed up and restless.

You must now follow the right teachings of the buddhas and practice with painstaking thoroughness until you arrive at a place where the self is at peace. One who has come to this state is like a man who has eaten his fill: although a king's meal may be offered him, he has no desire to eat more.

An impassable line divides Zen of little consequence and true just sitting. Zen of little consequence is Zen without content—zazen that is never accompanied by the experience of body and mind falling away or sudden awakening. If one wonders why there should be such a difference, I must point out again that the content of Zen meditation will differ depending on one's objective in practice. If you sit with ordinary Zen as your objective, you will arrive at ordinary Zen. If you sit with the conviction that it is unnecessary for body and mind to fall away—that it is enough to just sit—then that is precisely what will happen; no matter how long you sit, it is unlikely that your Dharma eye will open.

Whether the person is a beginner, a seasoned sitter, or an enlightened master, just sitting is called "the single greatest way to practice at the beginning, during, and after." It is the high road of Zen, its main thoroughfare. The buddhas and Zen ancestors, too, are engaged in this very practice at this moment. For a long time after Shakyamuni Buddha there was no Zen to speak of other than just sitting. Koan practice didn't emerge as an aid to instruction until the Chinese Tang Dynasty. In early days, however, koans were used to test the depth of a student's understanding, to measure whether the person's consciousness had matured or not. It was only later that koans were used to lead beginner students to a first Zen experience, that is, through the first barrier.

Looking at the way just sitting and koan study have been used in Zen instruction, we can make four general divisions:

1. A Zen where just sitting is the sole method of practice from beginning to end. This is Silent Illumination Zen, the practice promulgated by Dōgen Zenji.

2. A Zen where koans are the main practice, from the first barrier up to the final barrier and completion of formal study. This is the practice at most Rinzai training centers in Japan today.

3. A Zen where just sitting is the main practice, with koan study used as an adjunct to practice. This is the position taken by Keizan Zenji in his *Transmission of the Lamp* and his *Guidelines for Zazen (Zazen Yōjinki)*.

4. A Zen where koan study is the main practice, with just sitting used as an aid. In this type of training, just sitting is also taken up after completion of koan study. Some masters in the Rinzai sect use this method. In any case after great enlightenment, there can be no meditation other than just sitting in the process of becoming a bodhisattva, and koans become just so much useless furniture. This is why we refer to just sitting as Zen meditation's main thoroughfare.

According to Harada Roshi, the essential matter in just sitting is to just sit, with the mind as taut as a bowstring at all times. He also advises us to sit just sitting as if we were locked in mortal combat with a master swordsman: if we let up our guard for even an instant, the opponent's sword will come down upon our heads and we will be hacked to pieces. There isn't even a split second available for random thoughts. To truly "just sit" is to sit with such concentration.

In all other forms of Zen meditation, whether counting the breath, following the breath, or working on a koan, there is always some center that acts as the point of concentration. No such center exists in just sitting; the sitting itself is the practice.

Although I have defined just sitting as the single greatest thoroughfare in Zen for students at every level, it would be very difficult, especially for the beginner, to reach enlightenment through its practice without great perseverance and stamina. If a person using just sitting really breaks through, chances are that they will achieve a great seeing into their own nature without leaving even a trace of delusion. Nevertheless, for anyone other than the great Zen figures of the past, who had unremitting zeal, it is very hard to reach enlightenment through just sitting alone. This is particularly so for modern Zen practitioners who may not possess the intrepid spirit of the ancients.

Finding an Authentic Teacher 7

In his *Guidelines for Studying the Way (Gakudō Yōjinshū)*, Dōgen Zenji writes:

> If you do not find an authentic teacher, it is not worth practicing Zen.

He continues:

> You must be clearly aware that the truth or falsity of one's realization depends on the authenticity or incompetence of the teacher.

We cannot attain genuine enlightenment unless we practice under an authentic teacher; we will be led to a spurious experience if we practice under a false teacher. Nothing should be feared more than this. But how do we discriminate between an authentic and a false teacher?

It is nearly impossible, particularly for the beginner practicing Zen, to make this distinction. Addressing this problem, Dōgen advises us:

> Examine what they say and make a deduction, like scooping water from a stream to discover its source.

Just as we can judge the quality of water at the source by examining water downstream, so we can judge whether a person clearly sees the true fact based on what they say. Words spoken by a teacher who possesses a clear eye give forth a shaft of light. Examining the recorded sayings of the Zen ancestors contained in the *Gateless Gate*, the *Blue Cliff Record*, or the *Book of Equanimity*, we could say such a light permeates their pages. Almost every chapter of Dōgen Zenji's *Shōbōgenzō* brims with luminosity.

Passages that give off such radiance resist intellectual comprehension and are impossible to understand using common sense. Each line that emits such light could be a koan in its own right. When seen with an enlightened eye, however, their words are far from illogical; they are the most natural things in the world. Zen books that fail to emit any such light are like swords that have not been tempered in fire: they lack the sharpness of authentic steel. When someone with an awakened eye examines such books, they know at a glance that the author is not the real thing.

But for a student whose eye has yet to be opened, what criteria can they use to discern a true teacher? Dōgen goes on:

> A true teacher, regardless of whether or not he or she is old, is one who has clarified the true Dharma and received the Dharma-seal of a qualified master. He or she does not give precedence to the written word, nor put intellectual views first. He or she possesses ability beyond the ordinary, a spirit surpassing the commonplace. Not clinging to personal views, he or she does not get bogged down in emotions. Action and understanding are in agreement. This is an authentic teacher.

The foremost criterion is whether the person has clarified the true Dharma and received the seal of confirmation from a true teacher. Self-qualification is, of course, unacceptable. Only a real master—someone who has received confirmation from a qualified teacher—can determine whether someone has clarified the true Dharma. If we trace the line of qualified teachers back through each generation to the time of Shakyamuni himself, we see that this very continuity can rightly be called "the life of Zen Buddhism." The process of transmission may seem formalized, but this formalism has an important function in attempting to faithfully transmit the formless reality of awakening. As long as its form is preserved, there is less chance of misjudgment.

A Zen teacher can only examine a students' experience by drawing on his or her own experience—there is indeed no other way. If the teacher has authentic Zen experience, then he or she will be able to ascertain students' progress in practice, as well as their mental state. This allows the teacher to tailor instruction to best suit a particular student's needs at each step in training. Dōgen sums this up with, "You must be clearly aware that the truth or falsity of one's realization depends on the authenticity or incompetence of the teacher."

Dōgen goes on to say, "He or she does not give precedence to the written word, nor put intellectual views first." A true teacher values experience over concepts. Of course, one human being leads others in Zen, and must use words, concepts, and thoughts to do so. To make use of words is not wrong, but they must not take precedence over actual experience. Concepts and thoughts amount to nothing but empty theorizing, unless they are preceded by realization. Enlightenment never happens as a result of thinking.

Bodhidharma said:

Attain the Great Way and surpassing ability, be completely versed in the buddha-mind, and leave that level.

Dōgen echoes Bodhidharma with his advice that a true teacher "possesses ability beyond the ordinary, a spirit surpassing the commonplace"— advice that takes pity on beginning students who end up at the mercy of bogus teachers. "Ability beyond the ordinary" refers to capabilities that do not fit into the confines of everyday common sense. This kind of ability belongs only to someone who has clarified the self and penetrated to the true form of the universe—in other words, the ability that arises from seeing into one's own nature. The true master surpasses all standards or levels of practice because Zen enters directly into the ground of the Buddha. Unless a person possesses a keen determination to transcend all levels in a single leap and to progress forever along the path, he or she cannot be called a true teacher.

Next, Dōgen Zenji says of a true teacher: "Not clinging to personal views, he does not get bogged down in emotions. Action and understanding are in agreement. This is an authentic teacher." Here, "personal views" means the self-complacency or smugness that manifests as intellectual opinions and feelings based on dualistic opposition, and bears no relationship with enlightenment. In other words, they are delusions rooted in ego. As long as a person is still caught up in egotistical understanding and emotions, he or she is not a real teacher. The actions and understanding of the teacher must ultimately be in agreement. Bodhidharma says:

> When the source of buddha-mind has been clarified, actions and understanding are in accord. Such a one is called "ancestor."

Bodhidharma displays the image of a true Zen master. For actions and understanding to be in accord, the content of the realization experience and the general conduct of the person must have become one. It is extremely difficult to arrive at this state. Here, "understanding" does not mean a merely intellectual understanding; it means coming to a direct enlightenment experience. Although it is not easy to become enlightened, it is possible if we practice with utter earnestness. As the saying goes, "Beings of reckless courage can accomplish buddhahood in a flash." But it is very difficult to actually persist, embodying the content of enlightenment so that it becomes part of our daily lives. Examples abound of people who use high-sounding phrases, but whose actions do not measure up to their words, therefore disqualifying them as true teachers.

I hope the above has helped to clarify Dōgen Zenji's ideal teacher. As we know, people seldom live up to the ideal—the situation hasn't changed much from former times in this regard. How many of those respected as Zen masters and teachers who lead people in Zen practice today would pass muster with Dōgen Zenji? Which, then, of the above qualifications is absolutely indispensable, even if others are to some extent lacking? It is, naturally, "one who has clarified the true Dharma and received the Dharma-seal of a qualified master." What could be more wonderful for a Zen student than to encounter Dōgen's ideal teacher! If we cannot expect perfection, at the very least we must insist on the single condition above.

Any teacher who wishes to live up to the ideal of Zen master must strive to emulate this model, continuously and fervently practicing to approach that goal at all times. From the standpoint of Zen students receiving instruction, so long as the teacher has "clarified the true Dharma and received the Dharma-seal of a qualified master" the practitioner should turn a blind eye to other shortcomings in the teacher—as long as the teacher is not involved in harmful behavior—and believe, accept, honor, and follow his or her guidance.

There is no perfect Zen master. All teachers have their faults and bad habits (some have developed even worse habits than ordinary people). But as long as the person has clarified the true Dharma, he or she should be more aware than any one of those faults and be engaged in the arduous post-enlightenment practice of wiping them away. If the person is *not* making such an effort, then the true Dharma that was supposed to have been clarified becomes suspect. Dōgen clearly explains this point in detail:

> The most difficult thing for a person practicing the Supreme Way is to find a guiding master. Whether they are a man or woman is irrelevant; the person should be a great being, a person of suchness, belonging neither to people of past nor of the present.
>
> . . .
>
> After you encounter a master who can guide you, you must devote yourself to seeking the Way, casting aside all worldly attachments and never wasting a moment.
>
> . . .
>
> You must practice with mind, without mind, or with half mind. You must practice, therefore without hesitation, as if to put out a fire on your own head. You must practice your search for the Way as if standing on tiptoe for a week. If you practice in this way, those who slander the Way will not trouble you. You will realize that the ancestor who obtained marrow by cutting off his own arm is no one else—that the teacher who attained the fallen-away body and mind is already "I myself."
>
> Revering the Dharma means that whether one's guide is a pillar, a hanging lantern, buddhas, wild fox, a fierce deity, a man, or a woman, if it upholds the great Dharma and attains the marrow, you must make your body and mind its ground and serve it throughout innumerable eons. It is easy to obtain body and mind; many of them are there mixed in confusion throughout the world. It is rare to meet the Dharma.
>
> Shakyamuni Buddha says that should you meet a master who preaches the Supreme Way, give thought neither to class

nor to caste of features; despise not their shortcomings, nor judge their behavior. For by reason of the fact that we esteem wisdom alone, we should serve that person every day with a hundred *ryō* of gold. We should serve them offerings of heavenly food, honor them by scattering heavenly flowers, respectfully bow three times a day, and give no cause for worry or grief. If you act like this, you will surely find the way to supreme enlightenment.

From the standpoint of practicing and preaching Buddha-dharma, even if one's guide is a girl of seven years, she is a guiding master of four kinds of disciples, the compassionate father.

. . .

We should praise and honor her in the same way that we honor the buddhas. This is the traditional manner of the Buddha Way.

Harada Sogaku Roshi also spoke in minute detail about finding a true teacher:

Beginners or dabblers say that once a person has opened the Dharma eye he or she is now incapable of the slightest misconduct. They say that where there exists any misconduct one cannot claim to have opened the Dharma eye.

As a rule, those who speak such nonsense think that a monk is acceptable as a Zen master if he can spout views on the sect's doctrine and lives a clean life from a common sense point of view, even though he has neither experience, nor practice, nor realization. Even if they come across a clearly enlightened master, owing to this erroneous view, they will not go to that person for instruction. Instead, they approach the blind and make their wrong views all the more wrong.

This is the major reason that Zen has degenerated to the level of a Zen of letters and notions, which is pseudo Zen. However, even a Zen of letters is respectable, as far as the Dharma of understanding is concerned, so long as that understanding is right.

Depth of Enlightenment 8

The single word "enlightenment" covers endless degrees of depth and clarity of experience. Everybody is different: passing the koan Mu during one's first week-long period of intensive meditation is enlightenment; practicing arduously for thirty more years to break through the final layers of illusion and attain the deepest state of true freedom is also enlightenment. As Yasutani Roshi said, nowadays, true teachers that possess a clear eye are rare. Consequently, teachers who can give solid, detailed instruction on the Zen way are also rare. More than a few attain a bit of enlightenment and start to boast about their experience, not only deceiving themselves but influencing others, leading them down the same path of ignorance. So it is essential to have a correct understanding of the depth of one's enlightenment.

The first matter of importance here is the experience of enlightenment itself. Enlightenment means to directly see the essential world through one's own experience. But to bring the enlightened eye to complete clarity requires a long period of continued practice. The world of enlightenment, which transcends all phenomena and common sense, is called "the highest stage, where everything is of a single color" or "the world of emptiness alone." So long as we remain in this world, we are of no use in the everyday world, for this is the realm of "no other," where there are no sentient beings to save despite our vow to save them. Those who settle down here are called "elevated dead people." Buddhas and ancestors from every era have warned of the danger of falling into the trap of emptiness, something that often happens on the path of practice.

So after breaking through to the world of enlightenment, we must return to the ordinary world—the world of common sense. Having attained enlightenment, we have to wipe away every trace of it and understand that the line we thought existed between the ordinary world and the world of enlightenment never actually existed. From the very beginning what we thought to be two worlds was intrinsically one.

The next matter of importance is the motive for practice following awakening. Now we must allow the light of our intrinsic human character to shine forth more brightly by cleaning away the delusions and concepts that remain. The practice of doing this is the personalization of awakening. We awaken to the essential world and see the unity of all things when the eye of enlightenment opens. Nevertheless, passion and delusion, which arise from either basic habitual or instinctual illusions of dualistic opposition, don't go away overnight. The momentous task of wiping them away goes on both before and long after seeing into one's own nature.

We must also engage in the difficult process of cleaning away our so-called Dharma attachments—our views regarding Buddha, the Dharma, and everything that smells of Buddha or Buddhism. Occasionally in Zen records we come across expressions like "If you meet the Buddha, kill him. If you meet a Zen ancestor, kill her." which can be quite surprising to the uninitiated. These instructions, of course, don't mean we should literally kill the buddhas and Zen ancestors, but rather that we should kill our concepts about them. Then we can reach peace in the original self, as it is.

Referring to this point, Keizan Zenji says: "Zazen directly opens and clarifies the mind ground and brings us to rest in the essential." The "essential" is our essential nature, our True Self. When we "bring [ourselves] to rest" we can act with true peace of mind. At this point in our practice, the summit is not far away.

So what happens next? We make a spontaneous vow to save all beings and to repay our debt of gratitude by preserving and carrying out the teachings; we exert ourselves to the utmost to bring others to this true peace of mind. This is called the bodhisattva spirit or bodhisattva vow. It is both the vow and the practice of the first of the Four Great Vows: "Sentient beings are numberless; I vow to save them all." When we arrive at this final stage of practice the bodhisattva spirit arises naturally. It becomes a wheel of Dharma, turning without pause.

The koan "Kyūhō's Disapproval" (Case 96 in the *Book of Equanimity*) raises this important matter of the depth of experience. Kyūhō Dōken was among the disciples of Sekisō Keisho Osho and acted as his attendant. Sekisō inherited the Dharma of Dōgo Enchi and was therefore the Dharma grandson of Yakusan Zenji. He lived for twenty years at Mt. Sekisō in China's Tan province, where he built the temple known as Withered Tree Hall[27] and practiced meditation every day. The koan runs as follows:

> When Sekisō passed away, the assembly wanted to appoint the head monk of the meditation hall as chief priest. Kyūhō did not approve and so said, "Wait until I question him. If he understands our late master's spirit, I will serve him as I did our late master."
>
> Then he asked the head monk, "Our late master said:
>
>> Come to rest and go on.
>> Finish and go on.
>> Come to the cold and lonely place and go on.
>> Have one thought for ten thousand years and go on.
>> Become cold ashes and a withered tree and go on.
>> Become the incense burner in an ancient shrine and
>>   go on.
>> Become a strip of white silk and go on.
>
> Tell me, what sort of matter did he clarify with this?"
>
> The head monk said, "He clarified the matter of one color."
>
> Kyūhō said, "If that is so, you do not understand our late master's spirit."
>
> The head monk said, "Don't you acknowledge me? Prepare and bring incense to me."
>
> Kyūhō prepared some incense and brought it to the head monk, who lit it and said, "If I do not understand our departed master's words, then before this incense goes out I will die on this spot sitting in meditation."
>
> So saying, he sat down and died.
>
> Kyūhō patted him on the back, saying, "I do not deny that you can die sitting or standing. I only say that you do not understand our late master's meaning even in a dream."

The head monk's reply ("He clarified the matter of one color") indicated that he thought Sekisō had been talking about the world of enlightenment. "The matter of one color" means seeing things from the highest point where everything is of one color—the stage at which we have made the world of Mu our own. Let me draw on Yasutani Roshi's public teaching on this koan:

> To say "he has clarified the world of enlightenment" is a pitiful reply. To see only the world of equality and sameness is a shallow realization. He saw that all things are equal and the same—this is basic wisdom. He must go further and open up "wisdom that is subsequently attained." "Wisdom of wondrous observation" has to come into play as well. He must now use the eye of equality to look at the world of difference anew. To realize only the aspect of sameness is enlightenment sickness. Sekisō begins his Seven Departures by taking leave of that sick world wherein all things are seen as being of a single color, and gradually becoming clearer and more penetrating as his practice continues. Having polished his enlightened mind to clarity by letting everything fall away, he came at last to the original person of total ordinariness. This is what Sekisō was talking about. No wonder the attendant would not accept the head monk's answer![28]

Sitting down to consciously die at will is no easy thing to do. But it is a feat accomplished through mental concentration and is entirely different from enlightenment. It is possible to die seated or even standing by developing mental concentration. This head monk was certainly not the only example of someone with such powers, and his ability to die at will is no proof that he had achieved total enlightenment. I imagine that Kyūhō couldn't conceal his pity for the head monk, who had mistaken concentration of mind for the ultimate goal in meditation and had left this world without understanding his master's intent.

This koan addresses the question of the relative depth of enlightenment. In the private interview·room, Zen students must present their understanding of how experience deepens with each successive phrase. In general, we might use the following as standards for measuring of the depth of enlightenment:

1. How clear is the enlightened eye? How clearly have you seen the essential world?

2. To what extent has enlightenment died down and things returned to normal?
3. To what degree have you cleansed the emotions, concepts, and thoughts tied to enlightenment? That is, to what extent has enlightenment become visible as the light of your character?
4. How far have you "come to rest" in the essential? Namely, to what extent has true peace of mind become your own? More concretely, to what degree has awakening transformed your daily life?
5. How much do you manifest the bodhisattva's vow to save all beings?

Having said all this, how do we go about deepening and purifying the experience of awakening? As Dōgen Zenji tells us, there is only one way:

> . . . from the very beginning when you come to see the master it is not necessary to burn incense, make prostrations, pray to the Buddha, practice penance, or study sutras; just sit and let body and mind fall away.

Two different schemes for examining the relative depth of our enlightenment and activity in the world have evolved within the Zen tradition: Tōzan Gohon Daishi's two treaties on the Five Modes, and the Ten Ox-Herding Pictures.

TŌZAN'S *Five Modes of Endeavor and Accomplishment*

Tōzan Gohon Daishi, founder of the Sōtō sect, wrote two treatises on the five ranks—the *Five Modes of Essential and Phenomenal* and the *Five Modes of Endeavor and Accomplishment*.

In the *Five Modes of Essential and Phenomenal*, Tōzan analyzes the True Self according to the two aspects of equality and difference—or essential and phenomenal. Although we could call such an approach philosophical, it is not only theoretical, but an exposition based on a clear experience of reality.

The second treatise, the *Five Modes of Endeavor and Accomplishment,* is concerned with the relative depth of awakening. Using five stages, or modes, Tōzan shows the process whereby the content of Zen experience is gradually matured with practice. The five stages are as follows:

1. The Mode of Turning Toward It
2. The Mode of Serving
3. The Mode of Accomplishment
4. The Mode of Sharing Accomplishment
5. The Mode of Accomplishment without Accomplishment

The Mode of Turning Toward It

This is the level of facing in the right direction. In what direction must we advance? How clearly do we understand what we need to do in order to clarify our True Self?

Relying on the teachings of the buddhas and Zen ancestors and following the instruction of a genuine master, we understand that we must proceed in the direction that leads to realization of the Self. We also clearly understand the concrete steps that we should take in practice and are about to begin on our quest. This level is also known as "the mode of good resolution" or "the decision to embrace the Way." We could never attain the Buddha Way without entering this level. It is because of this fact that the buddhas and Zen ancestors since ancient times have valued this level most of all and have striven to make it their own. Facing the right direction is the first step toward achieving buddhahood; once we take that step we will inevitably accomplish the Supreme Way. The rest is just a matter of time.

In the Lotus Sutra's parable of the poor son of a rich man, the deluded person, who had been wandering aimlessly for eons in the dust of foreign lands, developed an understanding of the truth that all beings are intrinsically awake and took the first step on the road back to his original home. Undaunted by hardships along the way, he continued the long journey until he finally arrived at the gate of his true home. This is the stage of "orientation."

Consider Tōzan's verse for this stage:

> Sage rulers have always modeled themselves on Emperor Yao.
> Treating others with propriety, he bends his dragon waist.

At times he passes through the marketplaces and busy streets.
Throughout the land, the people rejoice in civilization and a
 peaceful reign.

A Zen practitioner who is "turning in the right direction" is compared to an outstanding and virtuous ruler. It may seem far-fetched to
compare an ordinary person at the first level to a saintly ruler, but we
must remember that ordinary people are intrinsically buddhas; they are
"infant tathagatas." If such people are baby buddhas, then it's not so
strange to call them saintly rulers.

Emperor Yao, the greatest of the illustrious rulers and saintly emperors of ancient China, is a mythical figure placed together with Emperors
Shun, Yu, and Shang. In ancient times, rulers who received the title
"sage ruler" or "holy emperor" were people who strove to govern by
following the example of the mythical Emperor Yao. Similarly, Zen
practitioners aspire to experience and embody unsurpassed awakening.
Faithful to the teachings of the buddhas and Zen ancestors, a student
takes the first step in the direction of the Dharma, following to the letter
the guidance of a qualified master.

The subject of the verse then turns from sage rulers to how such rulers govern. "Treating others with propriety" in its original sense means
that in order to bring peace to the people, the ruler gives himself entirely
to the task of directing his vassals. We can interpret the verse to mean
metaphorically that Zen practitioners bring all activities that pertain
to practice in their daily lives under their control. Just as the sage ruler
treats his subjects with propriety, the Zen practitioner carries out his or
her actions in the same spirit. Sincerity is the basis of propriety. When
praising him, Confucius's disciples express the essence of propriety:
"Our master is cordial, frank, courteous, temperate, and deferential."[29]
The "dragon waist" is the waist of the emperor. A truly outstanding
ruler, despite his or her high position, will bow from the waist, acting
with propriety, temperance, and deference. Similarly the Zen practitioner must interact with people faithfully, conscientiously, and humbly.

The enlightened ruler, modeling his or her actions on mythical emperors, goes out into the city's streets to inspect the life of his people. This is
how the Zen student should practice in daily life: the student should be
devoted to upholding the way of the Buddha, night and day.

But I would like to caution you here. People practicing the koan "Mu" are instructed to continue the practice at all hours of the day, without letting go of Mu. So they often ask me if they should continue to practice Mu even when walking on the street, studying, or working at the office. It is a reasonable question. My answer is that if you are walking on an uncrowded street, it is possible to continue the practice of Mu as you walk—this is good practice. If you are walking on a crowded street, however, or crossing a busy intersection, you must focus your attention to avoid bumping into people or being run over. Later in your practice you will realize this kind of focus itself is the living meditative absorption of Mu. When you study, you must put Mu aside and devote yourself single-mindedly to your studies. Once you sit down on your cushion and begin the practice of Mu, however, you must throw away all other concerns and become absorbed in Mu. At least for lay practitioners, this is the most realistic way to practice.

Looking at the closing line of the verse in terms of the practice of meditation, we see that the baby buddha is gradually maturing in practice and developing the power of absorption. The jewel of the original nature is clear enough so that the student can spontaneously act without being sidetracked by emotional ups and downs. Thus the verse refers to this stage as "the august dynasty." It would be well to continue this practice of quiet sitting for some months or a year. Even if you don't arrive at seeing into your own nature, your life situation will gradually improve and the problems of daily life will begin to resolve themselves. This is not theoretical; it is a fact. I'm sure this writer is not the only one to have experienced this.

The Mode of Serving

This level refers to the act of giving oneself in service or to a child honoring its parents with filial piety. From the perspective of the practice of Zen, it is the level wherein we set our sights on enlightenment without regard for life or limb, having determined to break through to the innermost source of the "single great matter." It was Yasutani Roshi's view that what passes as seeing into one's own nature today is still on the first stage of "Orientation." The Stage of Service, then, is the practice that follows seeing into one's own nature—where we work on koan after koan, polishing our understanding with each successive case, until we reach great enlightenment.

This interpretation, I believe, derives from the tradition of Harada Sogaku Roshi. This aspect had previously been explained as the stage wherein one practices with trepidation, in order to be in accord with the Buddha mind and to avoid acting contrary to it. But until we've clearly grasped what the buddha mind is, instructions to "follow the buddha mind" are just so much talk because we still haven't got a concrete idea of how to practice. All the same, we must try to assume the posture of real practice to the best of our ability in order to grasp buddha mind.

The verse for this stage:

> To cleanse the body and put on fine make-up:
> for whose sake is this done?
> The cuckoo's call urges you home.
> Hundreds of blossoms have fallen
> but there is no end to the call,
> as you move deeper and still deeper among the wild peaks.

The verse compares the Zen student's practice at this stage to the activities of ladies-in-waiting at the Imperial Court, who bathe and make up their faces. Who do the imperial maids beautify themselves for? Needless to say, they do it for their Lord, so that they will be presentable when they wait on him. From the standpoint of the practice of Zen, the Lord is the True Self. For Zen students who devote themselves to practice, it is important that the body be clean. Even if you can't take a proper bath every day, you can at least rinse with hot or cold water and towel dry. Your clothes should be simple and clean. When you wear fresh clothes, your spirit will naturally feel refreshed. Perfume or heavy make-up may be distracting to others, so you should avoid them.

But cleansing and making ready the heart is even more important than our external form. In addition to letting go of desires for fame and fortune or any depraved thoughts, you must throw away all thoughts about Zen and follow the directives of the teacher, as well as the teachings of the Buddha and the Zen ancestors. This is the way that leads to the essential buddha of the True Self. For those practicing Mu, if they wish to practice correctly, they should not have even the "s" of "seeing into one's own nature" in their minds.

"The cuckoo's call" urges us to hurry back to our true home and awaken to our True Self. But not just the cuckoo's call; anything we see or hear can urge us to return to our true home and sit down in peace. In his younger days Nakagawa Sōen Roshi wrote the following *waka* verse:

> In my seclusion, no end to musings on life and death.
> The sun sets on another day—a frog croaks.

This poem presents a vivid image of the youthful monk Sōen seeking the Way. The croak of the frog also urges us all to return home.

What is meant by "The hundred flowers have fallen"? Our years of painful practice are bearing fruit as the various delusions of self and other, illusion and enlightenment, ordinary and holy fall away, one by one. But the delusions of separation that stubbornly cling to us are not easy to sever. The subtle delusions of the final stages are most stubborn of all. At this point, we continue our efforts to move straight ahead on a thousand-mile iron rail, telling ourselves, "Not yet! Not yet!" This is the point where "the call is unending."

Though we think that all the "flowers" have fallen, the grime of endless eons of false knowledge and misperception has built up in thick layers like a range of mountains. We must continue to advance step by step, right in the midst of it, along the ever-more precarious pass, until we can remain in the meditative absorption of practicing with our whole being. This is what is meant by "as you move deeper and still deeper among the wild peaks."

The Mode of Accomplishment

This is the degree of perfect enlightenment, the stage at which our efforts have paid off. The long years of painfully practicing the previous stage have at last born fruit and we reach great enlightenment, where sweeping away everything, we clearly grasp the world where there is "not a speck of cloud in the sky."

The verse:

> A withered tree blossoms in the spring outside of time.
> Riding backward on a jade elephant, you chase the unicorn.
> You hide yourself high beyond the long shadows of the
>   thousand peaks.
> The moon is bright, the wind is fresh, a pleasant day is dawning.

When practicing meditative absorption in Mu or just sitting, the leaves and branches of our delusive sense of separation wither. But the trunk is slow to die. Even when the trunk finally withers, the roots still refuse to die back. Eventually they too shrivel, but some hint of green life remains. When that vigor too dries up completely, it is the time of great death, and with great death great life manifests for the first time. This is known as the "spring outside of time."

The original verse uses the expression "beyond eons" to denote timelessness. "Eon" translates the Sanskrit word *kalpa*, a term for an extremely long period of time, sometimes extending from the birth of the universe to its total extinction. It can also refer to ordinary time in terms of days and nights. At any rate, the "spring outside of time" exists on a different dimension from ordinary spring. When we have killed all of our discriminating delusions, suddenly timeless spring—the state of eternal peace—bursts forth.

Yasutani Roshi takes the expression "riding backward" to mean that you temporarily set up distinctions between self and other where there are actually none. "Jade elephant" refers to a gigantic elephant, the king of the herd. This is a symbol of our intrinsic buddha nature, the self that pervades heaven and earth. The unicorn (*kirin*) is a sacred animal or, as Yasutani Roshi puts it, "a symbol for all that is holy." I prefer to see it as "the other that exhausts the whole of heaven and earth." The other is a projection of self, just as the unicorn is the opposite of the elephant. Subject and object are not two from the beginning, but we temporarily set them up in the world where neither exists (riding backward), calling one "the jade elephant" and the other "the unicorn."

Looking at it this way, we see that the whole line refers to the totally free activity of our original self. In other words, we ride around with total control over both the world of the senses—color, sound, smell, taste, and touch—and the world of the five desires—wealth, sex, food, fame, and sleep. Yasutani Roshi explains that the line points to the same world expressed in the phrase: "When real Zen monks ride on sound and become one with color, everything is clear from moment to moment, everything is full of wonder from act to act." What, substantially, is this experience? Hearing, seeing, standing, sitting, drinking, eating: each is it. Raising a hand, stretching out a foot, arching an eyebrow, winking an eye, frowning or smiling: each and every one is "riding a jade elephant backward, chasing the unicorn."

"Now" is the point where time and space have become one, right now; it is any time, any place, always *now*. "Hiding high" means that the self has disappeared. As the second Zen ancestor said, "I have searched for my mind but have never been able to find it"—emptiness of self has been clearly verified. We have searched for the self but could not find it. Clearly awake to the emptiness of subject, we find that there is no trace of it to be found.

"Beyond the long shadows of the thousand peaks" means that we have leapt far beyond countless mountains. But what are these peaks, after all? We can take them as representing delusions of separation, such as self and other, deluded and enlightened, or ordinary and holy, but I prefer to see them more broadly as the entire objective world. We have clearly seen that all things are empty of self, but now even that emptiness has disappeared, without a trace.

As Yōka Daishi says in his *Song on Realizing the Way*:

> Truth and illusion are both void and without form,
> but this formlessness is neither empty nor not empty;
> It is the truly real form of the Tathagatha.

The last line of the verse, "the moon is bright, the wind is fresh, a pleasant day is dawning," celebrates the everyday life of the person who has attained this state of consciousness. It implies a succession of perfect days. Every day is a good day; every year is a good year. It is by no means easy to arrive at this state. Yasutani Roshi explains: "You must be able to demonstrate your appreciation of the verse in an intimate exchange with a qualified master in private interview. Make it your own and express it out of that personalization."

The first and second lines of the verse for this stage are easy enough to grasp. The third line is considerably more difficult, but if someone explains it, we will still understand it. We can only sigh in admiration when we reach the fourth line; the longer we practice, the more deeply this line impresses us.

The Mode of Sharing Accomplishment

This is the stage wherein we become free in the activity of teaching and saving all beings. We turn back from the essential world of one color and no dust to the world of distinctions. At the third stage there were no sentient beings to save, even if we wished to save them. Now, at the fourth stage, the bodhisattva spirit embodied by "Sentient beings are numberless; I vow to save them all" irresistibly wells up, and we do our utmost to carry it out.

At the third stage, we could only see the world of equality and still tended to feel proud of our understanding, but now the fever of enlightenment has subsided and we promptly give appropriate guidance to whomever seeks it. If a child appears, we become a child; if an elderly person comes, we respond appropriately. The same holds true whether the person is sick or well, man or woman. At the mode of accomplishment, those who were more active tended to make a show of their enlightenment, but they lacked true freedom. Those who were more passive tended instead to cling to the position that there are "no sentient beings to save" and stand aloof, no matter how much turmoil and suffering they saw in the world. They too could not act freely. Before the third stage, delusion kept us from being free, but when we reached the third level, it was enlightenment that hindered our freedom. It is only on the fourth stage of Sharing Accomplishment that we become free to save all beings.

The verse for this stage reads:

> Ordinary beings and the myriad buddhas do not intrude
>   upon each other.
> The mountain is naturally high, the water is naturally deep.
> Ten thousand differences, a thousand distinctions, what matter
>   do they make clear?
> Where the partridges chirp, hundreds of flowers bloom anew.

In Tōzan's *Five Modes of Essential and Phenomenal*, the stage called "Completion Amidst Both" applies to both the many beings and buddhas (enlightened ones). There is a strict distinction between master and servant, father and son, teacher and student, and so on, and there is no confusion of their roles. These distinctions are only natural from the standpoint of the essential world, and they make themselves apparent in the form of an orderly system. The verse teaches us that from the aspect of practice in the phenomenal world, things must be this way.

"Mountains are naturally high; waters are naturally deep" continues the import of the first line. Willows are green, flowers are red, the tall man is tall Dharma body, the short man is short Dharma body. There is a verse in the Pure Land sect of Buddhism: "The longness of the crane's legs saves it; the shortness of the duck's legs saves it."

"Ten thousand differences, a thousand distinctions, what matter do they make clear?" The endless changes and appearances of the phenomenal world, just as they are, are the perfect manifestation of the true fact. "Where the partridges chirp, hundreds of flowers bloom anew." Here, not a trace of reasoning remains. As Fuketsu Oshō says, "I constantly think of Konan in March, where partridges chirp among hundreds of sweet-scented blossoms." This line transcends both speech and silence. Yasutani Roshi adds, "Better not to say anything further. Go to private interview and understand the subtle points."

The Mode of Accomplishment without Accomplishment

The Mode of Accomplishment without Accomplishment is the eventual outcome of the former stage. The one who has attained the stage of Mode of Sharing Accomplishment and become capable of teaching freely must now take one step further—a step off the top of a one-hundred-foot pole. He must forget his spontaneous activity, have not the slightest awareness of self and other being one, or the thought that everything is unfolding naturally. This is the level of "no trace" and "no news." Awakening has vanished and the vanishing of awakening has also vanished. The seeker has become a truly ordinary person, returned to his or her ordinary state. This is the very completion of practice. Consider the verse for this stage:

If the head and horns appear even slightly, it is no longer bearable;
if you rouse your mind to seek Buddha, that's shameful.
In the vastness of the empty eons no one has ever known it—
why go south to meet the fifty-three sages?

Please remember that this verse refers to the state reached through unflagging practice after passing through the stages of Turning Toward It, Serving, Accomplishment, and Sharing Accomplishment; after this everything is forgotten.

What are the "horns" here? They are ideas about such things as Buddha and Dharma. As one saying puts it, "Even the word 'Buddha' is a stain on the pure ground of the mind." If anything remains that still smacks of awakening, smells of Buddha, or stinks of the lofty and profound, it is still as far removed as heaven is from earth. It is unbearable that even a bit of these dregs of thought remain.

Case 19 of the *Gateless Gate*, "Ordinary Mind is the Way," presents an exchange between Master Nansen and his student Jōshū:

Jōshū earnestly asked Nansen, "What is the Way?"
Nansen answered, "The ordinary mind is the Way."
Jōshū asked, "Should I direct myself toward it or not?"
Nansen said, "If you try to turn toward it you go against it."
Jōshū asked, "If I do not try to turn toward it, how can I
know that it is the Way?"
Nansen answered, "The Way does not belong to knowing
or not knowing. Knowing is delusion; not knowing is a blank
consciousness. When you have really reached the true Way
beyond all doubt, you will find it as vast and boundless as
outer space. How can it be talked about on a level of right
or wrong?"
At these words, Jōshū was suddenly enlightened.[30]

We could replace the word "Way" here with "Buddha." If we move our mind in the direction of Buddha even a little then we are "turning toward it," and it will no longer be "as vast and boundless as outer space." The verse is saying that this would be shameful for the fully enlightened person. The only way to understand this is through a lived experience of it, on our own.

To think in terms of the three-dimensional world of time and space is off the mark. Zen uses expressions like "Mu" and "your original face before your parents were born" to refer to this world in which there is no one who knows. Our intellectual thoughts are useless to understand it. It is the world that is gained in not gaining.

There is a chapter in the *Avatamsaka Sutra* called "Entering the Realm of the Dharma," which relates the story of a boy named Sudhana. He was one of five hundred sons of a rich man who lived in a place called the Palace of Wealth. Many precious objects appeared when he was born, so he was given the name Sudhana, which means "good fortune." Sudhana went to pay his respects to the bodhisattva Manjushri and resolved to seek the Way. After this he traveled south, where he practiced under fifty-three illustrious masters and "came to realization of the realm of the Dharma."

The fourth line of this verse cites the example of Sudhana, asking, "Why go south to meet the fifty-three sages?" In other words, since we are all intrinsically endowed with the Buddha Way, why search outside of ourselves? Hakuin Zenji ends his *Song in Praise of Zazen* with the line, "This very place is the Lotus Land, this very body the Buddha," which makes the same point. In the question, "Why go south to meet the fifty-three sages?" we have the natural, spontaneous body, without any smell of Buddha or Buddhism.

THE TEN OX-HERDING PICTURES

The Five Modes of Endeavor and Accomplishment help us to clarify the depth of enlightenment—the level of accomplishment in practice. But since the model divides the depths of enlightenment into only five stages, it lacks the detail of the ten levels of the Ox-Herding Pictures, which shine an even brighter light on the path of Zen practice.

Shibayama Zenkei Roshi's book *The Ten Ox-Herding Pictures* points out a number of iterations of the series that stand out as exceptional:

- Fumyō Zenji's *Pictures and Verses on Taming the Ox*
- Kakuan Zenji's *Ten Ox-Herding Pictures*
- *White Ox Pictures with Verses* (author unknown)

Among these three, Shibayama Roshi regards Fumyo Zenji's version as most Sōtō-like, and Kakuan Zenji's as having a distinctively Rinzai flavor. *White Ox Pictures with Verses* presents a combination of teaching and Zen. In Japan the version by Kakuan has received the most attention and is the version most people think of as "The Ox-Herding Pictures," and it is this version that I will use for the following discussion of the text.

One: Seeking the Ox

The "ox" referred to in the Ox-Herding Pictures is our true nature, our intrinsic buddha nature. At the first stage of Seeking the Ox we have already resolved to seek the Way and attain a state of peace, but we still don't know where to go or what to do; we read this book or that, and look into various different religions and teachings. Even if we chance upon a true transmission of Buddhadharma we continue to waver and are unable to grasp it.

> Introduction:
> The ox has never been lost. What need is there to search? It is only due to separation from my true nature that I fail to find it. In the confusion of the senses I lose even its tracks. Far from home, I see many crossroads, but which way is the right one I know not. Greed and fear, good and bad, entangle me.

> Verse:
> Pushing aside the grass, he looks for the ox.
> The water is vast, the mountains are far, and the road goes
>   deeper.
> His strength exhausted, he does not know where to search.
> He only hears the cicadas at evening chirping in the
>   maple trees.

Two: Finding the Tracks

On the second level we have been fortunate enough to meet a true teacher, learn the correct way to practice, and have set out on the right track in our Zen training. We have studied the sutras and their meaning has become clearer. We are intellectually convinced that "all beings are intrinsically awake," and "heaven, earth, and I are of the same root; the myriad things and I are of one body." We now have a conceptual grasp of the tracks of the ox—a picture of our True Self—and we've absorbed the basic principles of Zen practice. But we still lack an experiential grasp of it. We haven't yet set foot within the true gate. In other words, we have encountered only the tracks of the ox, but we haven't yet actually met the ox. Yet since the tracks are visible, there is nothing left to do now but to advance along the road.

> Introduction:
> Understanding the teaching, I see the tracks of the ox. Then I learn that, just as many vessels are made from one metal, so too are myriad entities made of the fabric of self. Unless I discriminate, how will I perceive the true from the false? I have not yet entered the gate, nevertheless I have discerned the path.

> Verse:
> There are many footprints at the edge of the water and
>   under the trees;
>   the fragrant grasses are hard to part; does he see it or not?
>   Even if it is the deepest part of the deep mountains,
> how can its nostrils, which reach heaven, be hidden?

The myriad phenomena of the universe are all, each and every one, the nostrils of the ox, and they are displayed before us, completely revealed to view. But until we see them, there is no help for us.

Three: Seeing the Ox

This is the level of awakening. We earnestly desire to have a living experience of the ox—our original face—and to rest in the essential world. We have been lucky enough to meet a true teacher and understand the key to practice. When we locate the tracks of the ox, joy wells up: our earnest seeking has been rewarded with a glimpse of the ox itself.

I want to emphasize again that although there is no difference in the actual substance of experience, its relative depth and clarity differs from individual to individual; no single experience is identical to another. Although everyone at this stage shares the experience of seeing the ox, some will have seen it face to face, while others will only have seen the tip of the ox's tail from a distance. The difference is one of degree rather than of substance, but the experience is qualitatively different from seeing only the tracks of the ox.

It is said that since ancient times few have ever reached perfect enlightenment with a single initial experience. Typically, in one's first experience a considerable sense of separation between oneself and the ox still remains, and that difference must be gradually lessened through the practice that follows the experience of seeing into one's own nature (kenshō), whether it is the study of koans or just sitting. Otherwise, the experience of seeing into one's own nature or "Seeing the Ox" will once more vanish because it was merely a glimpse. The memory of having experienced kenshō remains, and we retain it as a concept, as if holding on to a mere photograph of the ox. So we must dedicate ourselves to practice even more after having seen into one's own nature.

Is my feeling that the number of instances of the experience of kenshō has declined just personal prejudice? These days, many of the experiences that have been certified as seeing into one's own nature are mixed with some conceptual understanding. If a Zen master has certified such experiences as seeing into one's own nature with the clear intention to gradually get rid of those mixed-in elements, he is using an acceptable method of instruction. But if the master himself, unable to distinguish between a genuine and a false seeing of one's nature, has certified as authentic what is in fact an insufficient experience, that is a serious error. Distinguishing between sufficient and insufficient experience is a serious responsibility of the Zen teacher. In order to carry it out, the teacher must have clearly experienced seeing into his own nature. Otherwise the teacher-student relationship will be nothing but a case of "the blind leading the blind."

In the "Bendōwa" chapter of *Shōbōgenzō*, Dōgen Zenji says:

> If enlightened masters and enlightened disciples rightly transmit the subtle Dharma of the seven buddhas its true

significance manifests and can be experienced. This is beyond the ken of the priests who study only the words of the discourses.

Thus there must be a master who bears the seal of enlightenment in order for the teaching of the Buddha to be received or transmitted. A scholar who values letters will be useless as a master, like the blind leading the blind.

Introduction:
When one hears the voice, one can sense its source. As soon as the six senses merge, the gate is entered. Wherever one enters one sees the head of the ox! This unity is like salt in water, like color in dyestuff. The slightest thing is not apart from self.

Verse:
He hears the song of the nightingale.
The sun is warm, the wind is mild, willows are green
    along the shore,
Here no ox can hide!
What artist can draw that massive head, those majestic
    horns?

The stage of Seeing the Ox corresponds to Service, the second mode of the *Five Positions of Merit and Honor.*

Four: Catching the Ox

Here we take firm hold of the ox itself, no longer afraid that it might get away. This is truly seeing into our own nature, or the moment of great enlightenment. When we arrive here we finally gain true peace of mind. Our spiritual life has taken root, and we are no longer under the sway of any particular system of thought, theory, or philosophy, though we can clearly appraise the positions that they take. We stand on the summit of Mt. Fuji, able to identify the various rest areas along the way to the top.

Yasutani Roshi was of the opinion that, at present, at most two or three people in the entire world have reached this level of attainment.

Many Zen practitioners mistake a glimpse of the ox for having caught it, and then, when they try to teach their students, they are unable to discern in them the difference between these two stages.

We might think that when we reach the stage of catching the ox we would gain total peace of mind, but things are not so simple. Views of dualistic opposition, which linger as mental habits that have been with us from the beginningless past, still persist in the form of concepts and feelings, even though we may realize they are without content. In Buddhism we call such mental habits "seeds."[31] Although we have caught hold of the ox, its untamed spirit is more in evidence than ever and it still longs for the sweet grasses of the open plain.

Our cherished ideas about Buddha and Dharma are particularly difficult to get rid of, and arduous practice is needed before we can clearly see that "Even the word 'Buddha' is a stain on the pure ground of the mind." In order to arrive at a state where we are truly one with each thought and action, we must push on toward the goal, where both subject and object have been emptied.

> Introduction:
> It dwelt in the forest a long time, but today I caught it! Since the surroundings are so nice, it is hard to drive it out of there. Longing for sweeter grass, it wanders away. Its mind is still stubborn and unbridled. If I wish it to submit, I must raise my whip.

> Verse:
> Exhausting its high spirits, he grasps it.
> Its will is strong, its power vigorous and difficult to
>   subdue.
> Sometimes it nearly reaches the top of the table land;
> Other times it stays where the smoky clouds are thick.

Five: Taming the Ox

This is the stage where we finally begin to domesticate the ox via the difficult practice of clearing away ideas of Buddha, Dharma, and habitual dualistic views. Up until the fourth stage, Catching the Ox, we were talking about matters that anyone who practices ardently for twenty or thirty years can attain. But, as Yasutani Roshi used to say, this practice of taming the ox is no easy work even over two or three lifetimes.

Thick, stubborn clouds of delusion that obscure our essential nature remain as evidence of how tenacious our mental habits are. From one perspective the extent to which we can go on polishing our essential nature, to greater and greater luster, is without limit, and there is no way to fathom how long it will take.

Introduction:
When one thought arises even a little, another follows. In realization everything becomes true, and in delusion it becomes false. Being does not come into existence through the objective world but only from the mind. When the halter is held tightly, it does not permit doubts to enter.

Verse:
Never removing the tether,
he keeps the ox from going where it wants, into the dust
   and dirt.
When it has been tamed, it will become gentle and peaceful,
and naturally follow him, without bridle and chains.

The above has been an explanation of the Ox-Herding Pictures up to the fifth stage. The subsequent stages are so advanced, so removed from our actual practice, that it would be of little use for most students to examine them. I remember Harada Roshi saying that we can get at least some understanding up until the seventh stage, but that the stages beyond that would defy our imagination. Personally, I feel that I have no qualification to chatter glibly about matters of the sixth stage and beyond, so I prefer to end my explanation of the Ox-Herding Pictures here.

Cause and Effect as One 9

I n his *Song in Praise of Zazen* Hakuin Zenji says:

> The gate to oneness of cause and effect opens;
> neither two nor three, the path runs straight.

I would like to clarify the meaning of this passage, especially for those who are about to take up the practice of Zen.

Customarily, when we speak of cause and effect we are referring to the cycle of birth and death in the world of delusion, and we use expressions such as "retribution according to cause and effect," "good cause, good effect," "bad cause, bad effect." But what I call cause and effect here will be limited to cause and effect as it relates to the practice of Zen meditation: the cause and effect of awakening, so to speak.

Hakuin Zenji's verse says that cause and effect are not two but are rather one and the same. In other words, they are "stages with no stages, no stages in stages." We practice zazen to confirm buddhahood—that is, to experience the buddha ground of our own true nature. Looking at practice from its aspect of distinction, there are actually infinite gradations, from the moment we first decide to practice right up to the final stage. Viewed in terms of cause and effect, the meditation that we practice today is the cause of what we will realize tomorrow. Likewise, tomorrow's realization is the effect of today's practice. Tomorrow's effect in turn becomes the cause for the next day's effect. One day's worth of actual practice is one day's worth of effect. Practice over a month, a year, ten or twenty years will definitely reap commensurate results. We verify buddhahood in this way, but there are countless stages with a limitless range of depth and clarity along the way.

Even so, the content of zazen at each of these stages is exactly the same. Though the practitioner may be unaware of it, he or she is a complete manifestation of the essential world; we all experience the same single buddhahood. From the first step in our practice to the very last, even if there are billions of stages on the way, the content of the meditation at any two stages is exactly the same. We are forever treading the buddha ground and perfectly manifesting buddha nature. This is what "cause and effect are one" and "stages with no stages, no stages in stages" mean.

Let's think of our essential nature as being like a large crystal ball, the surface of which has been covered over with a hard, thick crust of dirt. Daily meditation is like the process of rubbing away, little by little, the dirty crust. Buddhahood is achieved when all the dirt has been removed and the transparent crystal ball is completely revealed. Yet our essential nature is transparent crystal, even from the very beginning. This is why Hakuin Zenji says that all beings are intrinsically awake. All distinctions and gradations are nothing more than the relative thickness of the obscuring crust. From the vantage point of the crystal ball "all beings are intrinsically awake" and are "intrinsically endowed with buddha nature," but from the side of the dirt encrusted on it we are all "deeply sinful, ordinary beings."

So if a person who has just taken up the practice of zazen today trusts in the teaching of an authentic teacher and practices as directed, even if they are unaware of it, they embody absolute virtue that is no different from that of Shakyamuni or Amida Buddha. There is not a hairsbreadth difference between the meditation of a complete beginner, the practice of someone who has been sitting for two or three years, the practice of a long-term student of thirty or forty years, or the meditation of Shakyamuni and Bodhidharma: each is the perfect embodiment and experience of absolute virtue, symbolized by the crystal ball. Zazen is the "gate to oneness of cause and effect, the path that is neither two nor three."

Dōgen Zenji was referring to this innate purity when he said, "A beginner's meditation is the complete expression of perfect enlightenment." Each person is "the very mind, the very Buddha" according to his or her level of attainment. How could this be possible? It seems too good to be true.

The allegorical tale of Enyadatta searching for her head, which appears in the *Surangama Sutra*, helps to clarify this point:

Long ago in the Indian city of Shri there lived a person named Enyadatta. (In most versions of the story Enyadatta is a young woman, although the sutra doesn't actually mention her gender.) Each day, as soon as Enyadatta woke, she would first sit at her mirror to gaze at her comely face. One day, however, when she sat at her mirror she was surprised to find that her face wasn't there. (Had the mirror been turned around or was something obscuring her vision? The sutra doesn't explain the reason, but at any rate she couldn't see her own face.) The astonished Enyadatta, thinking the devil was at work, rushed around the streets of the city like a crazed person in search of her head. With disheveled hair, she ran barefoot through the city, totally beside herself.

Seeing this, her friends asked, "What happened?"

"It's terrible! Last night a devil ran away with my head," she told them.

"Nonsense! Your head's right on your shoulders!" they responded.

But no matter how many times they assured her, she wouldn't listen and continued running through the streets crying, "How terrible! How terrible!"

Finally, because in her frenzy Enyadatta was unable to listen to them, her friends bound Enyadatta to a pillar and slapped her face to make her settle down. Having been bound, Enyadatta grows calm and regains her composure. When her face is slapped she suddenly notices that her face exists.

Filled with joy at finding her head again, Enyadatta danced around, crying, "Here is my head! Here is my head!"

Buddhas and sentient beings both are endowed with the same essential nature, with the same perfect wisdom and virtue. In this respect there isn't the slightest difference between them. Unaware of the treasure within us, however, we act out a foolish play in which buddha nature madly searches for buddha nature. Is it, then, a waste of time to search for the truth? Not at all. Although at first this search may appear to be idiocy, it is in fact a wonderful thing.

Christ said, "Seek and you shall find." Seeking is nothing other than the prelude to our awakening. We approach our search blindly at first. Until we find the right direction and the best method for reaching our goal, we make repeated attempts that seem like wasted effort. But even perceiving the need to search means we have taken the first step toward accomplishing the Way.

Although we already possess within ourselves something of absolute value, because delusion turns our world topsy-turvy, like Enyadatta we vainly try to find treasure outside of ourselves. Out of pity for our plight, the buddhas and Zen ancestors kindly revealed that all beings are intrinsically awake and are never parted from the meditative absorption of Dharma nature, and furthermore, that all sentient and insentient beings simultaneously attain the Way. Unable to believe this, like dogs chasing a clod of dirt, we continue to seek the Dharma outside ourselves.

The act of sitting down, folding the hands and legs, and beginning the practice of daily Zen meditation (zazen) is like binding Enyadatta. Bodily movement is restricted in meditation. Although mental turmoil may continue as before, various methods, such as counting breaths, following the breath, just sitting, or practicing Mu, are employed to restrain the agitated mind. In this way, even though we are still deluded, the mind begins to calm down. We begin to unify our spirit and enter into meditative absorption, but because we are not yet enlightened, we aren't aware that the practice in itself reveals the Dharma body of the perfect Self.

As our meditation grows purer and deeper, Enyadatta quiets down to the point where she is able to notice the existence of her own head. Then, she suddenly forgets herself, and her head, which contains the entire universe, appears. There is no set pattern that triggers this realization. For Shakyamuni Buddha it was the moment he looked up and saw the morning star twinkling in the eastern sky. Rei'un saw a peach blossom, Kyōgen heard the sound of a stone hitting a bamboo stalk, and Gensha cried out in pain upon stubbing his toe on a rock. In an instant, each suddenly lost awareness of himself and realized his own true nature—just as Enyadatta realized her own head.

The joy that Enyadatta experienced upon realizing that her head had never been lost was truly beyond expression. At that moment some are filled with an excitement that surprises the heavens and shakes the earth, for some the earth moves and dances beneath their feet, while for others, it's simply, "Huh. So that's it."

Yet we can't say that Enyadatta's madness has totally subsided so long as she dances around grabbing her head and crying, "Here is my head!" Likewise, even if we have seen into our own nature, as long as we run around telling people about it we are still the "nobly ill" and cannot yet be called "a person of no matter." When Enyadatta recovers from her madness and even the rediscovery of her head ceases to occupy her attention, she arrives at a state where "there is not even the memory of having incurred a disorder like awakening."

Bassui Zenji speaks of this:

> You should now continuously rid yourself of what you have realized. Go back to the very subject who realizes, to the very roots, and maintain that state. As your delusions fall away, your true nature will become ever more lucid and radiant, like a jewel becoming lustrous under continued polishing until it lights up the world in every direction. Don't doubt this!

We can divide the above story of Enyadatta seeking her head into three sections: the first being before she goes into a frenzy, the second when she frantically searches for her head, and the last being after she has realized that her head is still there and returns to normal. The head is of course right there on her shoulders throughout all three stages. Whether she is aware of it or not, her head is always one and the same head. Although she isn't aware of the presence of her head as she frantically searches for it, she seems perfectly whole to others. In a similar manner, although we ourselves aren't aware of it when in deep meditative absorption as we practice counting the breath, following the breath, just sitting, or a koan, we are always treading the Buddha ground. We are the complete manifestation of that clear, unblemished crystal. This is cause and effect as one, the oneness of cause and effect.

The doctrine of "cause and effect as one" may seem difficult, but once understood it is very simple. When we sit earnestly, every place at all times is the buddha realm. Because our practice embodies the buddha realm itself, our delusions and troubles simply fall away, gradually, day by day.

Deceptive Phenomena 10

INTRODUCTION

In order to practice Zen it is helpful to have an understanding of deceptive phenomena (*makyō*),[32] which are phenomena or states of mind that can become impediments to practice. Speaking from the highest standpoint—the standpoint of the essential world—every concept, thought, and feeling that even momentarily flashes into our awareness arises from the delusion of dualistic opposition and could thus be considered deceptive.

Buddhist cosmology divides the universe of sentient beings into ten realms. Among them, six are realms of delusion: the realms of hell beings, hungry spirits, beasts, violent demigods,[33] humans, and heavenly beings. The remaining four are the realms of enlightenment: the realms of those who attain enlightenment studying with a teacher (*shravaka*), those who attain enlightenment on their own (*pratyekabuddha*), bodhisattvas, and buddhas. Among the beings of these ten realms, delusion is most severe for hell beings, for in hell the delusion of dualistic opposition between subject and object is strongest and hell beings see things outside of themselves as enemies. Delusions progressively decrease in the realms of hungry spirits, beasts, violent demigods, human beings, and heavenly beings, and they decrease even further in the realms of those who attain enlightenment on their own, those who attain enlightenment studying with a teacher, and bodhisattvas. But even at the level of a bodhisattva, delusions are not completely gone; only in the realm of the buddhas do they totally disappear.

From the standpoint of actual practice, "deceptive phenomena" refers to all internal and external impediments to practice. Inner deceptive phenomena, traditionally called "inner demons," include excuses for giving up meditation and unusual states of consciousness that arise as practice progresses, especially if we cling to them, thinking them to have deep significance. They also include the pride that diverts us from practice, and fantasies, either pleasurable or fearful, that lead us to completely neglect our practice.

We can even consider external impediments that are well beyond our control to be outer deceptive phenomena, traditionally called "outer demons," such as illness or the pressure of work, for example, which can make it difficult to keep up our practice. To a certain extent, inner and outer deceptive phenomena disturb everyone; we must face them with courage when they trouble us. If we believe in the Three Treasures, trust in the teachings of a true teacher, and resolve to practice diligently, then deceptive phenomena can't ever deter us. We may also pray for the protection of the buddhas and ancestors.

In his *Prayer for Arousing the Vow* (*Eiheikōso Hotsuganmon*), Dōgen Zenji says:

> Even though the wicked deeds I've accumulated in the past obstruct my way, may the many buddhas and Zen ancestors who have already attained the Buddha Way still take pity on me and free me from the karma that I've accumulated, removing all obstacles to my practice of the Way. May they share with me their compassion, the virtuous power of which pervades the entire world of dharmas and prevails throughout the universe.

Here I will deal with impediments to practice in a narrower sense—namely, the inner deceptive phenomena that can affect us during meditation.

Deceptive Phenomena Prior to Seeing into One's Own Nature

Those who practice zazen for one or two hours a day probably will not encounter deceptive phenomena. Most people who participate in an intensive meditation retreat, however, and apply themselves assiduously to the practice for long hours will begin to experience at least some of them.

Visual deceptive phenomena are usually the first to appear: the space before your eyes, for example, may suddenly become black, and you won't be able to see any color no matter how wide you open your eyes; or everything may become as white as snow, or beautiful colored patterns may appear; the lines on the *tatami* mat may begin to undulate, the scene on the sliding paper door may begin to dance, or the pattern of the wood grain may suddenly turn into strange creatures; the Buddha may appear and pat you on the head. Then there are aural phenomena: you may suddenly hear the faint music of a *shakuhachi* flute out of nowhere, and no matter how you shake your head you cannot make the sound stop; or you may hear a loud explosion below yourself, as if a bomb had gone off. Deceptive olfactory phenomena may also occur: it may seem as if an ethereal, otherworldly fragrance fills the room. Of course, you will be the only one aware of these things—they have nothing to do with other people.

In short, these deceptive phenomena are myriad in variety, differ for each individual, and lack any predictable form. In his *Guidelines for Zen*, Keizan Zenji takes up unusual somatic sensations and says that they result from improper breathing:

> The body may feel hot or cold, taut or soft, heavy or light. All these unusual sensations result from not regulating the breath, and you must correct this. . . . It may happen that your mind feels depressed, or at peace, groggy, or alert. It may seem as if you can see through walls to the outside or into your own body. You may see the bodies of buddhas or bodhisattvas. You may have flashes of insight and understand the sutras. All of these unusual phenomena are disorders that happen due to faulty breathing.

According to this interpretation, things that appear at first glance to be supernatural phenomena are actually the results of improperly regulating the breath.

From the perspective of practicing meditation, we need to understand the substance of these deceptive phenomena in order to correctly treat them. They can become an impediment to practice if we make them into a problem that we attempt to control. But they present no problem to us if we ignore them and avoid getting tangled up in them. These phenomena are similar in a number of ways to dreams, which also have no actual substance. The images that appear in dreams are the contents of our unconscious mind assuming different forms, mingling by means of association, and manifesting on the surface of consciousness. But these images have no objective existence. In the same way, deceptive phenomena, even negative ones such as being bitten by a wild animal, have no real substance. Likewise, no matter how wonderful the phenomena may be, they will not necessarily result in good fortune. Just like dreams, they don't exist objectively and are nothing more than shadow-figures of the mind. We call them deceptive, or mental demons, by way of warning. Common sense is useless when it comes to understanding them. If we pay attention to them, give value to them, or become attached to them, they become impediments to our practice.

They resemble dreams in yet another way. We only experience dreams when we are about to enter into or just after we emerge from deep sleep. Similarly, deceptive phenomena don't occur when our minds are scattered and haven't yet settled down, nor do they appear after we have entered into deep meditative absorption. It is precisely when we are in a semi-deep state of meditation that they make their appearance. In other words, as the power of our concentration gradually increases and the intrusion of the six senses into our awareness finally begins to settle down, the previously submerged seventh consciousness, the afflicted mind, begins to act, and we start to experience various types of deceptive phenomena.

When they begin to appear, we can take them as proof that our Zen power of concentration[34] is gradually improving, at which point we must spur ourselves on and apply ourselves ever more fervently to practice. The treasure is near and the day approaching when we will unmistakably realize our primal face from before our parents were born. We should remember, then, that whatever delusion we experience and whatever phenomena appear, we should pay no attention to them, but simply continue our practice, becoming completely one with it, whether we are counting or following the breath, working with Mu, or just sitting.

DECEPTIVE PHENOMENA
AFTER SEEING INTO ONE'S OWN NATURE

Hallucinatory phenomena tend to be more prevalent prior to seeing into one's own nature, but they may appear even afterward. Developing an attitude of pride is a prime example of a deception that can occur after seeing into one's own nature. When we were in the middle of the nightmare of our delusive selves, we were unaware that we were in darkness or that we were living in a dream, but upon seeing into our own nature we see a world of light, even if only momentarily. We have half-awakened from a dream and become aware, however groggily, of the real world, a world that few people experience. Having glimpsed this world, we ecstatically imagine we have seen through to the very heart of the essential world. We may become proud of having seen into our own nature and stop practicing, or eventually lead others into error.

Even Hakuin Zenji, widely considered one of the greatest Japanese Zen masters of the past eight hundred years, had to go through arduous practice and trials after his first experience of seeing into his own nature in order to overcome the Zen sickness of a proud heart. Anyone who has a big head after some little experience of seeing into their own nature is liable to find themselves subject to the correction of the buddhas.

After having a confirmed experience of seeing into your own nature, you must devote yourself all the more ardently to meditation, go to private interview as often as possible, and be stern with yourself while being meek toward others. You must ceaselessly call upon the intercession of the buddhas and Zen ancestors. If you follow these instructions, your experience of seeing into your own nature won't become a form of delusion but will merely be the first barrier that everyone must pass through on the Way.

A second form of deceptive phenomena that can occur after kenshō is "ideas about emptiness." When you see into your own nature, you encounter an unexpected world of equality in which self and other are eliminated and you find peace in knowing that everything has always been all right. Resting in the world of nonduality, you can fall into self-deception, content with your own individual peace and unconcerned about the suffering of others. This is the delusion of seeing only a single aspect of nonduality, where there are "no sentient beings to save."

This problem is taken up in Case 2 of the *Gateless Gate*, "Hyakujō and the Fox":

> Whenever Master Hyakujō delivered a sermon, an old man was always there listening to the monks. When they left, he left too. One day, however, he remained behind.

The master asked him, "What man are you, standing in front of me?"

The old man replied, "Indeed, I am not a man. In the past, in the time of Kashyapa Buddha, I lived on this mountain (as a Zen priest). On one occasion a monk asked me, 'Does a perfectly enlightened person fall under the law of cause and effect or not?' I answered, 'He does not.' Because of this answer, I fell into the state of a fox for five hundred lives. Now, I beg you, Master, please say a turning word on my behalf and release me from the body of a fox." Then he asked, "Does a perfectly enlightened person fall under the law of cause and effect or not?"

The master answered, "The law of cause and effect cannot be obscured."

Upon hearing this, the old man immediately became deeply enlightened.

The expression "fox Zen," which means Zen that knows only the side of emptiness, has its origin here.

The law of cause and effect governs the phenomenal world, the world of distinction, but there is no place where it applies in the nondual world of equality. The monk's answer, "He does not," is thus not entirely wrong. But true reality has two sides: "Sameness is precisely distinction, distinction precisely sameness." To see just the single aspect of sameness and say "He does not fall under the law of cause and effect" is a one-sided view that goes against the truth. This is why the old monk was unable to escape from becoming a fox. He was only able to return to his original self when, taking the form of a monk, he told his story to Hyakujō, who supplied the other side of reality by saying, "The law of cause and effect cannot be obscured."

Another aspect of delusion after seeing into one's own nature is found in statements like, "Life is equally empty whether rich or poor, so it's enough to become one with your poverty and live with it if you are poor." Someone who sees only the side of emptiness and overlooks the benefits of sowing good fortune may look askance at anyone with wealth. Or someone might say, "If you are suffering from illness, just become suffering; when suffering, you become one with the whole universe, and then there is no more suffering." For one caught up in this one side of reality, the heart of compassion that seeks to relieve a sick person of their suffering closes. Such a person is a prisoner of one-sided enlightenment. The ancients warned against this, calling it "the deep abyss of liberation."

Before seeing into our own nature we cling to the dualistic view of subject and object as opposites. After seeing into our own nature we cling to the monistic view of equality, to "ideas of emptiness." These two attachments are alike in that they are both forms of delusion.

In his *Song of Realizing the Way* Yōka Daishi says:

> The great void banishes cause and effect.
> This chaos only invites disaster.
> The sickness of clinging to the void and rejecting the world of
>   being
> is like escaping from drowning by leaping into fire.

In the world of emptiness there is neither cause nor effect, neither good nor evil, neither God nor Buddha. Those who negate cause and effect fail to recognize humanity and ignore morality. Accumulating delusion in the present and straying onto paths of evil in the future, such people invite only disaster and suffering. In order to avoid being carried away by such delusion after seeing into one's own nature, students must regularly go for private interview, fervently recite the Four Vows after meditation, endeavor to develop the spirit of compassion, and keep polishing the Dharma eye. Along with this, they should study the sutras and records of the Zen ancestors, and resolve to model their actions on the examples of goodness and virtue set by the ancient sages.

Attachment to Dharma[35] is a third form of delusion after seeing into one's own nature. Although the expression "attachment to Dharma" refers to various levels of such attachment, here we are not concerned with the subtle attachments that remain in the final stages of practice, but with the coarser, more obvious ones. For example, speaking indiscriminately and elatedly about meditation in front of others, talking boastfully about the experience of seeing one's own nature, or going to great lengths to promote zazen, dragging people who aren't really interested to group Zen meditation sessions, are all forms of Dharma attachment. It's unlikely that true seekers of the Dharma would do such things, even if asked. But when still burning with fervor, people are apt to fall into these kinds of delusion. Not only do such actions damage our own virtue, they give others a false understanding of Zen and may cause them to dislike or make fun of it, which ultimately harms the efficacy of the Buddha Way. We should always keep our practice a secret from others. A passage in the final section of Tōzan Daishi's "Precious Mirror Samadhi" (*Hōkyō Zammai*) reads:

> Working alone, unobtrusively,
> Practice like a fool, like an idiot.
> Just to continue like this
> is called the host within the host.

Belief, Understanding, Practice, Realization, and Personalization 11

Although belief, understanding, practice, enlightenment, and personalization come together into a single whole on the Zen path, they are not unique to Zen—any authentic religion will possess them. But just what is it that we believe, understand, practice, realize, and personalize in Zen? It is, of course, our True Self. The True Self is exactly the same thing as the true fact. Although the words "True Self" sound more subjective and the expression "true fact" sounds more objective, Shakyamuni Buddha realized both aspects in his great enlightenment: our own essential nature is identical to the essential nature of the universe—this is none other than unexcelled complete awakening. This is the fundamental standpoint of Buddhism.

Harada Roshi provides a painstaking explanation of the five elements of belief, understanding, practice, enlightenment, and personalization in his *Essentials of Zen Practice (Sanzen no Hiketsu)*, on which I will base my explanation in this chapter.

BELIEF

Every religion probably begins with belief. Without some initial belief, most people will be unlikely to even want to spend time listening to religious teachings. From the standpoint of authentic Zen, belief means accepting the truth that the three classes of Three Treasures are one.[36] More directly, it means belief in the opening statement of Hakuin Zenji's *Song in Praise of Zazen*: "All beings are intrinsically awake." Some individuals, thanks to their fortunate karmic connection to the Dharma, are able to immediately believe this statement without argument. The Sixth Zen Ancestor Enō Zenji (Hui-neng), for example, attained enlightenment immediately after hearing the line from the Diamond Sutra, "Dwelling nowhere, the mind emerges."

Allowing for different levels in the depth of faith, we can say that when someone has faith, that belief can lead to a peace and salvation commensurate with their degree of faith. Thus we can say, to this extent, that they already "sit comfortably at home."

However, belief can easily become superstition or fanaticism if it is not accompanied by intellectual understanding. It doesn't matter how many times someone may exhort us to "just believe," if we lack real conviction in our hearts, we will never develop the decisive determination needed for practice. Furthermore, we will never reach a state of truth freed from doubt unless we practice and realize our True Self. Although we may believe in its reality, we need to actually see it with our own eyes before we truly know it to be true.

UNDERSTANDING

The two wheels that drive the vehicle of Zen practice are hearing the Dharma from a true master and practicing zazen. Dōgen Zenji explains these two wheels in his *Guidelines for Studying the Way*:

> There are naturally two aspects of settling the matter of body and mind: going to a teacher to hear the Dharma and practicing zazen. Hearing the Dharma lets consciousness go free. Zazen must make the two matters of practice and realization like the left and right hands. If you throw away either, you cannot attain realization.[37]

After developing belief, we must use the light of the intellect to accurately and clearly understand the Buddha Way. To do this it is essential to study authentic Dharma with a true master. If we mistakenly make arbitrary judgments or listen to heretical teachings, we will arrive at false understanding that could prevent the teachings from taking root. To practice under and study the Dharma directly with a true teacher includes participation in periods of intensive meditation, attending group meditation sessions, listening to the teacher's public talks, and receiving individual instruction in the private interview room.

In order to correctly understand the Dharma, however, we must also read and study the teachings. This is absolutely essential for students who do not have access to a true teacher. I would recommend first of all, among all the works on Buddhism, the teachings of Shakyamuni Buddha as recorded in the sutras, followed by the records and writings of early Zen founders, as well as the public talks of enlightened masters. In the beginning we may struggle to understand such texts, but if we repeatedly read them we will in time be able to appreciate, however dimly, the world they discuss.

Our understanding increases in proportion to our level of training and perceptiveness. As we progress in practice our understanding and appreciation deepens, so we don't need to exhaust ourselves trying immediately to grasp the meaning of an unclear passage. It is enough to savor the passages that we don't understand. At least once or twice a year, however, we should find an opportunity to see a true teacher and hear his or her public talks or lectures. Otherwise we may misunderstand the teaching and acquire a complacent attitude toward Zen.

At least before seeing into one's own nature, one should avoid reading books that discuss Zen. Outsiders to Zen with only a smattering of knowledge and no real experience of sitting have taken advantage of the recent boom of interest in Zen to write a variety of books that explain the subject. It is best for beginners not to read such books at all. Reading such books might enhance your general knowledge of the subject after you have seen into your own nature, when your understanding is more accurate and your discernment of the Dharma clearer. But until then such books might actually be harmful.

The publication of books with titles like "This-or-That Zen" or "Zen Such-and-Such" supposedly address a blind spot for modern readers, who are easily impressed and drawn in by the printed word. Such books may sell extremely well. It is quite common to find this sort of ill-informed, "popular" take on Zen among Zen books authored by non-Japanese authors. For the most part, these people are not at all aware that there is a side to Zen that clearly sets it apart from philosophy and psychology. This is why beginners are better off sticking to original texts authored by worthy masters of ancient times. I can confidently recommend the following works to beginning students of Zen:

- ▸ *Prajnaparamita Heart Sutra*
- ▸ *Principle of Practice and Enlightenment* [38]

- ▸ *Song in Praise of Zazen* by Hakuin Zenji[39]
- ▸ *Recommending Zazen to All People* by Dōgen Zenji[40]
- ▸ *Guidelines for Studying the Way* by Dōgen Zenji[41]
- ▸ *The Book of Rinzai*[42]
- ▸ *The Teachings of Bassui Zenji*
- ▸ *Guidelines for Zazen* by Keizan Zenji[43]
- ▸ *Spurring Students through Zen Barriers* by Unsei Shukō Zenji[44]
- ▸ *The Ten Ox-Herding Pictures* by Kakuan Zenji
- ▸ *Talk on Wholehearted Practice of the Way* by Dōgen Zenji[45]

We deepen our correct understanding of the practice of Zen meditation and nurture an attitude of belief through direct contact with the teachings of the ancient saints and sages. This is known as "ancient teachings illuminating the mind."[46] We prevent ourselves from straying onto false paths by examining our mental states and actions in the light of the words of the Buddha and Zen ancestors.

PRACTICE

Once we have gained a foothold in belief and understanding, our next step is to begin to practice. "Practice" here doesn't refer to intense ascetic hardship but to the practice of meditation. At the beginning of his *Talk on Wholehearted Practice of the Way*, Dōgen Zenji writes:

> All buddhas and "ones who have thus come" have together transmitted the wondrous Dharma in a single unbroken line. In realizing unexcelled, complete awakening, they possess the highest and most wondrous, uncaused skill—a skill that has been transmitted from buddha to buddha without deviation, because the criterion for its transmission is meditative absorption, freely received and used. In order to delight in this meditative absorption, we take sitting upright and practicing zazen to be the true gate.

Dōgen Zenji tells us that Zen meditation is the way to the wisdom of unexcelled, complete awakening, that zazen itself is the true gate.

Without meditation there can be no understanding of Zen, much less any understanding of the workings of Buddha.

There are too many people today who have never felt the pain of sitting in their legs yet who speak with supposed authority on the subject of Zen. The mere mention of the word "Zen" seems to be enough for such people to delude themselves that they are speaking about some mysterious truth that is beyond the understanding of others. Such deluded people only end up deceiving and misleading others. Even some Zen monks who are supposed to be specialists on the subject eagerly devour the ancients' words that "Doing is Zen, sitting is Zen," or cling to just one side of statements like "Rites are the same as Buddhadharma, ceremonies the same as the Zen sect," and basing their authority on inadequate understanding, use such statements as an excuse to avoid actually practicing zazen. It seems as if traditional Zen might just be disappearing!

These types of errors occur because when belief and understanding are incorrect, one's attitude toward practice will also be wrong. Since there can be no realization or personalization without actually practicing Zen, such people end up losing their ability to save all beings. It is my personal feeling that all the harmful influences in the world of Zen today have their origin in this. It is a regrettable situation and those who seriously seek true Dharma must be careful about this.

REALIZATION

Realization means awakening—the core of the Zen way of Buddha-dharma. But there are differences of opinion as to what the actual nature of satori is. This can confuse practitioners and lead them to practice incorrectly. Since this confusion can have such negative consequences, I will take up this problem in some detail here.

The Japanese word for realization is *shō*, which literally means "proven" or "authenticated." But the word *kenshō* ("seeing into one's own nature") can also mean realization. Confusion arises from this use of the word *kenshō*. But some members of the modern Sōtō sect use statements that Dōgen Zenji made in the *Shōbōgenzō* and other writings to claim that he denied the existence of seeing into one's own nature.

It does seem that Dōgen made statements that could, at first glance, be interpreted as denials of the need for realization:

> Only when one casts body and mind into Buddhadharma and practices with no further hope of anything—even the hope to realize and attain the Dharma—can one be called an undefiled practitioner. This is what is meant by, "Do not stay where there is Buddha; run quickly away from where there is no Buddha."[47]

> To continue sitting upright with nothing to attain or nothing to realize is the Way of the Zen ancestors. Although the ancients encouraged both koan Zen and just sitting, they principally encouraged meditation as such. Although there have been some who awakened by practicing koans, their awakening was actually due to the merits of sitting. The true merit of the practice is in the sitting itself.[48]

If we take such statements out of context they could be interpreted to mean that sitting itself is the whole of practice, and seeking realization is wrong. The "sitting itself" that Dōgen speaks of in this passage is what we call "just sitting" in modern language. We may be tempted to take his statement to mean that it is enough *just* to sit, that sitting is the totality of Zen. But is this really true?

The word realization is usually used synonymously with the phrase "seeing into one's own nature," but using it this way creates a problem. According to Dōgen, there is an important difference between seeing into one's own nature (*kenshō*) and authentication (*shō*) or realization of the Way (*godō*). Seeing into one's own nature is usually interpreted as equivalent to the stage of "Seeing the Ox," the third in the series of Kakuan's *Ten Ox-Herding Pictures*. This is clearly not the entirety of Buddhism. When Dōgen uses the term, he is speaking from the position of having transcended even the tenth stage in the ox-herding series—in other words, from the level where both practice and enlightenment have been transcended.

However, the phrase "seeing into one's own nature" is sometimes used to refer to the entire process, from "Seeing the Ox" up until the tenth stage, "Entering the Marketplace with Helping Hands." I feel that Bassui Zenji's use of the phrase "seeing into one's own nature," for example, is of this type, because he sees any lack of maturity in a practitioner as the result of "incompletely seeing into one's own nature."[49] Other Zen masters, like Iida Tōin Roshi, for example, who said, "There is no Zen without seeing into one's own nature," also stress the importance of seeing into one's own nature. If the self-realization that occurs when both body and mind truly fall away during a sudden awakening is truly seeing into one's own nature, then the experience of "body and mind fallen away" that Dōgen had under Nyojō Zenji must also be a case of what Iida Tōin Roshi referred to as "the experience of kenshō." Usually, however, this initial experience refers to nothing more than the stage of "Seeing the Ox." Would it even be possible to realize and attain the whole of the Buddhist path in a single leap, without passing through the various stages of seeing into one's own nature? I would have to say, "No." With the possible exception of Shakyamuni Buddha, such cases haven't even occurred among illustrious Zen ancestors.

Dōgen Zenji spent nine years studying under Eisai Zenji and Myōzen Zenji to master the teachings of the Rinzai sect before traveling to China to study under Nyojō Zenji. During that period he had undoubtedly passed beyond the stage usually referred to as "seeing into one's own nature." Not satisfied with this, he resolved to go to China to practice further. When studying with Nyojō Zenji of Tendō-San Temple, he finally came to full realization of the Buddhadharma. That was when he experienced "body and mind fallen away." At that point he finally realized "there is not even a trace of Buddhadharma" and confirmed for himself that he had "completed the matter of a lifetime's practice." It would only be natural for Dōgen Zenji, given the depth of his experience, to reprimand anyone who thought their practice was finished merely upon seeing into their own nature.

Dōgen was evidently not in favor of the phrase "seeing into one's own nature," but he never denied realization. His "authentication," however, was not the seeing into one's own nature spoken of by the Zen masters of the Sung Dynasty, which was probably little different than the seeing into one's own nature spoken of today. Dōgen used various expressions to refer to realization:

> ▸ *Authentication*: to authenticate the Supreme Way;[50] to authenticate and attain Buddhadharma; to become one with and realize the mind; to attain and realize the Way.
> ▸ *To attain the Way*:[51] to attain the Way and clarify the mind.
> ▸ *To realize the Way*:[52] to realize the Way and attain the Dharma; to hear sounds and realize the Way.
> ▸ *To see colors and clarify the mind.*[53]

Dōgen seemed to prefer "authentication" out of all of these as his term for awakening. We can see "authentication," "attaining the Way," and "attaining the Dharma" as practically synonymous. The experience of authentication that he speaks of also means "authenticating the Way," "realizing the Way," and "attaining the Way." It means realizing unexcelled, complete awakening or the Supreme Way.

The Zen of Dōgen Zenji has its roots in his absolute conviction, based on experience in actual practice, that "practice encompasses authentication." Authentication necessarily means gaining clear realization in self-awakening. It is for this reason that Dōgen says:

> If we were to attain realization without practice, how could we understand the Buddha's teaching on delusion and enlightenment?[54]

Dōgen Zenji teaches that if we wish to reach true peace of mind so we can serve others, we must first see into our own nature and realize the Way. Yet the true form of the Buddha Way is "stages with no stages." "Stages" and "no stages" are merely two aspects of the same reality. Thus far in this chapter we have looked at seeing into one's own nature and authentication from the viewpoint of levels or stages of practice. But we should not forget the other viewpoint—that of the essential world, where all beings are intrinsically awake. Speaking from the side of no stages, Dōgen said:

> If one were to impress the Buddha-seal upon the three types of action[55] and sit in meditative absorption, even for a short time, the entire universe of dharmas would become the Buddha-seal and all of empty space enlightened.[56]

Both Harada Roshi and Yasutani Roshi deplored how, in modern Zen, the Rinzai sect tends to cling to the aspect of stages in practice and forget the solemnity of "no stages," and the Sōtō sect is content with the "no stages" Zen of little consequence and neglects the arduous stages of practice.

PERSONALIZATION[57]

Personalization is the final step where the experience of awakening is totally embodied in our own flesh and blood and in every aspect of our daily lives. The fourth stage of the *Five Modes of Endeavor and Accomplishment*, "Sharing Accomplishment," is the first step in this process. This is where we return to our original self—where the excitement and pride that follow the enlightenment experience are extinguished and traces of delusion, such as dualistic views, are done away with. We return to the state of the ordinary person without complaints or objections. But at this stage traces of pride about our enlightenment still remain—"the spirit tortoise cannot avoid leaving the traces of its tail on the sand."

We must press on from here to the fifth of the five positions, "Accomplishment without Accomplishment," where the traces of awakening are totally wiped away and we attain true liberation. At this stage we finally enter the marketplace with helping hands—in other words, we stand in the midst of the everyday world to fulfill the vow of saving others. This is the fifth stage, "Practicing and Repaying the Debt of Gratitude," in Dōgen's *Principle of Practice and Enlightenment*. For someone like me, this is a far distant state, and I have the feeling of viewing the gate of my ancestral home from a distance of ten thousand miles.

Thus, the Buddha Way is comprised of nothing other than believing in, understanding, practicing, and realizing our essential nature of intrinsic buddhahood—where in one sense there is not one thing, but in another our essential nature is complete, perfect, and limitless—and then personalizing that realization.

Eight Great Tenets of Mahayana Buddhism 12

In his *Essentials of Zen Practice*, Harada Sogaku Roshi lists the eight great tenets of Mahayana Buddhism. These tenets examine, from eight different angles, the absolute self, the true Fact. The eight tenets are one, and each one of them is eight, which means that any one tenet fully contains the other seven. If you can truly accept any one of them, then the other seven will be natural and self-evident. The eight tenets are as follows:

1. All Beings Are Intrinsically Endowed with Buddha Nature
2. Unenlightened Beings Cling to the Illusion of a Self
3. Life Continues
4. Cause and Effect Are Inevitable
5. Buddhas Actually Exist
6. Sentient Beings and Buddhas Mutually Interact
7. Self and Other Are Not Two
8. All Beings Are in the Process of Becoming Buddhas

To believe in and understand these eight tenets is to trust in Mahayana Buddhism. What I have written so far in this book has been, more or less, an elucidation of matters concerning these eight tenets. Now, to sum up, I would like to provide a brief explanation of each of them.

ALL BEINGS ARE INTRINSICALLY ENDOWED WITH BUDDHA NATURE

The tenet that all beings are intrinsically endowed with buddha nature is also sometimes phrased "all beings are intrinsically awake." To clearly come to a direct, lived understanding of buddha nature, to attain the spiritual state of great peace of mind, and to make it part of one's daily life is to correctly transmit the Zen of the buddhas and Zen ancestors.

On the other hand, to intellectually study buddha nature and to offer theories and proofs concerning it is to work with Buddhist doctrine or philosophy.

UNENLIGHTENED BEINGS CLING TO THE ILLUSION OF A SELF

Usually we think of our individual body and mind as our "self," and cling to this idea of who we think we are. But this belief is a kind of superstition or delusive attachment; it is not the actual truth. Most people immediately resist the idea that our sense of self is an "inverted illusion." In fact, this universal belief in the individual self is itself the very source of dualism and the cause of suffering. To actually experience the total emptiness of this self is "awakening" in Zen.

When we speak of our original buddha nature, we are speaking from the perspective of our essential nature. From the perspective of the world of phenomena, however, the normal condition of ordinary, unenlightened people is one of attachment to an individual self, which is perceived to be a solid mass, but which is in fact illusory. As long as we fail to open the eye of enlightenment, we will be unable to see that what we usually think of as our "self" has never really existed.

The brighter our intrinsic buddha nature becomes, the more clearly we will see the shadow of the illusory self. In this sense, the degree to which we are aware of our delusory attachment to the self is determined by the extent to which our intrinsic buddha nature manifests itself. Ordinary beings, without any exception, suffer from delusive attachment to an individual self. The various differences that exist in the relative strength and intensity of this delusion depend on the depths of personal practice and the extent of one's karmic relationship to the Dharma. It is no exaggeration to say that the entire practice of ethics and morality boils down to the means of decreasing this delusory attachment to an individual self.

LIFE CONTINUES

In the simplest terms, "life continues" means that life is eternal and indestructible. According to the natural sciences, when a life form, human being or otherwise, dies, the materials that comprise its body disintegrate into their basic elements and disperse; death is final, and any talk of subsequent lives after death is nothing more than superstition. Buddhism rejects this as a nihilistic view.[58]

Even before Shakyamuni Buddha's time, currents of thought that denied the continuity of life after death were prevalent. In regard to such views, Dōgen says:

> Some say, "When a person dies, he definitely returns to the ocean of True Nature. If one naturally returns to the ocean of enlightenment, even if one doesn't practice Buddhadharma, then there is no further cycle of birth and death. Thus there is no subsequent life." This is a nihilistic view held by non-Buddhists. Although some who propound this view may wear the garb of Buddhist monks or nuns, if they hold such false views they are non-Buddhist and not disciples of the Buddha."[59]

Although the ideas about returning to the ocean of True Nature expressed in this passage differ from the views of the natural sciences, both deny subsequent lives after death and are thus types of nihilistic view.

Another view recognizes that life continues but asserts that when a person dies, a spiritual entity (the soul), which had been dwelling in the body until then, departs one fleshly body to enter a new life, like a cicada sloughing off its chrysalis. This is called a view of continuity or an eternalist view.[60] Dōgen also takes issue with this perspective:

> What you have just said is certainly not Buddhist Dharma, but rather the view of the followers of the nonbeliever Shrenika[61] (a school of naturalism in India), which holds that we have in our bodies a spiritual intelligence that distinguishes good or bad, right or wrong, pleasurable or painful, and bitter or sweet. When the body dies this spiritual intelligence parts from the body and is reborn somewhere else. So although the body dies the spiritual intelligence lives on in another place, never perishing. Such is the teaching of the nonbeliever Shrenika. If you think such a theory constitutes the Buddhist

teaching, you are even more foolish than someone who mistakes a roof tile for a gold coin.[62]

According to Dōgen, then, the relative understanding that a soul remains while the form is destroyed contradicts Buddhadharma. But how exactly do eternalist views, which seem to agree that life goes on, differ from the correct views of Buddhism? Dōgen gives a painstaking explanation of this matter:

> Buddhism has taught, from the very beginning, that body and mind are one, and that form and essence are not two different things. Be certain that this was taught in both India and China, without any deviation. Furthermore, when Buddhism teaches immutability it means that all things are unchanging; it does not make a distinction between body and mind. When it teaches annihilation from moment to moment it means that all things are destroyed; it does not make a distinction between form and its essence. So how can one say that the body ceases but the mind is unchanging? Wouldn't that go against the truth?
>
> Buddhism preaches that the fact of being born and dying, just as it is, is nirvana. Nirvana has never been spoken of outside of that. Moreover, those who mistakenly think that the mind is unchanging and has no connection to the body, and consider it to be the wisdom of the Buddha that is beyond life and death, should recognize that the very mind they use to think that thought is bound to the cycle of life and death. This is hopeless, isn't it?[63]

In order to make the Buddhist tenet on the continuation of life a little clearer, I will make use once more of my fraction $\alpha/\ominus$, wherein the numerator α is divided by the denominator $\ominus$, an encircled infinity sign. When we see into our own nature, we clearly realize the world of the denominator $\ominus$—this is our self, which is zero but possesses infinite capabilities, without beginning or end. However, the phenomenal self, represented by the numerator α, continues to undergo an endless process of change from birth to extinction. The force that propels this process of birth and rebirth is called "the power of karma,"[64] and the continuation of life is technically known as "continuity of the power of karma."[65] But the continuity of the power of karma is related only to changes in the world of the numerator α. Of course the numerator α always exists together with the world of the denominator $\ominus$, but since the five senses are completely unable to grasp the world of the denominator, what superficially appears to perception are changes in the forms of the phenomenal world of the numerator α.

If you throw a pebble into perfectly still water, waves form on the surface and spread out endlessly. But since gravity is working on the surface of the water, gradually the ripples become increasingly smaller, and the water eventually returns to its original state of perfect stillness. The world of the denominator, however, is without mass, so that gravity has no effect, and waves, once produced, ripple on forever. We can think of the power of karma like this. The working of our own minds, our own thoughts, creates the first wave. Positive thoughts produce positive waves; negative thoughts produce negative waves. In this way, the infinite changes that develop as a result of the intertwining of endless positive and negative thoughts appear as the numerator in the phenomenal world. But it is the fraction as a whole ($\alpha/\ominus$) that forever reincarnates, and not merely the numerator that changes according to the power of karma.

A person dies and is born again. Birth and death, leaving and arriving: *Abhidharma Treasury* and other texts explain this cycle of rebirth in great detail. Those who are interested in such matters should bear in mind that such explanations deal only with the phenomenal world. If you truly wish to concretely understand that life continues, then you must intimately see into your own nature.

In his younger days Harada Roshi wrote long letters to three of the greatest Japanese Zen masters of the time to seek their advice in his search for the ultimate solution to the problem of life and death. He received the following answer from Shaku Sōen Zenji: "Can we call one who does not know that life continues 'a disciple of the Buddha'? If you see into your own nature, this problem will be as simple as pie." Harada Roshi recorded in his autobiography how this reply brought him to his senses and strengthened his resolve to begin actual practice and attain awakening. In other words, if you realize your own nature, all doubts concerning not-leaving or not-arriving will totally disappear.

The *Shōbōgenzō* chapter "Life and Death"[66] contains a careful description of how we should view life and death from the point of view of the continuation of life:

> Trying to find Buddha outside the domain of life and death is like pointing your cart north when you want to go south, or facing south to look for the North Star. By doing so you gather more causes for life and death and lose the way of liberation. Accept life and death as nirvana; do not turn away from life and death and do not seek nirvana. Only then can you truly be detached from life and death. . . . Life and death is itself the life of the Buddha. If you despise and reject it, you lose the life of the Buddha. Consequently, if you are attached to life and death, you also lose the life of Buddha, left only with his outer form. Only when you are not disgusted by life and death nor attracted to nirvana will you enter the mind of Buddha.

The life of the Buddha spoken of here is eternal and indestructible; by no means is it just the perpetuation of the power of karma.

I would like to close this section with a passage on life and death found in Dōgen's *Extensive Record*:[67]

> Engo Zenji said, "Coming and going within life and death is the true human body."
>
> Nansen said, "Coming and going within life and death is the true body."
>
> Jōshū said, "Life and death is precisely the true person."
>
> Chōsha said, "Coming and going within life and death is exactly the true body of all buddhas."
>
> The teacher (Dōgen) said: These four worthies each set forth the spirit of their sects. What they say is well said, but it is not yet there. If it were I who said it, I would not say it thus, but rather: life and death is just life and death.[68]

CAUSE AND EFFECT ARE INEVITABLE

Most people would agree that natural phenomena, including our physiological bodies, are governed by the principle of cause and effect: if you eat too much, your stomach becomes upset; if you drink too much, you impair your judgment. However, some might disagree if we say that cause and effect govern all human affairs. Few people are willing to accept that good and bad fortune, calamities, and natural disasters necessarily arise due to this principle. Of course, expressions like "actions and consequences," and "good cause, good effect" are common, and it seems that everyone believes in cause and effect at least to some extent, but almost everyone will mix in hazy ideas about chance and fate. Correctly transmitted Buddhadharma, however, states outright that all phenomena are the inevitable manifestations of cause and effect. No other teaching presents such a thoroughgoing doctrine of causality.

Dōgen explains the matter as follows in the *Shōbōgenzō* chapter "Believing Deeply in Cause and Effect":[69]

> To study Buddhism, it is first necessary to clarify cause and effect. If one ignores cause and effect one will develop false views and sever the roots of goodness.
>
> The principle of cause and effect is very clear and there is no "I" in it: those who create evil will fall and those who practice good will rise, without a hairsbreadth of disparity between the two. If cause and effect had perished and ceased to be, then the buddhas would not have appeared in the world, the founding teacher would not have come from the West, and sentient beings would never have met the Buddha and heard the Dharma. People like Confucius or Lao-tse do not propound the principle of cause and effect. Only the buddhas and Zen ancestors have made this clear.

The second paragraph of the above quote also appears in *The Principle of Practice and Enlightenment*. We do find scattered passages that contain reference to the principle of causality in the writings of Confucius and Mencius. For example:

Households that accumulate virtue will definitely have good fortune; households that accumulate evil will definitely have calamity.[70]

He who does good in secret will definitely be rewarded in public.[71]

The merit of study is in that study itself.[72]

People like Confucius and Lao-tse were undoubtedly aware of the extent of cause and effect, but only Buddhadharma actually teaches the view that all phenomena appear and develop according to the principle of causality.

Even though we may hear the Dharma and study the Buddha Way, we will remain unable to believe in the principle of causality until our practice matures. This is to be expected. Since cause and effect is the activity of buddha nature, until we clearly experience buddha nature, we will not be able to accept the principle of causality without reservation. The following appears in Harada Sogaku Roshi's *Essentials of Zen Practice*:

> There is a very ardent Buddhist living in Tokyo who has done ample study of *Abhidharma Treasury*, *Treatise on Mind Only*, *Awakening of Faith in the Mahayana*, as well as the three main sections of the *Lotus Sutra*. He has also practiced meditation for several years, and having come to a thoroughgoing realization of the Way, his Dharma eye is quite clear at present. When he asked me the following question, however, he was still not completely clear. He asked, "Is *Record of the Hōkyō Era*[73] the work of Dōgen Zenji?" To which I replied, "Yes, it is."
>
> When I met him again about a month later, he asked me the same question and I gave the same answer. After another month had passed we met again, and he asked the same question for a third time. I asked him why he wanted to know the same thing over and over. The man then took out a copy of *Record of the Hōkyō Era* and said, "Please look at what is

written here." It was the section where Dōgen asked Nyojō Zenji, "Do we inevitably experience cause and effect?"

"Ah, so this is it," I said with a little surprise, and was able to answer that this was truly the writing of Dōgen Zenji. . . . It was quite natural that, until he clearly realized the fallen-away body and mind, Dōgen too had a thin veil of doubt concerning the principle of cause and effect. I must say that it was the absolutely unrelenting and painstaking nature of Dōgen's way for him to take even such a doubt to a true teacher.[74]

Nyojō Zenji's reply to Dōgen in *Record of the Hōkyō Era* was as follows:

Cause and effect cannot be negated. This is why Yōka Daishi said, "The great void banishes cause and effect. Yet this just invites dissipation and woe." If I speak about rejecting causality, those who reject it are people that sever the roots of goodness in the Buddhadharma. How can they be descendants of the buddhas and Zen ancestors?

So unless we see the principle of causality from the standpoint of past, present, and future, we won't be able to clearly understand it. In the chapter of the *Shōbōgenzō* entitled "Karma of the Three Times," Dōgen teaches that we are able to encounter the karmic effects of our actions, whether good or evil, in three periods: during this life, in the next life, or in a life beyond the next. This perspective helps us to overcome nihilistic views of karma, for we can understand that karma is still operating in situations where good people encounter misfortune and bad people prosper.

I would like to add a few words about three categories of cause and effect: small causes that have big effects, causes that have simultaneous effects, and causes that have effects that happen later. Small causes that have big effects are cases wherein the effect of a particular cause grows larger with the passage of time. This is why it is important to confess as soon as possible when you do something wrong in order to purify the action. Unless you prune a tree in its infancy, it will become so large that it will be difficult to cut down. Similarly, if you have performed a good act, it is best to keep it to yourself for as long as possible in order to nurture and prolong its effect. This is partly why Buddhism encourages us to keep our good deeds to ourselves.

Causes that have simultaneous effects are cases wherein one encounters the effect at the same time as one creates the cause. For example, we may feel happy when we're doing something good, even though others may not know about it. Likewise, we may suffer from pangs of conscience when we're doing something wrong, even if others don't know about it. However, causes that have effects that are truly simultaneous occur when we give in to uncontrollable anger, or when we experience the virtue of a bodhisattva and this world becomes the Pure Land while we are having compassionate thoughts. Causes that have effects that happen later are cases wherein an interval of time occurs between the cause and the effect.

Many will remain unconvinced of this for the time being, but to believe in, accept, and practice according to this unambiguous truth is the Buddha Way.

BUDDHAS ACTUALLY EXIST

The tenet that "buddhas actually exist" states that at this very moment myriad buddhas and bodhisattvas actually exist, not as abstract concepts but in reality. If we believe in the previous tenets, then we should be able to believe that buddhas actually exist. When a Zen practitioner vows to achieve the wisdom of enlightenment and to practice determinedly in this world and beyond, it's hard to imagine what a wonderful character might develop from this intention. Since the future extends thousands, millions, and billions of years into eternity, such a person will inevitably attain buddhahood. Given this tenet, how many people in the past must have already attained buddhahood?

The bodhisattvas Manjushri and Samantabhadra, attendants of Shakyamuni Buddha who stand at his right and left in Buddhist iconography, represent the two aspects of the perfected character of the Buddha: great wisdom and great compassion. But these bodhisattvas are not merely symbols in our consciousness, and thinking them to be unreal is a mistake. Likewise, buddhas such as Vairochana, Baisajyaguru, and Amitabha, as well as the myriad buddhas mentioned in the *Sutra of the Three Thousand Names of the Buddha* are not only names of the infinite potential of our essential nature, but are actual buddhas. In the *Shōbōgenzō* chapter "Making Offerings to the Buddhas,"[75] Dōgen Zenji quotes from *The Deeds of the Buddha*[76] and the *Buddha Treasury Sutra*[77] to show how Shakyamuni honored and served the countless buddhas until he attained buddhahood:

The Buddha said:

> If there were no past ages, there would not have
> been past buddhas.
> If there were no past buddhas, there would not have
> been becoming a monk and receiving the precepts.

You must understand that myriad buddhas exist in the three times. When speaking of the buddhas of the past do not say that they had a beginning and do not say that they had no beginning. Calculating in terms of beginning and end is not something that comes from studying Buddhadharma. Those who make offerings to and revere the buddhas of the past will become monks and receive the precepts, and will become buddhas without fail. They achieve buddhahood due to the merit from revering the buddhas. How will those who have never made offerings to a single buddha achieve buddhahood? One does not achieve buddhahood without a cause.

He continues:

The Deeds of the Buddha says:

> The Buddha said to Maudgalyayana, "I recall that in the past I planted myriad roots of goodness, training under limitless buddhas and sought the Supreme Way. O Maudgalyayana, I recall that in the past I attained the body of a wheel-turning king[78] and met the thirty billion buddhas all sharing the same name, Shakya. I paid respect and showed obedience to all, from buddhas to their disciples, serving and making offerings of the four necessities to them: namely, dress, food and drink,

bedding, and medicine. At that time those buddhas predicted my future: "You will attain unexcelled, complete awakening and attain the rank of knower of the world, teacher of gods and humans, Buddha, World-Honored One, and will accomplish true realization in a future life."

. . .

In the first uncountable period of eons, Shakya Bodhisattva met and made offerings to 75,000 buddhas: the first named Shakyamuni, the last was named Ratnashikhin.

In the second uncountable period of eons, he met and made offerings to 76,000 buddhas: the first named Ratnashikhin, the last named Dipankara.

In the third uncountable period of eons, he met and made offerings to 77,000 buddhas: the first named Dipankara, the last named Vibhashi.

In the ninety-one eons wherein he practiced maturing the various kinds of karma, he met and made offerings to six buddhas: the first named Vibhashi, the last named Kashyapa.

If you can believe and accept these passages, you have begun to believe that the buddhas actually exist.

SENTIENT BEINGS AND BUDDHAS MUTUALLY INTERACT

Mutual interaction (*kan'ō*) occurs when two minds meet and intermingle. All sentient beings in the universe are sensitive in this way. But there is a mutual interaction that occurs between buddhas and sentient beings that is particularly important in the search for truth.

As I have said, all sentient beings are endowed with the wisdom and virtuous power of the buddhas and possess perfect and complete original nature. The latent drive to awaken to our essential nature is a natural part of this original nature. Eventually all human beings grow dissatisfied with animalistic or materialistic life, and when the time is right, they begin to seek out the equilibrium of a spiritual life. This is known as "the spirit of seeking the Way."[79]

The point at which we begin the search is known as "Seeking the Ox," the first stage of the Ten Ox-Herding Pictures. Usually we begin our quest by looking into a particular system of thought, philosophy, or theology. We may come to believe in some religion, and through our belief find a temporary satisfaction that lasts for years or even across lifetimes. But when the spirit of seeking the Way really begins to blaze forth, we won't be able to rest until we attain a true and unshakable peace of mind. At that point, only a lived understanding of infinite and immovable truth will satisfy us.

This search for spiritual peace is the natural expression of our buddha nature at work, an expression of the wondrous power of our own nature. This type of intrinsic activity is known as "sensitivity."[80] At the same time, innumerable buddhas who have been polishing their innate buddha nature through bygone ages without beginning radiate out the light of their great compassion and wisdom so that all sentient beings may awaken to buddha nature. Their activity occurs without us ever knowing about it. The salvific power that the buddhas transmit to us is known as "response."[81]

When a sentient being who has been seeking the Way meets the power of the response of myriad buddhas, they realize the resolve to traverse the Way, to practice, and to attain enlightenment and the Dharma body. The *Principle of Practice and Enlightenment* says:

> When one's sensitivity interacts with response, one will definitely acquire the merit of devoting oneself to Buddha, Dharma, and Sangha. Whether one is a heavenly being, human, an inhabitant of hell, or an animal, when one's sensitivity interacts with response one will definitely return, filled with devotion, to the Buddha, Dharma, and Sangha.

The subject of the interrelation between sensitivity and response can be divided into four aspects. There is a sensitivity to response where:

1. neither the sensitivity nor the response are apparent
2. the sensitivity is not apparent but the response is

3. the sensitivity is apparent but the response is not
4. both the sensitivity and the response are apparent

In this context "not apparent" means faint and obscure—in other words, not apparent in the phenomenal world. "Sensitivity" refers to signs that the spirit of seeking the Way has begun to work in the heart of a sentient being.

The first aspect—sensitivity to response where neither the sensitivity nor the response to it are apparent—refers to that stage wherein no indication of seeking the Way has yet dawned in our awareness, nor has the light of the buddhas appeared in the phenomenal world. Nevertheless, this is the most fundamental type of interrelation between sensitivity and response, and we could say that it is the basic driving force for achieving the Way of the Buddha. Myriad buddhas have endlessly been sending out their compassionate guidance since time immemorial. Simultaneously, all sentient beings have been unconsciously seeking the Supreme Way. During this first stage sentient beings receive transformative guidance from the buddhas without being aware of it at all. The situation resembles that of a dormant seed that hasn't yet sprouted, hidden underground, where the force that drives it to sprout pulses with life; the sun, concealed behind clouds, doesn't shed its light directly on the ground, but warms the air, which then penetrates the earth nurturing the seed, without it ever knowing that it's there.

The second aspect—sensitivity to response where the sensitivity is not apparent but the response is—refers to the situation where a sentient being, still mired in darkness, has resolved to seek and practice the Way, despite not being aware that they have done so. However, the buddhas have extended the hand of salvation into the phenomenal world. An enlightened teacher, for example, may give Dharma talks that one hears, but the spirit of seeking the Way remains dormant and one has absolutely no interest in the talks: the sensitivity is not apparent but the response is. It's as if the sun, freed of obstructing clouds, shines brightly, but the seedling has yet to sprout from the ground.

The third aspect—sensitivity to response where the sensitivity is apparent but the response is not—refers to the situation where a sentient being has resolved to practice Buddhism and earnestly seeks the Way, yet gropes about in darkness, having not been blessed with the karma to come into actual contact with the teachings of the Buddha or Zen ancestors. In reality, such beings receive teachings in an unseen world, but they do not notice it given their present circumstances. It's as if the seed has finally sprouted and emerged above the ground but cannot receive direct sunlight because the sun is obscured by clouds.

The fourth aspect—sensitivity to response where both the sensitivity and the response are apparent—refers to the most substantial form of interrelationship between sensitivity and response. At this stage the spirit of seeking the Way clearly appears, and one is able to actually receive guidance from buddhas and Zen ancestors. It's as if the seedling has finally broken through the ground to show its head and the sun is shining brightly.

We must understand that this process of interaction is constantly occurring in the relationship between buddhas and sentient beings. Thus, we can clearly understand that we are continuously treading a single path toward attainment of the Buddha Way.

Self and Other Are Not Two

The concept of dualistic opposition is the most fundamental of our delusions and the source of all our troubles. Usually we think of ourselves and others as two completely different things; our self-interest and the interests of others are intrinsically at odds. If this feeling of opposition is strong enough, we will think that if we act for the benefit of others we will lose something, and that in order to gain something for ourselves, others must make sacrifices. This is delusion.

Furthermore, based on this sense of opposition, we come to believe that the environment and the circumstances of our lives operate independently of us. When things don't go the way we wish and we're faced with difficulties, we blame circumstances rather than ourselves. This is also delusion. We cannot help but think of ourselves and others as separate because the phenomenal world is the only thing we know and we form our view of the world based on that knowledge, considering our surroundings to be external, in opposition to ourselves. This is how the world is according to everyday common sense. But because self and other are, in reality, naturally one, this too is delusion.

In order to clearly realize the essential unity of ourselves and others, we must open the eye of enlightenment to clearly see that subject and object are empty—that the subjective and objective worlds are empty. When we realize that both worlds are empty, we clearly experience the universe as one. This is what "self and other are not two" means. To practice Zen is to realize this fact, be dissolved by it, and live it.

Dōgen Zenji says:

> It is the foolish man's idea that his own profit must decrease if he gives precedence to profiting others. But this is not so. The act of benefitting is one and it benefits both oneself and others.[82]

Please impress this upon your hearts. When we perfectly realize that self and other are not two, not only will we see ourselves and circumstances as one, but we will see ourselves and everything in the universe as one body. A commentary on the *Avatamsaka Sutra* says:

> There is not a hairsbreadth difference between oneself and others in the limitless universe.

The *Treatise of Seng Chao* says:

> Heaven, earth, and I are of the same root; the myriad things and I are of one body.

These passages all proclaim the principle that self and other are not two.

When we are dreaming we take the mountains, rivers, flowers, trees, roads, houses, and people we see to objectively exist, but when we wake, we realize that they were all products of our minds. In the same way, as long as unenlightened beings remain deep in the dream of delusion, they will only see things in the world as objectively existent, no matter what we might say to them. But once they awaken to their True Self, they realize that the entire universe is the brilliant light of the self. Referring to this the sutras say, "The three worlds are only products of the mind"; "Above all and below the heavens, I alone am honored"; "Only one in the entire universe"; "All sentient beings are the Buddha radiating out light without obstruction in every direction"; and "Total self and and total other."

I am a complete outsider to the teachings of Christianity and don't know how the essence of original sin is explained, but I wonder if it is tied up somehow with the concept of dualistic opposition. A newborn baby has no concept of separation between itself and others. As the baby begins to experience the world, he or she becomes aware first of the self, then of others in opposition to that self. This dualistic consciousness grows stronger over time until it becomes an impregnable wall. Negative emotions such as jealousy, antagonism, hatred, and enmity arise out of this idea of dualism. When we harbor such feelings toward others, it's only natural that others return them, which leads both parties to suffer. The Japanese saying "Curse another and you dig two graves" is related precisely to this.

Needless to say, the feelings we have for others are not strictly negative. Humanity brims with positive feelings such as affection, sympathy, kindness, love, and mercy. Why is this so? Because we are all essentially one. Just as sunshine breaks through clouds, the light of our essential nature shines through the cracks in our delusion. Buddhism teaches that absolute and universal love emerges when we eliminate the delusion of dualistic opposition.

This love is the mercy of the undifferentiated body known as "compassion bound in three ways" and is divided according to its degree of perfection. There is:

1. compassion that is bound to sentient beings
2. compassion that is bound to things
3. compassion that is unbound

The compassion that is bound to sentient beings is a tenderness that cannot help but feel compassion toward the suffering of all creatures, human and animal. The Buddhist injunction against eating meat and fish has its roots in this type of compassion.

The compassion that is bound to things (*dharma*) is compassion toward everything. Here the word "things" refers to all phenomena, everything that exists. Compassion that is bound to things feels pity and mercy toward every tree, every blade of grass, every speck of dust, and every stone. Everything has life. When we see things with enlightened eyes, then even a scrap of paper, a pencil, or a cigarette butt is a manifestation of life. Each thing is the ever-present buddha mind and should be treated with care. It is important to treat each and every thing in the spirit of taking care of its life. This is compassion.

Compassion that is unbound naturally flows out when subject has been eliminated and object has been transcended. It is an absolute and universal love, the compassion of the one, single body. As we gradually clarify the heart's eye—the eye that sees the absolute—we more and more clearly experience this unbound compassion and come to fully understand that we love everything with an infinitely deep love, and that all things completely love us. What discontent could there be? Where is antagonism, hatred, jealousy, or anger? A life of infinite gratitude and peace naturally opens.

ALL BEINGS ARE IN THE PROCESS OF BECOMING BUDDHAS

"All beings are intrinsically Buddha," as Hakuin said, means that all sentient beings are endowed with the wisdom and virtuous power of the Buddha and are, without exception, gradually advancing along the path of liberation. It is inevitable that all human beings will perfectly realize their essential nature. Each of us, as perfect and infinite existence, is of necessity on the path to buddhahood, even when in the phenomenal world. This is what we call "the process of becoming a buddha."

To sum up this process: (1) We are intrinsically endowed with buddha nature, and although (2) we cling to the illusion of a self, (3) life continues. Also, (4) cause and effect are inevitable, (5) myriad buddhas actually exist, and (6) sentient beings mutually interact with them. It is also a real fact that (7) self and other are not two. Since all of these conditions are already perfectly met, (8) it is only a matter of time before we will, without fail, break through the deluded dream of self, awaken to our intrinsic buddha nature, and achieve the wisdom of supreme enlightenment. When one believes and understands these, one correctly believes and understands Buddhism. If we condense these tenets further, they all boil down to the eighth tenet, that all beings are in the process of becoming buddhas. In other words, we believe that all sentient beings attain the Way of the Buddha. This is true faith in Mahayana Buddhism.

The *Brahmajala Sutra* says:

> O all you people, believe unmistakably in your hearts that you are accomplished buddhas. "I am already an accomplished buddha." If you believe always in this way, then you are already endowed with the precepts.

Dōgen Zenji says:

> Buddhas and ancestors were once like we are; we shall come to be buddhas and ancestors.

Since the buddhas are people who have already accomplished the Buddha Way, they are "accomplished buddhas." And since we are already on the way to achieving the Buddha Way, we are known as "future accomplished buddhas." The buddhas and ancestors were originally ordinary beings like us, and at some point we too will definitely become buddhas and Zen ancestors. Developing faith in this is known as "developing true faith" and is called the "stage of true determination and not retreating."

To believe and practice in this way is the Zen of the Buddha Way—it is Mahayana Zen. If a person truly believes in Mahayana Buddhism, then whether they are monk, nun, or layperson, the whole of his or her life will be directed toward the ultimate objective expressed in the final verse of the bodhisattva vow: "The Way of the Buddha is unsurpassed; I vow to attain it." At mealtime we recite the verse that begins, "Fifth, we accept this food to achieve the Way of the Buddha," and which contains the line, "The first taste is to cut off all evil; the second taste is to practice all good; the third taste is to save all beings; may they all attain the Way of the Buddha." If we were to sum up the aim of Buddhism in a single phrase, it would be this: may all beings attain the Way of the Buddha. Or more simply: become Buddha. The eight great tenets are a step-by-step exposition of the contents of this Buddha Way. The Great Way, whereby we achieve the ultimate and most fundamental goal of humanity, is the Zen that has been correctly transmitted from the buddhas and Zen ancestors.

When I say that the aim of Buddhism comes down to "become Buddha," what do these words mean? The sutras tell us, "All things return to one" and "The three worlds are products of the mind alone." So we could say that "become Buddha" has its origin in oneness, or the mind alone. But what does oneness or mind alone return to? Any speculation here is futile. Recall Case 45 of the *Blue Cliff Record*:

> A monk asked Jōshū, "All things return to one. Where does the one return to?"
>
> Jōshū replied, "When I was in Seishū I had a robe; it weighed seven pounds."

Here I must shut my mouth.

On Private Interview 13

"**P**rivate interview" (*dokusan*) means receiving one-on-one instruction from a Zen master. Without the private interview it is impossible to lead people to true Zen. Although we cannot guarantee that authentically transmitted Zen exists in every zendo that holds private interviews, we can conclude that true Zen isn't being taught if private interviews aren't being conducted at all. Such is the importance of private interview in authentic Zen.

WHY PRIVATE INTERVIEW IS NECESSARY

We can compare the act of leading people in Zen practice to a doctor examining a sick person and administering the appropriate cure. For a cure to be effective, the doctor must meet with the patient to investigate their problem. A doctor who settles on a specific remedy without ever seeing the patient or questioning them about their illness is most likely a fraud. Likewise, even the greatest doctor in the world cannot cure someone simply by lecturing on health. A Zen master's lectures and public talks are, in the end, like lectures on health. It is impossible to give individual students of Zen appropriate guidance with public talks alone. Just as there are a great many kinds of physical ailments, so too are there a great variety of mental ailments—delusive thoughts, ignorance of the truth, and so on—and because people differ according to the type and extent of their illnesses, individual instruction is essential.

It is said that private interview was already practiced during the time of Shakyamuni Buddha. Chisha Daishi of the Tendai sect made a skillful classification of the teachings used by Shakyamuni during his lifetime, including "secret teachings," which Harada Roshi says were what we would today call "private interviews." Even Shakyamuni Buddha himself could not expect to completely instruct his disciples with public teachings alone.

There is also a reason why individual instruction should be carried out in privacy. We ordinary people tend to defend ourselves with the outer garment of our egos. The private interview gives us the opportunity to remove this garment. People of wealth, high social status, or refinement, in particular, are concealed within a thick outer garment of defensiveness, which they just can't remove if others are watching or listening. Even though they may have questions about their practice, in front of a group they will worry about the reactions of others and feel too ashamed to ask. Instead they will pretend to understand and say nothing. Wrapping themselves more tightly in the garment of a prideful self, they refuse to bare their souls. As a result of this hesitancy on the part of the student, they will only receive an incomplete teaching on the topic and real Zen instruction will be impossible for them. This is why the meeting between master and disciple must be conducted in private.

Even though instruction given in the meeting between teacher and student is meant to be private, people sitting close to the private interview room might think that listening in could help their own practice. This is comparable to trying to learn math by looking up the answer, without understanding how to solve the problem. Particularly after a student has begun koan study, to observe and listen to the proceedings of another person's private interview can be nothing but harmful. It is equally important to keep what goes on in the private interview room to oneself. Telling another practitioner about the content of a private interview can actually damage his or her practice. In a strict zendo, where authentic Zen is taught, it's unlikely a student would talk about a private meeting with a teacher. But if the training center is somewhat loose, senior students may reveal details of a private interview and even give out answers to koans. People who listen to them may then try to imitate the same response in an attempt to fool the master. If Zen teachers accept this fakery and pass the student on the koan, we can only call it the tragedy of the Dharma's final age. What goes on in the private interview is between the student and teacher. No one else should even inquire about it.

Attitude toward the Teacher

Students should trust and follow the instructions that their teachers give in private interview. Although there is nothing wrong with listening to other teachers' public talk, Dharma talks, or lectures on Buddhism (provided the content isn't in error), you shouldn't listen to a single word from anyone other than your teacher when it comes to instruction on individual practice. In authentic Zen practice, the living Zen master is the highest authority on Buddhism. When it comes to instruction on practice, you shouldn't accept the interference of even Shakyamuni or Amitabha Buddha.

One's first private interview will be preceded by a ceremony of first meeting (shōken), which establishes the bond between student and teacher. It is a solemn ceremony in which the student offers to respect and faithfully follow the teacher. It is customary to offer a small amount of money and incense at that time. We shouldn't enter into the relationship lightly, or we may fail to value the Dharma or to honor the teacher. Once the relationship between disciple and teacher is formally established, we may receive instruction from that teacher.

Students who are still practicing prior to seeing into their own nature should go only to one teacher for private interview. As each teacher will vary in terms of their style of teaching, students who simultaneously practice under two teachers will receive signals from two different directions. Not knowing which to follow, students may end up losing the purity and focus of their practice. Practice can easily become a case of "chasing two rabbits and catching neither" if it isn't unified.

Once you've selected a teacher, you may wonder if you are allowed to change to another. The answer is yes. It is essential in the practice of Zen that the teacher and student be on the same wavelength. If the teacher and student do not have good rapport, the process of instruction can be unpleasant for both. If you have been practicing with a certain teacher, but then meet another whom you feel to be vastly superior to the current one, there is no reason—even feelings of obligation or respect toward your present teacher—to refrain from changing. Of course such changes should not be taken lightly. However, if after careful consideration you feel it to be the best thing to do, you need not hesitate.

You should pay a respectful farewell to your former teacher, as a matter of courtesy, but ordinary sentiments do not apply when it comes to matters of Dharma. The correct course is to make a clean break, and start practicing under the new teacher. It is important to keep in mind, however, that once you do so, you should forget the teaching of the former and place absolute trust in the teaching of your new teacher, wholly submitting yourself to his or her guidance regarding the Dharma.

The above advice is intended for those who are practicing prior to seeing into their own nature and is limited specifically to the teacher you study with in private interview. After seeing into one's own nature, it is all right to practice under several teachers at the same time, but it's preferable to complete koan study under one teacher before going to a private interview with another.

HOW TO GO TO PRIVATE INTERVIEW

The form for going to private interview is strict. Even though teachers may have human faults, when receiving others in private interview—so long as their Dharma eye is correct and clear—they stand in the place of the Buddha and Zen ancestors in bestowing the teaching. The teacher needn't show deference toward the student, but the student should go to the private interview with a true feeling of trust and respect, just as if the teacher were the Buddha or a Zen ancestor. People of wealth, high social status, or learning and culture may find it difficult to be totally open. Internal resistance is not surprising, but if we wish to attain to the great Dharma we must overcome it.

When going to private interview we should dress appropriately. Monks should wear formal robes, while laypeople should wear modest, dark-colored clothing (white is acceptable during the summer). The important thing is to dress respectably.

In principle, private interview should consist of questions and answers about the first principle of the Dharma. People who haven't yet seen into their own nature usually ask about how to practice in order to come to a direct experience of this first principle. No matter how trifling a question may be, if it concerns actual practice, it must be resolved. For example, students may ask what to do when leg pain makes it impossible to concentrate, or what to do when they are sleepy and doze off during meditation. These may seem like trifling questions, but for the questioner they are important and should be asked without reserve. On the other hand, lofty queries on intellectual matters or philosophy are discouraged.

Also, questions such as "What is buddha nature?" "Is there really a heaven and hell?" or "How do the Buddha of Buddhism and the Christ of Christianity differ?" aren't appropriate for the private interview. Such intellectual questions can be covered amply in a lecture or public teaching or brought up when having tea with the teacher. But they aren't matters for discussion with the teacher during the private interview. We should also avoid personal questions—questions about health, for example—unless they are connected to our practice. Idle talk has no place in the private interview, where the teacher is expending every effort to lead the student to an authentic Zen experience.

The exchange in the private interview room should be clear and concise. When working on a koan, for example, to begin by saying, "My koan concerns Jōshū's question as to whether a dog has buddha nature or not," when we could simply say, "I'm working on Mu," adds unnecessary words and time to the process. Many people may be waiting in line. Also don't sit before the teacher thinking of what to say or waiting for the teacher to begin; you should thoroughly prepare ahead of time and speak without hesitation.

When ringing the bell before entering the private interview room, strike the bell twice; be careful that the interval between the two strikes is neither too long nor too short. If you take a little care, this will come naturally. Your movements upon entering and leaving the room should be done in the same spirit, neither too fast, nor too slow. They should be natural and fitting. Your bows before the teacher should not be carelessly done, but it is also out of place to put on a show of excessive politeness.

In short, every movement and every word reveals our character, depth of concentration, and level of aspiration, so we must be attentive at all times. This is living Zen practice.

Three Necessary Conditions for Zen Practice 14

The ancients spoke of three essential conditions for Zen practice:

> First: great faith;[83] second: great doubt;[84] third: great determination.[85] These are like the three legs of a tripod.

It is uncertain if we can accomplish the Dharma if one of these three legs is missing. If all three are present, however, we would be more likely to miss the ground with a hammer than we would be to miss enlightenment.

The first condition, great faith, means believing, without any doubt, that you are intrinsically awake, that "all beings are intrinsically awake." You also believe that seeing into your own nature means discovering something that you have already been using from morning to night without even realizing it. Because seeing into your own nature is you discovering yourself, you cannot fail to experience it. Great faith also means believing that every person is in the process of eventually achieving supreme enlightenment[86] and trusting that if we ask for help from the Three Treasures, we will definitely get it. Lastly, great faith means that we believe in the teaching of our Zen teacher.

This great root of faith is not just a tepid faith. It is a thoroughgoing belief that will settle for nothing less than complete awakening and is rooted firmly in the ground like a huge tree, immovable in the face of even the strongest gale. When the root of faith is present, there is nowhere for demons to get a foothold.

Now, what is great doubt? The type of doubt being referred to here is not intellectual doubt, such as we have when asking about the meaning of a koan. Instead, we can think of great doubt as utterly becoming one with our practice—whether we are counting the breath or practicing with the koan "Mu"—to the point that our entire body and mind are like a single mass of inquiry. When practicing with Mu, for example, as long as we think that there is something called "ourselves" that is practicing, we have not quite achieved great doubt. When we become truly meditatively absorbed in Mu, then Mu itself is practicing Mu. But if we are still aware of this, it is still not fully great doubt. Harada Roshi used to say, "Mu mu-s Mu." We shouldn't think about the meaning of the word "Mu"; just the sound is enough: "Mu-u-u, Mu-u-u, Mu-u-u." Nothing else—no thought of becoming enlightened or of not becoming enlightened—there is only Mu, completely naked and exposed. We must continue to practice like this, urging ourselves on, asking ourselves why we can't understand it, even though it's plainly in view. Our whole being must completely become a single moment of Mu. We must become a ball of Mu, our spiritual energy solidified into an immovable mass of questioning.

The great root of faith naturally activates this great ball of doubt. If the root of faith appears, the great ball of doubt will arise without fail. Spurred on by great doubt we continue the practice of Mu, without seeking or expecting awakening. The quickest way to awaken when completely absorbed in Mu is to throw away all thoughts about it. Awakening has nothing to do with any kind of intellectual knowledge or discrimination.

Ekai Oshō, author of the *Gateless Gate*, practiced at Manjuji where he received the koan, "Does a dog have buddha nature?" from his master Getsurin Shikan Zenji. He worked on this koan for six years and, at the end of the most painful practice, he finally achieved great enlightenment. His commentary on the first case of the *Gateless Gate* is an account of his own experience, expressed in words that are filled with conviction:

> Concentrate your whole self, with its 360 bones and 84,000 pores, into Mu, making your whole body a solid lump of doubt. Keep digging into it day and night, without pause, but don't mistake it for "nothingness," "being," or "non-being." It must be like a red-hot iron ball that you've swallowed, which you try to vomit out, but can't. You must extinguish all delusive thoughts and feelings that you have cherished

until the present. After a period of such efforts Mu will bear fruit, and inside and out will naturally become one. You will become like a dumb man who has had a dream: you will know yourself and for yourself only. Then Mu will suddenly break open, astonish the heavens, and shake the earth.

When the great root of faith and the great ball of doubt are present, great determination will arise. Great determination is a strong resolve that wells up from the bottom of our gut and spurs us on. We already believe that we ourselves are intrinsically awake; we only need discover what is within us. We ask ourselves why we can't realize it. It must be possible! With great determination we continue to practice Mu single-mindedly, but mountains of silver and walls of iron rise up before us and we can't break through. Still, we must continue to goad ourselves on, "There's no reason I can't do what others have done!"

Bassui Zenji says:

What obstructs realization? Nothing but our own half-hearted desire for truth. Think of this and exert yourself to the utmost.

The sixteenth chapter of the *Lotus Sutra* says:

And when the living have become faithful,
Honest and upright and gentle,
And wholeheartedly want to see the Buddha,
Even at the cost of their own lives . . .[87]

To meet the true Buddha within us, we must be ready to give up our lives.

People often tell me that although they have participated in many intensive Zen retreats and seem to have progressed in their practice, they find it impossible to take the final step. Although there is nothing to be afraid of, they are afraid in spite of themselves, wondering what might happen next, fearing that perhaps their awareness of themselves will be destroyed. Here is the dividing line between success and failure. You must summon up a reckless resolve to break through, no matter what, and throw yourself away. When you break through, you realize great life. I have never heard of anyone who died from practicing Mu. Remember that great determination is the deciding factor.

When deep faith, unbounded practice, and great determination are present, there is in fact already no self; our entire bodies are just Mu. When self and Mu have truly become one, then Mu suddenly appears and we finally come face to face with our original selves.

No matter how high the mountains of the great Dharma are, no matter how deep the sea of ignorance is, they will be as nothing before a boundless spirit of determination. Regardless of what happens, your self is, from the beginning, the spontaneous self-nature of Buddha.[88]

Zen Practice for People of Other Religions 15

There have been an increasing number of people from other religious traditions, especially Christianity, who have a serious interest in the practice of Zen meditation. Many of these are specialists who have dedicated their lives to religious activity—priests, nuns, and pastors. Why have so many Christians, especially Catholics, developed an interest in Zen at this particular moment? One reason may be the trend toward increased philosophical precision in theology—among both Buddhists and Christians—paired with a gradual impoverishment of the content of religious experiences.

Genuine religious experience is the heart of any religion, providing its source of vitality. Ideas can never be substituted for experience. In other words, philosophical speculation and logical deduction cannot make up for lack of religious experience. This is true for Christians, as it is for Buddhists or anyone else. Those truly seeking salvation, or religious advisors who wish to lead others to spiritual salvation, are looking for more than a theory and won't be satisfied with merely intellectual explanations. In the end, ideas are only ideas, thoughts are only thoughts, and we cannot gain true peace of mind without directly experiencing the source of reality, no matter how strongly we cling to an idea.

Devout Christians are drawn to Zen meditation, hoping that seeing into their own nature, or awakening, will somehow help them to directly experience God. Christians who come for instruction in meditation often ask me whether they can practice zazen while retaining their faith as Christians. Realizing that this is an urgent question for them, I answer, "Don't worry. It's fine to practice zazen so long as you have a heart and mind." I explain that zazen is not religious in the same sense that Christianity is. I imagine most Christians who show up at our San'un Zendo in Kamakura go through a lot of private agony when harmonizing their faith with the practice of Zen. This is a truly noble thing to do. A priest, nun, or pastor who practices Zen meditation can only become a better priest, nun, or pastor. Christians, almost without exception, tell me that they feel that the quality of their prayer deepens after beginning to practice zazen. This is so regardless of whether they have realized their own nature or not. This is nothing unusual; I would say that it is quite natural.

A certain result will necessarily appear in a person's mind, if provided with the right conditions. Whether that person is Buddhist, Christian, or an atheist makes no difference whatsoever. However, when seeking to produce the right conditions in the mind, it is possible that ideas associated with one's religion can become obstacles that make it difficult for one to practice single-mindedly. The conditions that zazen requires of the mind are concentration of attention and forgetting oneself. Once one sits down in zazen and begins to practice with Mu, for example, if one is Buddhist one must put aside buddhas and bodhisattvas, and if one is Christian one must put aside God and Christ, and plunge one's entire body and mind into the practice of Mu.

I am a complete outsider to the teachings of Christianity, but I know that Christ said, "The Kingdom of God is within you." So couldn't it be that the "heaven" spoken of when Christians pray to "our Father who art in heaven" actually means the unseen realm that Zen calls the essential world? I'm not qualified to speak lightly about whether the essential world that is confirmed in great enlightenment is the same as the Kingdom of God mentioned in the Bible, or whether there is a relation between the Pure Dharma Body and the God of Christianity. It may just be that Christians use meditation and deep prayer to directly experience God. In any event, we can't resolve these matters at the level of conceptual thought. We must only compare experiences in both traditions after having reached the level where neither words nor ideas are of any use.

Father Enomiya Lassalle was a pioneer among Catholic practitioners of Zen. When he first visited Harada Sogaku Roshi at Hosshinji in Obama to ask permission to practice meditation, he inquired whether he, too, could see into his own nature. The roshi's reply was, "So long as you have a body." I heard this story from Father Lassalle himself.

In Case 32 of the *Gateless Gate,* it says:

A non-Buddhist in all earnestness asked the World-Honored
One, "I do not ask about words; I do not ask about no-words."

The World-Honored One just sat still.

The non-Buddhist praised him, saying, "The World-
Honored One in his great benevolence and mercy has opened
the clouds of my delusion and enabled me to enter the Way."
Then bowing, he took his leave.

Ananda asked Buddha, "What did the non-Buddhist realize that made him praise you so much?"

The World-Honored One replied, "He is just like a fine
horse that runs at the shadow of a whip."[89]

During the time of Shakyamuni Buddha a number of seekers who
weren't members of the Buddha's group came to practice with him.
Shakyamuni would immediately give them unadulterated Dharma and
didn't refuse private interviews to outsiders. If there had been Christians
at the time, the Buddha would certainly have received them as well.
Some of the non-Buddhists, like the person in the koan, would amaze
Shakyamuni with their lightning-fast perceptivity. Likewise some of the
Buddha's own fold were like Ananda, who, even though he never left the
Buddha's side, took a long time to grasp the whole of his great teaching.

Zen is truly like a great ocean: any boat—whether it is a great battleship, a tanker weighing a million tons, a small fishing boat, or a
tiny sailboat—can maneuver freely on its surface without restriction.
I also think of Zen as like the air: any living thing—a human being, an
animal, a plant, even invisible life like bacteria or viruses—can live in
that air. Zen is also like empty space: anything of any size, shape, or
form—including the sun, the moon, and the stars—can exist there in
perfect freedom, sometimes amid ordered harmony, sometimes amid
what looks like chaos.

The Actual Practice of Zazen 16

The real life of meditation lies in the practice itself. The somewhat theoretical material I have presented thus far can be thought of as preparatory knowledge for the actual practice of zazen—as nothing more than a rather lengthy introduction. Even with a clear intellectual understanding of this material, these are all so many wasted words unless one actually begins to practice zazen. It is sitting that brings the theory of zazen into being.

For those of you planning to practice zazen, the following section will be most important: please read it with particular care. Since each of us are unique individuals with our own particular set of circumstances, the optimal course would be to seek out a qualified teacher, before anything else, who can discern what kind of instruction is best suited to us. When you find such a teacher, you should drop any preconceptions about Zen and follow the teacher's instructions to the letter. If you don't have the opportunity to practice under a qualified teacher, however, faithfully following the methods outlined below will enable you to come to rest in the essential world. The instructions below are mainly a summary of Harada Sogaku Roshi's *Matters of Immediate Importance*.[90]

The practice of meditation can be divided into three parts: adjusting the body, regulating the breath, and preparing the mind.

ADJUSTING THE BODY

Preparing to sit

First place a thick mat, called a *zabuton* (sitting futon), at the place where you usually sit. It is best to use as thick a mat as possible. If the mat is too thin your legs will hurt and it will be difficult to concentrate, which will be an obstacle for both body and spirit.

Place a round meditation cushion, called a *zafu*, preferably one filled with kapok rather than cotton on the mat. With continued use kapok tends to flatten, which necessitates refilling it periodically to keep it at the desired thickness. If the zafu if too high, it will be difficult to come to equilibrium when sitting; if it is too low, it will quickly become painful for the legs. Persons with short legs require a higher zafu than those with longer legs do.

Sitting postures

Traditionally, there are three styles of sitting on the floor: full lotus,[91] half lotus,[92] and Japanese style.[93]

In the orthodox, full-lotus posture, you place your right foot on your left thigh and your left foot on your right thigh. The tips of your toes should be flush with the outer edge of your thighs, and your heels should lightly touch your abdominal region. This is the most stable position for sitting because the largest area of the body is in contact with the ground, creating a wide triangular foundation. Since the purpose of meditation is to bring the spirit to rest, we need first to bring our bodies to a state of rest. We make a point of placing the right leg under the left leg because the right side is usually more dynamic than the passive left. Aiming to bring the unsettled spirit to a state of rest, we place the static, quiet element over the active, dynamic element of the body. Therefore this position is also known as "overcoming delusion sitting posture."[94]

Images of the Buddha in Buddhist iconography, however, show him seated with his right leg over the left. This posture is the posture of one engaged in the act of "instructing all beings,"[95] and therefore, the active element is on top. This posture is also called "the sitting of good omen."[96] Our meditation posture, with the left leg over the right, is called "the posture of one still in the process of becoming a Buddha."[97]

If full lotus is the orthodox method of sitting, then half-lotus is its simplified form. In half-lotus, you place your left foot on your right thigh and your right foot underneath your left thigh. If you come to feel pain in the legs, it is acceptable to change the order, placing the right foot on left thigh and left foot underneath right thigh. In principle, however, it is recommended to keep the left leg on top.

Sitting in full or half lotus relieves the lower back area of excessive weight, which leaves only the problem of pain arising from sitting with folded legs. If you can get used to sitting in one of these two positions, they will prove, with time, to be more comfortable and stable and thus more suited to longer sitting.

Those who are unable to sit in either full or half-lotus position are advised to sit in Japanese style, the position that many Japanese use when sitting on the floor. Sit with both legs under you, with only the toes on top of each other, right above left. In this position the entire weight of your upper body comes down on the folded legs, so they tend to fall asleep faster than they do in either the full- or half-lotus posture. You may put a thin *zafu* or folded cushion between the legs and the buttocks to lighten the pressure on the legs and raise the trunk, which makes it easier to achieve the correct posture and sit for longer periods. The knees should be slightly apart, about the width of two fists. Some Westerners use a variation of this position by straddling a high zafu placed between the legs.

Students who find all of these positions extremely painful may find relief by sitting with the legs crossed in front of them on the floor, tailor style, and then gradually practice sitting in one of the other above described styles over a period of time. It is also possible to practice zazen seated on a low meditation bench with your legs tucked under it, or if necessary on a chair or stool. When sitting on a chair or stool, knees should be apart slightly and legs perpendicular to the floor to maintain stability. It is important to make sure the back is straight when using a chair.

If the zendo is cool, you may place a blanket over your legs.

It would be best for practitioners to try to sit in the orthodox, full lotus posture from the very beginning. Although it may be rather painful at first, if you persevere you will eventually be able to sit comfortably in this position.

Clothing

Your clothing should be clean, neat, and appropriate for what you are doing; shoulders and legs should be covered. While we advise students to wear loose-fitting clothes, this does not mean that careless dress is acceptable. Wear clothes that are comfortable to sit in and not so tight that they constrict your body. Wear plain dark or neutral colors. If you wish to wear a Japanese robe[98] or similar loose robe, it should be worn with a skirt,[99] as is done in Japanese martial arts.

It's not necessary to be so particular about dress when sitting at home. Nevertheless, just as our environment can affect our spirits, our clothes can also affect our psychological state. If we get into the habit of wearing neat clothes whenever we sit, it will help bring our spirits into a proper state for sitting. Thus, when sitting at home, we should also make sure we are wearing clothes that are at least presentable.

Position of the hands

The hand position used in meditation is called the *dhyāna mudrā* or "sign of the Dharma Universe." It symbolizes meditative absorption in our buddha nature and is the hand position most conducive to bringing the spirit to rest.

Place your right hand in your lap with the palm facing upward. Then put your left hand on top of it, also with palm facing upward. Bring the tips of your thumbs together so that they lightly touch and point your thumbs upward toward your chest, so that they form an oval in the shape of a chestnut or jewel.

Checking bodily posture

It is important to sit up straight, for when our bodies are erect, everything else falls into place: the chest, abdomen, and inner organs will all be in healthy alignment, and our circulation and respiration will be unobstructed. Harada Roshi suggests that when sitting down, we push the buttocks as far as possible to the rear and then let the upper torso bend forward toward the floor. Then, leaving the lower part of the trunk in position, we sit up erect. Another way of achieving the same result is to lean back as far as possible and gradually return to an erect position. Check that you are not listing to the right or left, or leaning forward or backward. The head should also be erect, with the nose and navel in alignment and the chin slightly tucked in. Check that your head is not bending forward as this could detract from the alertness of spirit needed for meditation. At our training center, one of the zendo leaders periodically checks the students' posture. Try to remember how the adjustment feels in order to get in the habit of sitting properly.

Although some methods of meditation teach the student to sit with closed eyes, a crucial point of the practice of Zen in Mahayana Buddhism is to keep the eyes open at all times, with the gaze lowered to an area about a yard in front of you. It might seem easier to concentrate with the eyes closed, shutting out the outside world and thereby decreasing distractions. However, when we do this, it is easy to fall into a dreamy stupor and fail to always reach a state of ever-alert, flexible-but-taut concentration of mind that is needed for true practice. Such alert concentration enables us to cut through the stream of delusions and concepts in our minds. Practice will be of no use to us in our everyday lives unless we can concentrate with our eyes open.

In *Recommending Zazen to All People*, Dōgen has the following to say regarding these matters:

> Your clothing should not be carelessly loose but at the same time should be comfortable and not too tight. Next, put your right hand facing up on the top of your heel. Put your left hand facing up in the palm of your right hand. Put your thumbs together lightly so that the tips mutually support each other. Sit erect. Do not lean to the left or to the right. Do not bend forward or lean backward. Your ears and shoulders should be in a straight line with each other. Your nose and navel should be in a direct line with each other. The tip of your tongue should be in contact with the roof of your mouth. Your mouth should be closed with lips and teeth together. Your eyes should always be open. You should breathe quietly through your nose. Adjust your posture. Take a deep breath quietly through your mouth and then let it all out through half-closed lips. Rock your body back and forth from left to right and then sit as unmoving as a mountain.

Adjusting the breath

When practicing zazen we should always breathe quietly through the nose and avoid breathing through the mouth. However, I sometimes advise students, when practicing Mu alone in their room, that saying "Mu" in a low voice may be helpful to achieve meditative absorption. But this shouldn't be done when practicing in a group.

Once you have adjusted your posture, take a deep breath and let it out. Then take another deep breath with your mouth open, as if yawning, and exhale. Harada Roshi says that letting out all the reserve air in the entire body several times expels restlessness and settles the spirit, as if wiping the slate clean. Take a few more ordinary deep breaths, exhaling through the mouth. This serves to correct any irregular breathing and prepares the way for regulating the mind. Then breathe normally through the nose with the mouth closed. Next, sway from side to side like a pendulum, beginning with large oscillations that gradually grow smaller until you come to rest in the center. Then begin your practice.

Before standing up at the end of a period of meditation, rock sideways again for roughly the same number of times as when sitting down, beginning with small oscillations and gradually increasing them in size. This is the way to gently emerge from a state of deep concentration. It isn't necessary to do this if you've only been sitting for a few minutes. Harada Roshi and other past Zen teachers also recommended rocking from side to side on the cushion. Dōgen Zenji says, "Rock your body from left to right, then sit as unmoving as a mountain."

An important caution: when practicing meditation never put undue force or pressure in the abdominal area. Harada Roshi writes about damaging his health as a result of his own experimentation with applying force in the abdomen for some fourteen or fifteen years. He advises that "force should be limited to that which arises naturally in the course of breathing." Harada Roshi says that in premodern times the question of whether exerting force in Zen practice was a problem or not hadn't been mentioned. We find no references to it whatsoever in Dōgen Zenji's works, in Keizan Zenji's *Warnings for Zazen*, or Bankei Zenji's *Treatise on Zazen*. Such discussions may have begun around the time that Hakuin Zenji wrote *Leisurely Talk from a Night Boat*,[100] wherein is proposed a method for directing attention internally[101] to areas in the lower half of the body as a means of leading the physically ill back to health.

But this wasn't meant to be instruction for the practice of meditation. Aside from possibly injuring one's health, consciously thinking about applying force in the abdomen while practicing Mu will divide one's attention in two, such that one would lose the complete concentration needed to purify the mind. Even in the practice of just sitting, as long as one attempts to exert force in the abdominal area, one is not "just sitting" in the real sense of the word. The true way to practice Zen is that which the Buddha and Zen ancestors have transmitted from generation to generation down to the present.

ADJUSTING THE MIND

We can divide the methods for adjusting or settling the mind in meditation into four categories: counting the breath, following the breath, just sitting, and working on a koan. As students should receive a koan from their teacher and practice it only under his or her guidance, I will forego discussion of koans to give a general explanation of the other three methods of practice.

Counting the breath

Counting the breath is a suitable method for anyone beginning the practice of zazen. There are three ways of counting: to count both the inhalations and exhalations, to count only exhalations, or to count only inhalations.

Count from one to ten, counting the breath in your mind—not out loud—keeping the mouth closed as you count. Begin by counting both the inhalation and exhalation, assigning both its own number. Inhale "O-o-o-ne" and exhale "Two-o-o-o." Then inhale "Thre-e-e" and exhale "Fo-o-o-ur," up to ten, and then start again at "one."

Next practice counting only exhalations: watch the breath on the inhalation and then count "O-o-o-ne" on the exhalation. Watch the next inhalation and count "Two-o-o-o" on the exhalation, and so on up to ten.

Finally, practice counting inhalations only—from one to ten—and simply watch the exhalations. We practice this method last because counting inhalations is slightly more difficult than counting exhalations.

It is important to stay aware of the breath with your mind's eye during the time when you're not counting, so that random thoughts don't arise in the interval. Once you've gotten the knack of all three methods, you may choose which one to use at any particular time, altering your practice depending on conditions. The most important thing to remember with all three methods is that you should totally concentrate on only counting itself, without concern for anything else.

Although you intended to return to one after reaching ten, you may catch yourself going on to eleven, twelve, thirteen, and so on—or losing count altogether as you drift off into thought. When this happens, as soon as you notice you have lost count, simply bring your attention back to one and begin again. Don't worry about losing count or drifting off. Just come back to one.

The practice is to concentrate the mind by counting each breath with undivided attention. Although this might seem to require great effort, it isn't so. At times you may have to arouse a spirit of determination to stick with the method, especially if distracted or sleepy. But if you try your best to keep your attention on counting, your mind will naturally become concentrated. No other special effort is necessary. Counting the breath is unification of mind in itself.

Following the breath

Following the breath means to direct your mind's eye to your breathing, being completely aware of each inhalation and exhalation. Since you are no longer counting, there may be a tendency to become distracted or sleepy if you do not practice with fixed attention. Stay determined to follow each breath without wavering.

Both counting the breath and following the breath are methods given to beginning students of meditation. At the same time, both practices are in and of themselves the complete actualization of the Supreme Way and should by no means be considered inferior. You should know that it is possible to come to great enlightenment through counting the breath alone.

Just sitting

"Just sitting" is the English translation of the Japanese word *shikan-taza*. *Shikan* means "only" or "just." The *za* of *taza* means "to sit," and the syllable *ta* is a verbal intensifier. Whereas both counting the breath and following the breath use the breath as their point of focus, just sitting consists of just the sitting itself. In this sense, it is the purest form of meditation, the original meditation practiced by the buddhas and Zen ancestors. If you are sitting to penetrate the innermost recesses of yourself, just sitting is the ideal form of meditation. Dōgen Zenji broke through to complete enlightenment when practicing just sitting. At San'un Zendo in Kamakura Zen practitioners who have finished the formal course of koan study in the private interview room usually take up the practice of just sitting.

It is not an easy practice for beginners, however. There is no focal point of attention as an aid to rely on in just sitting. If one is not completely alert, the mind will be taken over by random thoughts and one will no longer be practicing true zazen. If one's environment is conducive to meditative concentration and the practitioner is of outstanding spirit, just sitting may be the ideal way to break through to enlightenment. Laypeople with secular jobs, however, find it extremely difficult to come to a real breakthrough with just sitting alone. For many, the practice may sink to the level of dreamy, aimless sitting with no real content.

Furthermore, a teacher guiding someone in this practice will find it difficult to ascertain that person's progress, so that both teacher and student may find themselves without reference points. Therefore, here at San'un Zendo, I nearly always assign koan practice to those who have come with the intention of attaining realization. Nevertheless, I feel it important for my readers to have an understanding of just what we resolve to do when we undertake the practice of just sitting, so I will excerpt here a section from Harada Roshi's *The Key to Zen Practice*[102] that touches on this subject.

> When practicing just sitting the mental condition of "just sitting" is very important. You must sit as if you were Mt. Fuji, towering above the surface of the sea; your sitting cushions are the earth and you are the only one in the entire universe. In this spirit, sit regally and immovably on your cushion with complete alertness. To use another simile, sit as if you were a balloon about to burst, or, better yet, a swordsman who has locked blades with an opponent and is about to make a final decisive thrust.

Here I must add some words of advice which apply to all forms of Zen meditation and should be kept in mind at all times. No matter how absorbed you become in counting or following the breath, your eyes should be open so that whatever is in front of you is visible. Likewise, your ears should not be plugged, so you can hear the sounds around you. Your mind should not be asleep, and you should be aware as random thoughts arise one after the other. Whatever sights or sounds you see or hear, whatever thoughts may come into your head, none of them are harmful and you needn't consider them to be obstructions. At the same time, however, know that these sights, sounds, or thoughts are in no way beneficial to your practice, and you should strictly avoid following them. By "following" I mean consciously engaging in looking at or listening to something, or to willfully follow a thought that pops into your mind. To do so will definitely obstruct your meditation.

Both beginning and experienced students often tell me they are troubled because random thoughts arise or they can't reach a state of non-thinking. But this is in fact nothing to worry about. Just don't pay attention to what you see or hear or to the thoughts that arise. Don't do anything at all. Leave matters as they are and simply continue wholeheartedly with your practice. When you find that your attention has strayed, immediately bring it back to the practice, without stopping to chide yourself for having wandered off track.

Dealing with random thoughts when practicing just sitting doesn't differ fundamentally from what I have outlined above. However, given that there is no focal point of concentration, if random thoughts do arise and we worry about them, they are all the more likely to persist. This is a real point of difficulty in the practice of just sitting for the beginning student. The self that was lost in random thoughts is not a false self; it is none other than your original True Self. But you will be unable to accept this fact until you come to a living experience of that True Self. There is a proverb: "Catch a thief and discover it's your own son." If you wish to catch that thief, single-mindedly continue your practice.

Since the actual method of practice in Zen meditation is so simple, some people might find it difficult to practice with sustained fervor. While the very simplicity is, to be sure, a source of difficulty, lying beneath the surface of this simplicity is an infinitely noble and profound truth. In practicing any of the methods outlined above, you should realize that each one of them is a noble path whereby you can achieve total enlightenment. Be convinced of this and practice with complete fervor.

Practical Matters 17

When we actually begin zazen, we find that we have numerous other questions about the practice. In the following section I will take up some related issues to keep in mind regarding your practice of Zen.

Sit facing the wall

It is customary in Sōtō Zen and in our Sanbō Zen line to sit in meditation facing a wall or similar flat surface such as a door or folding screen. Bodhidharma, who was known as the "wall-gazing Brahmin," always sat facing a wall. Ideally you should sit about three feet from the wall in order to cut off the view of distant objects, so as not to be distracted by them. Therefore choosing a place to practice meditation because of the fine view entirely misses the point.

In Rinzai Zen centers, practitioners sit facing each other, and there may also be good reason for this. If someone is sitting across from you, you are probably less prone to slacken in your practice or fall into a drowsy state. At any rate, follow the directions of the master at the zendo where you practice. When sitting alone, sit facing a wall or similar surface.

Where to sit at home

Although the best place to practice at home will vary according to individual circumstances, if possible choose a quiet place that you can dedicate solely to zazen. Though it may be very quiet to sit on your bed, it could also lead you to feel sleepy. But don't worry about matters beyond your control, and just try to create the best atmosphere you can. It may be helpful to practice in the innermost part of the room, away from the door, and to create an altar-like area where you can light a stick of incense or place a flower.

The light in the room should be neither too bright nor too dim. If it is too bright, it may be difficult for you to settle into practice. If it is too dark, your mind may become dull and lack the alertness needed for true practice. Use a curtain or blind to filter the light in a very bright room, so that the light gently bathes the room. In other words, avoid extremes of brightness or darkness.

The temperature of the room should be neither too hot nor too cold. A slight chill in the air is preferable to stuffy warmth. When people are truly one with their practice, however, they will be able to meditate even in conditions of extreme cold or heat. Make sure that the room is sufficiently ventilated and the air as fresh as possible. This is especially important when a large group sits together over a period of time. It is the responsibility of the person in charge of the room to see to it that it is well ventilated.

Meal times and zazen

It is best to refrain from meditation for about thirty or forty minutes after eating. We sit better when the stomach is empty, but this doesn't mean we should fast. From days of old, masters have warned against fasting while meditating. On the other hand, sitting with a full stomach tends to make us sleepy. An old saying in Japan warns, "When the skin on the belly is taut, the skin on the eyelids droops." If we sit when our stomach is full, we will feel drowsy and our practice may be less effective, unless we sit with exceptional earnestness. If we sit too often when we're sleepy, it becomes a habit and we find ourselves getting drowsy whenever we sit down in zazen—hardly a suitable situation for coming to realization. At home, when we feel sleepy, it would be better to lie down and go to sleep. Thirty minutes of sharp, alert sitting is far more beneficial than an hour of sleepy, dull zazen.

These remarks are directed to beginners in the practice of zazen. Those who are ardently practicing in order to clarify "the matter of great importance" for themselves can ignore the warning against sitting after meals. On the contrary, I encourage them not to let up for even a moment from morning until night, and to continue their practice even while sleeping.

Warding off sleepiness

Quite a few beginners in Zen meditation find themselves getting sleepy as soon as they sit down to practice. At such times you should perk up your spirits and make every effort to keep yourself sharp and alert. Rock right and left on your zafu and summon up your energy. If drowsiness persists, try splashing cold water on your face or doing some light exercise. Of course you are not free to do these things when you are sitting with a group, but you can request the warning stick (*kyōsaku*) to wake you up. It may also help to recite to yourself the following:

> To have attained a human form is difficult indeed: I have attained it. To meet up with the Buddha Way is rare indeed: I have encountered it. If I do not save myself in this life, when will I do it? Life and death are serious matters; life passes quickly away. I have not yet achieved the Way; what am I doing dozing off?

You can also light incense and pray earnestly to the buddhas and Zen ancestors, asking that hindrances to attaining the Way be removed, in the spirit of atoning for karmic obstructions.

If you are still unable to overcome sleepiness, it might be good, momentarily, to give in to it. In other words, allow yourself to fall asleep while sitting for five or ten minutes. Then rouse yourself again, and sit with renewed fervor and attention. This will help to make the ensuing zazen clear and concentrated.

Optimum length of a sitting

Many people wonder about the optimal length for a period of zazen. Sitting a short period of time is by no means less effective than a longer period. Zazen has worth and merit in itself, no matter how long one sits. Sitting from morning to night is not necessarily the best meditation. If you sit for a short period of time, you receive benefit from that sitting, and if you sit for a long period of time, you also benefit.

What is more important than the length of time in determining the effectiveness of the meditation is the ardor with which you sit. If you consistently sit with fervor, however, the results will differ depending on whether you sit five minutes, an hour, or all day. It is a great mistake to think of short periods of zazen as meaningless, just as it is mistaken to assume sitting all day is in itself sufficient. Regardless of the length of time, if the person sits earnestly there will definitely be benefits, and we should consider any available sitting time to be precious. If we continue to meditate, the effect of those times of practice will add up and produce great results.

Conversely, if we sit for overly long periods of time, our spirits may slacken so that we lose the intensity needed for effective sitting, despite our determination to sit with great fervor. Our psyches are not made to endure long, uninterrupted periods of intense concentration. Beginners who sit on their own should start with periods of five minutes and gradually work up to about twenty-five or thirty minutes for a single sitting. Here at San'un Zendo in Kamakura, the practice has always been to sit for twenty-five minutes, followed by walking meditation. In many temples in Japan the monks sit for as long as forty to fifty minutes at a time. But, again, this doesn't necessarily mean that the longer you sit, the better the meditation is. The length of sitting time ultimately depends on individual circumstances, and it should always be limited to what the individual can reasonably undertake.

Sitting for longer periods of time

When you have more free time and wish to attempt sitting several periods of zazen, be sure to allow time for movement and rest. Seated meditation, walking meditation, and rest are known respectively as *shijō*, *kinhin*, and *chūkai* in Japanese. *Shijō* means "to stop and be still" and refers to sitting in zazen without moving. *Kinhin* is meditation in motion. *Chūkai* means "to bring forth release" and refers to a rest period or a time to leave the zendo to go to the toilet or take care of other necessities.

If you are careful to divide your time up in this way you will be able to sit as long as you wish. But as I have said, you should take care not to make individual periods of meditation too long. In particular, it is not easy to sit more than thirty minutes when sitting alone, even for long-time sitters. Sitting for about twenty minutes is good at first for beginners sitting on their own. You should do walking meditation for about five to ten minutes after sitting a period of zazen, followed by rest for another five or ten minutes. You can consider the three divisions of a proper meditation period to be a single unit that can be repeated as many times as your schedule allows. Your sitting should always be alert and concentrated.

If you think that sitting for long periods in a pleasant dreamy state is good zazen, you are missing the point.

Walking meditation

Walking meditation is getting up and walking after a period of seated meditation. The objective is not just to limber up or take a stroll around the zendo, but to practice Zen in motion. Because walking meditation is the connection between the still practice of sitting meditation and the dynamic practice of Zen in motion, it should be done with total concentration of mind.

We continue our Zen practice as we walk: those who count breaths should single-mindedly continue counting; those working on the koan Mu should continue unabated their practice of Mu as they walk; the same advice applies to those practicing just sitting or following the breath. In other words, as we walk quietly we continue the same practice that we do during seated meditation.

Walking meditation is a crucial element of Zen practice. Earlier in this book I listed the three aims of Zen: the development of the power of concentration, seeing into one's own nature, and perfection of character. In particular, the regular practice of walking meditation together with seated meditation is essential to the development of the power of concentration. Developing this power of concentration helps us to become "master of any situation." Rinzai Zenji said, "If you can become the master of any situation, then wherever you stand is true." In other words, no matter what the situation, you will not be at the mercy of circumstances and will be able to act effectively. To develop this power of mind, it is crucial not only to practice while sitting still but also to practice Zen in motion, dynamic Zen.

Mental peace is easy enough to achieve in a quiet setting, but when we are caught up in the activities of everyday life, composure of mind may quickly vanish and we may find ourselves controlled by our surroundings, unable to take effective action. This is why, apart from the practice of zazen, we must also develop the ability to concentrate in everyday situations. The ancients said: "Zen practice in motion is a million times greater than still practice."

When walking in walking meditation the hands are folded against the chest. Make a fist with your right hand, place it lightly on your chest, and cover it with your left hand. Just as when we fold our legs, we cover the dynamic right side with the less active left. The forearms should be in a straight line parallel with the floor. Make sure your back is straight and that your head is erect, not bending forward or backward. The gaze should rest on a place about two yards ahead as you begin to walk slowly around the room. At temples in the Rinzai sect, the monks tuck up their kimono in back and walk very quickly, almost at a run, around the room or outside the dojo. In contrast, monks of the Sōtō sect practice what is called "one step, half a foot":[103] they advance half the length of the opposite foot with each step, walking very slowly. Unless you look carefully the monks don't appear to be walking at all.

Both methods of walking meditation have their particular logic. Rather than going into a comparative analysis here, though, let me advise you to take a step every two or three seconds, which is the speed we use during walking meditation in our training center. In addition to the advantages mentioned above, walking meditation also serves to relieve pain in the legs and to chase away drowsiness.

Keeping track of time during zazen

Always make sure you have a way of measuring how long you have been sitting when you meditate. Some students may wish to sit for twenty, thirty, or forty minutes. In the beginning stages of practice time will seem to go slowly and you may continually wonder when the period will end. You may worry about the time and find it hard to settle into practice, particularly if you have something to do afterward. A visible clock, watch, or a stick of burning incense can be used to mark the time and ease your anxiety.

On occasion we might set out to sit a short time and find we have been sitting much longer than planned. Conversely, sometimes we might plan a long sit and find that only a little time has passed. Here a time-piece becomes helpful too. Using a clock or watch is probably the simplest method, but burning a stick of incense is another way to keep time. It produces no sound, is not a visual distraction, and the fragrance of the incense may aid the meditative state. When using incense, break off a length equal to the period you plan to sit and light it when you begin. You can also use a flashing or vibrating timer.

Number of sittings per day

The ideal number of sitting periods in a day will depend on individual aspiration and circumstances. If we decide that one of our periods of sitting will be thirty minutes, then sitting four periods of zazen in a day would already amount to two hours. At the very least, everyone should be able to make time for one period each day, and most people should be able to sit at least two, for a total of an hour a day. People with high aspirations should be able to sit three or four periods a day, although maintaining such a schedule every day is hardly easy.

Sometimes people complain they are too busy to meditate, but their complaint comes from misunderstanding what zazen is. If they really understood how zazen works, they would realize that the busier they are the more they need to sit.

Zen meditation is a means to health for body and spirit, for it restores and renews both. After returning home following a day's work, finishing dinner, and relaxing a little, we are overcome by weariness and don't feel like doing anything. If at such a time we resolve to go and sit for twenty minutes, after some minutes we can almost hear the stiffness in our body gradually crumbling. I don't think I am alone in this experience. After sitting, we find we have energy to read or do additional work. Zazen restores us both mentally and physically, so that people who do intellectual work, as well as those working with their hands, will discover an increase in general efficiency. If someone sits in meditation for thirty minutes and works for seven-and-a-half hours, that work is far more efficient than eight hours of work without sitting.

The merits of meditation are not limited to our bodies and minds. If we continue to practice zazen, our circumstances in general—social, economic, and domestic—improve by themselves. We will experience this not as an abrupt change but as a gradual improvement that seemingly happens of its own accord. When we practice zazen, our essential nature, which is perfect and totally virtuous, manifests itself in both body and mind. If we sit each day without slackening, a shift occurs in our lives. Nonetheless, even if we intellectually accept this, the proof is in the pudding. I urge you to try to put it into practice and see for yourself.

Practice as many periods a day as is reasonable given your aspiration and circumstances, and make sure you faithfully stick to your schedule every day. Say you are sitting three periods a day. What is the best time to do so? This will also depend on circumstances. The ideal scenario would be to sit one period after rising and getting dressed, one period during the day, and one period before going to bed. Those who work full time may find it impossible to sit a period of meditation during the day, in which case they could incorporate that time as part of their morning or evening sit. Once again, the important thing is to practice as much as your circumstances allow.

Using a notebook

I advise keeping a small notepad by your side when you sit in zazen. When your mind is busy you are apt to forget even important things that demand attention. As soon as you settle down on your cushions, however, you begin to remember them. Often, once you are sitting, problems that demand attention, and for which a clear solution has eluded you, will suddenly become transparent. Creative ideas may also suddenly appear. Trying to remember these will interfere with your practice, but if you have a notepad at hand, you can jot down a few notes and return to your practice. This might appear to be a trifling matter, but it can in fact be important.

Checking on progress

How should you check on your progress in Zen practice? Since the benefits of zazen are intangible, even though you may practice earnestly, you might be unaware of the benefits and feel that practice isn't having an effect. Your resolve could weaken, and you might come to feel that zazen is a foolish waste of time and give it up altogether. So it is important to check on your progress in order to avoid becoming frustrated.

If you have been sitting two or three twenty-minute periods each day for a month, three months, or half a year, you should compare your physical and mental condition at the end of that time with what it was when you began. You will surely notice a change for the better. Your stomach, for example, may no longer be giving you trouble. You may have been having difficulty getting to sleep, or would often wake in the middle of the night, unable to get to sleep again. Now you find that you readily doze off and sleep soundly through the night. Or perhaps you frequently felt irritable and lost your temper, but now you realize you hardly ever get angry. Or again, you might notice you can concentrate better on the content when you're reading. The change might be small but you should definitely recognize some improvement.

When you notice these changes, your confidence in your ability to practice will increase and you'll find yourself able to sit with increasing fervor. At the same time, you should realize that what registers consciously is only a tiny part of what takes place beneath the surface; what you notice is only a fraction of the actual effects.

Setting goals

When you begin to practice zazen, you should set a goal of sitting for a specific period of time: a period of weeks or months. From the standpoint of the Mahayana Zen Way, the extent to which we follow this path should be limitless. The ideal would be to always hold the intention of following the path, without any break, never retreating, and never flagging. But this is too high a goal to expect from ordinary people, and those who begin with the intention of never stopping may give up after only a few weeks; this is always regrettable.

I urge beginning practitioners to set up a time goal for themselves with the firm resolution of continuing until they reach it. If the goal is too long, however, it will differ little from setting no goal at all. Likewise, if the goal is too short, the time will be up before you have had a chance to become aware of any of the benefits of practice. It's best to set your sights somewhere between six months and three years. When you set up your time goal also set an intention to sit a certain number of periods each day. Resolve to persist until your goal is reached.

People who feel a strong pull toward Zen practice may, in place of a time goal, resolve to continue practicing until a certain beneficial effect appears. For example, some people might decide to practice until their complaining attitude disappears, or until they can keep their temper. Some may decide to continue until their religious faith deepens, or until they truly see into their own nature. But unless the person is of an unusual temperament, this will prove difficult to carry through. For most of us it is best to set up a goal in terms of time: a goal of months or a few years at most. If you check your progress regularly, you will definitely notice the benefits of practice, and will naturally want to continue.

When you reach your goal, set a new one for yourself and continue to practice.

Fervor

The practice of zazen aims to achieve a great internal revolution, so the effectiveness of the practice depends on whether we practice with fervor or as if we were half asleep. If we walk for an hour in a leisurely manner, looking at the sights along the way, we'll be lucky to cover two or three kilometers. But if we walk at a lively, directed pace, we can easily go twice that distance. And if we go it at a dead run we'll advance even further. Given that such differences in outcome are possible when walking, imagine the possible outcomes on the great spiritual journey of Zen practice, where we propose to travel from the dim world of illusion into a world of shining brightness and clarity.

You have set aside precious time for the practice of meditation. You should sit as fervently as possible, aiming at the highest possible effect. Whether you practice for five or ten minutes or for a whole hour, sit single-mindedly with all your might; put aside everything else and boldly do your zazen.

Continuity

Suppose someone has decided to practice zazen for three years, sitting two periods of twenty to thirty minutes each day. He practices for a week but then has to stop for ten days because of work. After that period away from zazen, he starts again and practices for four or five days but then takes a week break, because he is once again very busy at work. With this on-and-off approach, his progress will be slow. Of course that doesn't mean there is no progress at all—he is surely advancing—but because his progress is slow, the changes that are taking place don't dawn in awareness, so he will be unaware of them. He may well eventually lose interest in practice and give up.

Of course, there will be days when circumstances prevent us from sitting; there is nothing we can do about this. But as much as possible, even if we have to go out of our way, we should try to faithfully keep our sitting schedule. Continuity is extremely important, as the above example shows. If we sit earnestly every day, we will become clearly aware of the effects of meditation and gain increasing enthusiasm for the practice. A person who absolutely believes in and practices in this way from the beginning will press forward without retreating for a moment, until he or she reaches the final goal of total perfection of character—the accomplishment of the Buddha Way. But such a person is truly one in a million and quite extraordinary, having nurtured deep karmic relationships with the teachings over several lifetimes. But the relative depth and ripeness of our relationship to the Dharma differs from person to person, and the average person seeking the Way cannot expect his or her practice to be so straightforward.

At the same time, you should know that the effects of even one period of zazen make an impression on the subconscious mind. When you decide to practice zazen and sit with complete fervor, whether for an hour or just five minutes, you perfectly and fully manifest your unstained essential nature. The effects of that meditation—even though you may not be aware of them—will never disappear from your personality. Additionally, since the nature of the essential world is "One is all; all is one," if you reveal that peerless self-nature, even for a moment in the world, then the entire universe is also rendered pure and unsurpassed.

In his *Talk on Wholehearted Practice of the Way* Dōgen Zenji says:

> Because zazen—done even by one person for a short time— unifies everything in the universe and harmoniously becomes one with every instant of time in the entire flow of time, it ceaselessly works in infinite worlds in the past, present, and future to accomplish the salvation of all sentient beings. . . .

Even if all of the innumerable buddhas in the entire universe combined their efforts and attempted to measure the merit of one person's zazen, they could never fathom it.

Once an experience has been stored in our hearts, it lives in every moment of our lives, in every thought and action, whether we are aware of it or not. Our individual personalities are formed from the sum total of past experience stored in the unconscious; they are in effect a crystallization of those experiences. The personality operates throughout our every waking moment, as will, emotion, speech, or gesture.

Buddhist teachings refer to our personalities as karma. Modern psychology seems to agree with Buddhist doctrine in viewing personality as the sum total of past experience. Psychologists limit their study, however, to traits stemming from inherited characteristics, prenatal experience, and life experience. Buddhism goes a step further and includes all experience—over countless eons from the beginningless past. Of course, we're not conscious of all these experiences. The events we can call to mind are a minute fraction of the total. Nevertheless, all of those experiences have come together now to form a single personality that lives and acts, every minute of the day.

As I mentioned before, our True Self, our original face, is colorless and transparent, pure and stainless, without a speck of dirt. In the phenomenal world, however, that True Self is encrusted with delusion. In contrast to the delusive state of our personalities, the Buddha is spotless and free of delusion. As mentioned earlier, the process by which we progress from the pitch black world of delusion to the world of stainless purity is divided into ten levels in Buddhist cosmology: the levels of hell beings, hungry spirits, beasts, warring demigods, humans, heavenly beings, those who hear and proclaim the teachings, those who attain enlightenment on their own, bodhisattvas, and buddhas. This division is made for convenience's sake, however, and though all of us exist on the level of human beings, there are myriad individual differences in attainment.

Having resolved, at least to some extent, to purify our delusion-encrusted personalities, we take up zazen as a means of chipping away at the layers of delusion. Each period of meditation can be thought of as another stroke in this process of wearing away our delusions. Sitting for one minute will produce a minute's worth of result, an hour's sitting will bring an hour's worth, and a day's sitting will produce a day's worth. Most important of all: each period of meditation, whatever its length, brings us that much closer to the stainless purity of buddhahood.

Suppose we have a bucket filled with dirty water and pour a glass of clean water into it. Although we will see no difference when we look at it, the addition of that glass of water has made the water in the bucket that much cleaner. Likewise, when we sit for even a single period of zazen our personality becomes purified in proportion to the length of that sitting. Although we may not be the least aware of it, we can be certain we have moved a step closer to the realization of our essential nature.

Some readers may think that I am belaboring a small point here, but you should understand this clearly. Otherwise if you try to do zazen for a week, or for a year, and feel that it has had no measurable effect, you may come to view the whole practice as a waste of time. In reality, if you sit even one or two periods of meditation, your personality will definitely be affected to a degree proportional to that sitting.

These remarks on the effects of Zen practice come from the standpoint of the aspect of practice in the phenomenal world.[104] When considering the merit of zazen from the standpoint of the essential world, we would do well to consider Dōgen's words in the above quote from *Talk on Wholehearted Practice of the Way*:

> Even if all of the innumerable buddhas in the entire universe combined their efforts and attempted to measure the merit of one person's zazen, they could never fathom it.

Translator's Afterword

I am delighted that Kōun Yamada Roshi's introduction to Zen is finally appearing in English. It is high time this towering figure in the history of Zen becomes more widely known to Western readers.

Yamada (1907–1989) was born and raised in Nihonmatsu in Fukushima Prefecture, a region that has become a place of global concern since a tsunami hit it in the spring of 2011. His immediate ancestors had been engaged in the lucrative silk trade. In the Yamada family shrine housed in San'un Zendo in Kamakura one could see photographs of these bearded or mustachioed gentlemen from the Meiji Era. The young Yamada Kyōzō occasionally attended services in the nearby Sōtō Zen temple along with local residents who recited Buddhist texts, including the Zen poem "Song of Enlightenment" (Shōdōka), which made a lasting impression on the boy, perhaps influencing his later resolve to begin Zen practice in earnest. Many years later as a Zen teacher, he gave a series of Dharma talks on this poem.

In 1923 Yamada entered the prestigious prewar First Higher School of Tokyo, having successfully passed the "examination hell" of its entrance tests. There he became the roommate of fellow freshman Nakagawa Motoshi, the future Nakagawa Sōen Roshi. An artist at heart who later became one of Japan's most respected haiku poets, Nakagawa had a profound influence on Yamada. The two entered Tokyo Imperial University together in 1927, Yamada majoring in English law and Nakagawa in Japanese literature. After graduation in 1931, Nakagawa took orders as a Rinzai monk while the young Yamada found employment with Chiyoda Life Insurance Company and later gained a position in the Manchurian Mining Company.

In 1938, after having married and started a family, Yamada was transferred to Shinkyō, the capital of the Japanese puppet-state of Manshukoku (Manchuria). It was a tumultuous time—with Japanese expansion into China, Korea, Taiwan and elsewhere, paving the way for the

Pacific War and Japan's subsequent defeat. These events formed the dramatic background to Yamada's first serious attempts at Zen practice.

Yamada, through his voracious reading, had acquired an extensive knowledge of Buddhism and Zen, as well as German neo-Kantian philosophy. Steeped in the Confucian classics and armed with an intellectual understanding of Buddhism and Western philosophy, Yamada began formal Zen training amid the rigors of the Manchurian winter under the Rinzai master Kōno Sōkan Roshi. Nakagawa Sōen, then still a young monk, had also been transferred to Shinkyō as the attendant to the Rinzai master Yamamoto Gempō Roshi, so the two former roommates had an unexpected opportunity to renew a friendship that continued until Sōen Roshi's death in 1984.

In the chaos of the postwar months, which included fear of Russian retaliation after Japan's defeat, the Yamada family was unable to return to Japan. During this period of fearful and impatient waiting, Yamada continued his inner search, whiling away the desolate hours reading works of German philosophy, often to the consternation of his family and friends.

After finally arriving back in Japan in 1946 and settling in the seaside town of Kamakura, Yamada, now nearing middle age and the father of three, eventually found employment. It was a time of unrest, and Yamada seemed to share the mood of disillusionment and despair reigning in postwar Japan. His daughter Mitsuko, oldest of the three children, recounted how her father, beset by worries, would often mutter to himself, "What will become of us now?"

But it was precisely this inner unrest that goaded him to continue Zen practice. Through his extensive reading, he realized clearly that philosophy alone, no matter how profound, could not resolve his basic questions or quell his anxiety. This led him to practice under Asahina Sōgen Roshi in nearby Engakuji Temple. Eager for Zen practice and guidance, Yamada would ride his bicycle at the crack of dawn to early morning meditation (*zazen*) with the monks at the temple, often seeking private interviews (*dokusan*) with the roshi. From there he boarded the train for Tokyo to put in a full day's work. On the way back he would alight again at Kita-Kamakura station to attend evening meditation and private interviews at the temple before pedaling homeward in what must have been an exhausting schedule. During this period he also studied under Hanamoto Kanzui Roshi, who had a temple at the foot of a hill in Kamakura's Ōfuna district on which a huge statue of the Bodhisattva Kannon (Kuan-yin) would later be erected.

In 1950 Yamada received the Buddhist precepts from Harada Daiun Roshi at a ceremony in Tokyo. It was Yasutani Haku'un Roshi, the dharma successor of Harada Roshi, who later became the true master Yamada had been searching for. Like Yamada, Yasutani Roshi finally found his true teacher, Harada Roshi, after practicing under various teachers when he was already in his forties.

During his discipleship with Yasutani Roshi, Yamada had the especially profound enlightenment experience recounted in *The Three Pillars of Zen*. Although he had been "passed" on the koan "Mu" under Asahina Roshi and had been working on subsequent koans, in retrospect he did not feel he had actually "broken through the bottom of the bucket." His persistence provides a fine example for all serious Zen students not to become smug or lax in their practice after an initial experience of awakening. Yamada's own deep experience led to his appointment as Yasutani Roshi's dharma successor, with the teaching name Kōun Roshi. In 1970 Yasutani Roshi asked Kōun Roshi to take over his Zen line, Sanbō Zen (Sanbō Kyōdan, as it was then called, meaning "religious foundation of the three treasures"). Kōun Roshi accepted this responsibility while maintaining his work as a businessman and built the small San'un Zendo—Three Clouds Zen Hall—on his own property in Kamakura; it would soon became a center for spiritual seekers from around the world.

My first encounter with Yamada Roshi was in October 1971 at Koko-An Zendo in Honolulu. Robert Aitken had arranged for Yamada Roshi's first visit in October, during which he led two seven-day periods of intensive meditation (*sesshin*) back-to-back. The roshi saw all of us in private interviews daily and delivered an hour-long public teaching every day, reading in English from a typed manuscript he had prepared himself. Having had little experience with intensive Zen practice, I found the first period of intensive meditation a grueling but totally convincing experience. Yamada Roshi returned to Hawaii to lead periods of intensive meditation a number of times after that, until Robert Aitken became a Zen master in his own right. Eventually I moved to Japan to practice more intensively at San'un Zendo, little realizing that I would be spending almost seventeen years of my life there.

In the spring of 1976 Yamada Roshi approached me with the idea of translating his introduction to Zen, which had yet to be published in Japanese. I agreed to the request without knowing exactly what I was getting myself into. The roshi presented me not with a book but a stack of handwritten manuscripts wrapped Japanese-style in a large, colored *furoshiki* cloth. They were written on the *genkō-yōshi* manuscript paper still popular at the time. It was printed with squares, typically two hundred or four hundred per sheet, each square designed to accommodate a single Japanese character.

I dutifully embarked on the translation, the first of any length I had ever attempted—first drafting by hand my translation for each chapter, then correcting it, and typing a final copy to present to the roshi. The project suffered its share of setbacks. Yamada Roshi had quoted freely in his own book from original texts of Dōgen Zenji and other Zen ancestors, not to mention works of Japanese literature or even books written in Japanese on nuclear physics. At times I felt myself up against the proverbial "silver mountains and iron walls" that confront every Zen student, this time facing the mountain not on my sitting cushion but sitting in front of my typewriter, attempting to make sense of thirteenth-century Japanese texts and create felicitous English equivalents.

Toward the end of the project Roselyn Stone checked the manuscript for general style and kindly offered me the use of her new Macintosh computer, still quite a novelty in those days. We set up camp on the second floor of the San'un Zendo, retyping texts into the computer while smoothing out grammatical and stylistic flaws.

For many years, the finished translation existed solely as a printout. Copies of it went through many hands, with several people offering assistance in getting the text into shape for printing, which proved to be an elusive goal. Over the years I have referred time and again to the manuscript in preparing my own public teachings or talks, discovering precious pieces of pure gold not found in other modern Zen books. I was thus overjoyed to hear of Joan and Henry's plan to create a slimmed-down version of the original Japanese book, presenting the essence of what Yamada Roshi has to say for modern readers and seekers.

Yamada Roshi repeatedly emphasized how books written by persons having an authentic Zen eye are different altogether from those written by persons lacking such an eye. They sparkle with a special light, he often said. This couldn't be truer regarding the present work, which presents the essence of Zen in direct, uncompromising terms. It fills a gap that has existed for many years, during which countless books on Zen and spirituality have appeared, all interesting in their own right, but for the most part lacking the authoritative voice that speaks so stirringly in these pages.

I bow in gratitude to my late master and to Joan and Henry for their tenacity in making this publication possible.

Paul Shepherd
Sigriswil, Switzerland

Table of Japanese Names

Arai Sekizen Roshi	新井石禅老師	1864–1927
Asahina Sōgen Roshi	朝比奈宗源老師	1891–1979
Chisha Daishi	智者大師	538–97
(Ch.: Zhiyi)	智顗	
Eka Daishi	慧可大師	487–593
Enō (Ch.: Hui-neng)	慧能	638–713
Engo	圓悟克勤	1063–1135
Hakuin Ekaku	白隠慧鶴	1686–1768
(Hakuin Zenji)	白隠禅師	
Harada Sogaku Roshi	原田祖岳	1871–1961
Hideyoshi	秀吉	1537–98
(Toyotomi Hideyoshi)	豊臣 秀吉	
Iida Tōin Roshi	飯田欓隠老師	638–713
Isan Reiyū Zenji	潙山霊祐	771–853
Keihō Shūmitsu Zenji	圭峰宗密	780–841
(Ch.: Kui Feng)	圭峰	
Keizan Zenji	瑩山禅師	1268–1325
Koizumi Shinzō	小泉信三	1888–1966
Kyōgen Oshō	香厳和尚	?–898
Kyūhō Dōken	九嶺道虔	n.d.
Myōzen Oshō	明全和尚	1183–1225
Nakagawa Sōen Roshi	中川宋淵	1907–84
National Teacher Bukkō	仏光国師	1226–86
National Teacher Echū	南陽慧忠	675–775
National Teacher Shōichi	聖一国師	1202–80
Nyojō Zenji	天童如浄	1163–1228
Rinzai Zenji	臨済禅師	died 866
Seigen Gyōshi	青原行思	died 740
Sekisō Keisho Oshō	石霜慶諸和尚	807–88
Keihō Shūmitsu Zenji	圭峰宗密	780–841

Taiso Daishi (Keizan Zenji)	太祖大師	1268–1325
Tokusan Senkan Zenji	德山宣鑑禅師	780–865
Tōrei Zenji	東嶺禅師	1721–92
Toyoda Dokutan Roshi	豊田毒湛	1840–1917
Toyotomi Hideyoshi	豊臣秀吉	1537–98
Tōzan (Dongshan)	洞山	807–69
Yakusan Zenji	藥山惟儼	745–827
Yasutani Roshi	安谷白雲	1885–1973
Yōka Daishi	永嘉大師	665–712

Notes

1. This is an example of *senryū* 川柳 verse.
2. Bassui 抜隊, *Hōgo* 法語 (Dharma Talks)
3. *Shōbōgenzō*, "Genjō Kōan" 正法眼蔵，現成公案
4. *Zazen Yōjinki* 坐禅用心記
5. *shushōhen* 修証辺
6. *anuttara samyak sambodhi* 阿耨多羅三藐三菩提
7. Nata: Son of the Brahman King. A great demon-king with three faces and eight arms, Nata here represents the Original Face.
8. *tendō mōzō*, literally, "upside-down delusions" 顛倒妄想
9. *shūshōhen* 修証辺
10. *honbunjō* 本分上
11. *mokushō* 黙照
12. *kanna* 看話
13. *kūge*, literally "empty flower," or "a particle floating in the vitreous humor of the eye" 空華
14. 1941
15. Translated by Thomas Yuho Kirchner in *Dialogues in a Dream*, forthcoming from Wisdom Publications.
16. *sankikai* 三帰戒
17. *sanju jōkai* 三聚浄戒
18. *sassho* 拶所
19. *gongo dōdan* 言語道断
20. *furyū monji* 不立文字
21. *kangai kenkon* 函蓋乾坤
22. *shuru setsudan* 衆流切断
23. *zuiha chikurō* 随波逐浪
24. The above koans are found in the *Entangling Vines, Gateless Gate*, and *Blue Cliff Record* koan collections.
25. See chapter 8 for treatment of the *Five Modes of Endeavor and Accomplishment*. Yamada Roshi did not take up the *Five Modes of the Essential and Phenomenal* nor the Ten Grave Precepts for discussion in this book. —The editors
26. From the "Bendōwa" chapter of *Shōbōgenzō*.
27. *Koboku-dō*
28. *Shōyōroku-Dokugo* 従容録独語
29. *The Analects of Confucius*, translated by Arthur Waley.
30. Translation from Kōun Yamada's *The Gateless Gate: The Classic Book of Zen Koans* (Boston: Wisdom Publications, 2004).
31. Japanese: *jikke*; Sanskrit: *bija* 習気
32. *makyō* (literally "demonic consciousness") 魔境

33. *asuras* 阿修羅
34. *jōriki* 定力
35. *hosshū* 法執
36. Absolute, Manifest, and Maintaining Three Treasures
37. *Gakudō Yōjinshū* 学道用心集
38. *Shushōgi* 修証儀
39. *Zazen Wasan* 坐禅和讃
40. *Fukan Zazengi* 普勧坐禅儀
41. *Gakudō Yōjinshū* 学道用心集
42. *Rinzai-roku* 臨済録
43. *Zazen Yōjinki* 坐禅用心記
44. *Zenkan Sakushin* 禅関策進
45. "Bendōwa" 弁道話
46. *kokyō shōshin* 古教照心
47. *Sayings of Dōgen Zenji, Shōbōgenzō Zuimonki* 5:21   正法眼蔵 随聞記
48. Ibid., 5:23
49. *kenshō futettei* 見性不徹底
50. *shōdō* 証道
51. *tokudō* 得道
52. *godō* 悟道
53. *kenshiki myōshin* 見色明心
54. *Gakudō Yōjinshū* 学道用心集
55. Physical, verbal, and mental
56. "Bendōwa" 弁道話
57. *nyū* 入
58. *danken*, Skt. *uccheda-drsti* 断見
59. *Shōbōgenzō*, "Believing Deeply in Cause and Effect" [*Jinshin Inga*] 深信因果
60. *jōken*, Skt. *sāsvata-drsti* 常見
61. This refers to the "Śrenika Heresy." See Buswell and Lopez *The Princeton Dictionary of Buddhism*, p. 852.
62. "Bendōwa" 正法眼蔵, 弁道話
63. Ibid.
64. *gōriki* 業力
65. *gōriki sōzoku* 業力相続
66. "Shōji" 生死
67. *Eihei Kōroku* 永平広録
68. Kōshō Temple Chapter, Part 1
69. "Jinshin Inga" 深信因果
70. *Ekikyō Bungen-den* 易経文言伝
71. *Huainanzi* 淮南子
72. *Confucian Analects* 論語
73. *Hōkyōki* 寶慶記
74. p. 61
75. "Kuyō Shobutsu" 供養諸仏
76. *Buddhacarita*
77. *Butsuzō-kyo* 仏蔵経

78. Cakravarti-raja 転輪王
79. *gudōshin* 求道心
80. *kan* 感
81. ō 応. Yamada Roshi is providing an etymology for the term *kan'ō* 感応, which generally means "sympathy" or "divine response" in colloquial Japanese. But here *kan'ō* refers specifically to the interrelationship between the innate buddha nature of sentient beings, the expression of which makes them "sensitive" recipients of the inconceivable wisdom and compassion of fully enlightened beings, which is itself expressed as a salvific "response" that naturally emerges from their own buddha nature when it has been fully purified.
82. *Principle of Practice and Enlightenment* 修証儀
83. *dai-shinkon* 大信根
84. *dai-gidan* 大疑団
85. *dai-funshi* 大憤志
86. *mujō-bodai* 無上菩提
87. Translation by Gene Reeves in *The Lotus Sutra* (Boston: Wisdom Publications, 2008), p. 296.
88. *Tennen Jishōbutsu* 天然自性仏
89. Kōun Yamada, *The Gateless Gate* (Boston: Wisdom Publications, 2004), p. 157.
90. *Chokusetsu no kokoroe* 直接の心得
91. *kekka fuza* 結跏趺坐
92. *hanka fuza* 半跏趺坐
93. *nihonza* 日本坐
94. *gomaza* 護摩坐
95. *kōgemon* 向下門
96. *kichijōza* 吉祥坐
97. *kōjōmon* 向上門
98. *yukata* 浴衣
99. *hakama* 袴
100. *Yasen Kanna* 夜船閑話
101. *naikan* 内観
102. *Sanzen no Hiketsu* 参禅の秘訣
103. *issoku hampu* 一足半歩
104. *shūshōhen* 修証辺

Index

· *Page numbers followed by "(2)" indicate two discussions.*
· *Page numbers followed by "q" indicate quotations.*
· *Page numbers followed by "+q" indicate discussions plus quotations.*

A
abdominal force in zazen, 182–83
academic approach to Zen, 42–43
Accomplishment mode (Tōzan), 106–9
Accomplishment without Accomplish-
    ment mode (Tōzan), 110–12, 141
the actual world. *See* the true fact
actualization of enlightenment, 12
    See also personalization of the
    Supreme Way
Akutagawa Ryūnosuke, 4+q
all beings:
    as becoming buddhas, 160–62
    as Buddha/awake, 64, 120–21,
    143–44
    saving, 109–10
    the ten realms, 125
all things:
    awakening by, 24
    emptiness, 26, 31–33
"All things...as if a dream...," 6
"All things return to one...," 162
American couple practicing Zen,
    young, 49–52
angst/anxiety. *See* suffering
annihilation, 146
Arai Sekizen Roshi: *Essentials of Zen*,
    71
ardor. *See* fervor
Asahina Sōgen Roshi, 73, 202, 203
attachment to Dharma, 131–32

attaining the Great Way, 93
    See also authentication...
attention, paying, 186
authentication of the Supreme Way,
    139–40
    See also attaining...
authenticity of the teacher, 91, 92–93
    criteria for judging, 92–95. *See also*
    under depth of enlightenment
authority of the teacher, 164–65
Avalokiteshvara, 26, 34
Avatamsaka Sutra, 112, 158
awakening (realization/enlightenment),
    12–13, 16–17, 25–26, 35, 42–53,
    137–41, 144, 158
    actualization of, 12. *See also* person-
    alization of the Supreme Way
    all beings as awake, 64, 120–21,
    143–44
    by all things, 24
    through breath counting/following,
    184
    of the Buddha, 19, 61, 133
    clarity, 55
    concentration and, 41, 52
    conditions for, 15, 169–72, 174
    deepening, 101. *See also* personaliza-
    tion of the Supreme Way
    depth. *See* depth of enlightenment
    differences in experiences of, 115
    to emptiness, 35

four realms of enlightenment, 125
and freedom, 22, 23
great. *See* great enlightenment
joy of, 21, 33, 48
through just sitting, 85–86, 88–89;
  Dōgen, 84–85
as kenshō. *See* seeing into our true
  nature
"No trace...remains...," 24
one-sided. *See* stuckness in ideas of
  emptiness
perfect enlightenment, 55
practice after, 54, 73, 98, 104–5,
  129; great enlightenment, 66, 88,
  106–12, 116–18. *See also* personalization of the Supreme Way
practice with the expectation of, 43,
  60, 111–12
as release from suffering, 21, 26, 31,
  34
ridding yourself of what you've
  realized, 123
satisfaction with our level of, 82
Sōtō notions re, 52–53
as unattainable through concepts,
  43–53
wiping away all traces of, 97
zazen and, 21; Dōgen on, 53, 64, 86,
  101, 120, 136–37, 137–38; Keizan
  on, 34, 98
See also seeing into our true nature

B

Baso, 77–78q
Bassui Zenji:
  on awakening, 21–22
  on great determination, 171
  on mind, 16–17, 30
  on ridding yourself of what you've
    realized, 123
  on seeing into one's own nature, 139
Batsudabara: awakening, 61
belief:
  great faith, 169
  in "I"/self-delusion, 27, 144
  initial, 133–34

"Believing Deeply in Cause and Effect"
  (Shōbōgenzō), 149
"Bendōwa" *(Shōbōgenzō)*, 46–47,
  64–66, 115–16
benefitting (generosity), 158
"Blow Out the Candle," 43–46
Blue Cliff Record, 67, 72, 79, 91–92
  "Bokushū's Thieving Fool," 19
  Jōshū cases, 80, 162
  "Seppō's Grain of Rice," 19
  Unmon cases, 79, 80–81
Bodhidharma, 71q, 93q
  and Eka Daishi, 4, 29–30, 31, 45
  on seeing into one's own nature,
    60–61
  on true teachers, 94
"Bodhidharma Puts the Mind to Rest,"
  4, 29–31, 45
bodhisattva practice, 98
bodhisattvas, existence of, 152–54
"body and mind fall away," 24, 33, 60,
  86, 87
body-related practices in zazen, 177–83
"Bokushū's Thieving Fool," 19
Book of Equanimity, 67, 79, 91
  "Kyūhō's Disapproval," 98–100
books on Zen, 135–36
Brahmajala Sutra, 161
brain: mind and, 30–31
breaks from zazen (rest periods), 190
breath counting/following, 183–84
breathing practice in zazen, 181–83
  counting/following the breath,
    183–84
  improper practice, 127
"Bring me your mind...," 4
the Buddha:
  all beings as, 64, 120–21, 143–44
  awakening, 19, 61, 133
  private interviews with, 163, 175
  "...this very body the Buddha," 112
  "'Buddha' as a stain on the pure
    ground...," 111, 117
buddha nature. *See* true nature
Buddha Treasury Sutra, 153
the Buddha Way, 37, 141

intellectual understanding of, 134–36
"the spirit of seeking the Way,"
    154–55
"stages with no stages..." of, 119–20,
    140–41
"To study...," 24
See also the Supreme Way
buddhas:
all beings as becoming, 160–62
existence, 152–54
sensitivity of sentient beings to
    response of, 154–57
Buddhism:
aim/function, 16, 24, 161–62
eight great tenets of Mahayana Bud-
    dhism, 143–62
source, 19
See also Zen
Buddhist precepts. *See* the precepts
buji Zen, 84, 87
Bukkō Zenji, 34–35+q
awakening, 62
busyness complaint re zazen, 193

C
"Catching the Ox," 116–17
cause and effect, 149–52
categories, 151–52
the law of, 129–31
as one, 119–23
See also karma
chair sitting practice, 179
character, 56, 57
See also perfection of character
China: Dōgen's travel to, 84, 139
Chisha Daishi, 163
Chōkei: awakening, 61
Chōsha, 148q
Christ, 121–22q
Christianity: salvation in, 20
Christians: Zen practice for, xi, 173–75
Chūhō Oshō, 68
clarification. *See* seeing into our true
    nature
clarify-with-words koans, 79–82
clarity of enlightenment, 55

cleanliness, 105
clothing for zazen, 179–80
*Collected Discourses from the Well-
    spring of Zen* (Shūmitsu), 59, 60,
    62
*Commentary on Transmission of the
    Lamp* (Yasutani), 85–86
"compassion bound in three ways,"
    159–60
composure in the face of death, 35
concentration (power), 15, 39–41
and enlightenment/realization, 41, 52
in everyday situations, 191–92
walking meditation and, 191
concepts. *See* intellectual understanding
conditions for zazen, 187–88, 189–94
conditions for Zen practice/awakening,
    15, 169–72, 174
Confucius, 149–50
the contemplative approach vs. the
    scientific approach, 23–26
continuation of life, 144–49
continuity in Zen practice, 196–99
counting the breath, 183–84
"the cuckoo's call," 105, 106
cushions for sitting, 177–78
"cutting off myriad streams," 81

D
daily practice of zazen, 120, 122,
    193–94
Daiō Kokushi, 75q
Dairyū, 78q
death (mortality):
composure in the face of, 35
denial of/ignoring, 5–6
dying at will, 99, 100
"elevated dead people," 97
great death, 107
life after, 144–49
deceptive phenomena, 125–32
from breathing improperly, 127
dreamlike hallucinations, 127–28,
    128–29
after seeing into one's own nature,
    128–32

before seeing into one's own nature,
126–28
decline of morality, 6–8
The Deeds of the Buddha, 153–54
degeneration of Zen, 96
delusion (illusion), 56, 82
dualistic opposition/consciousness,
125, 157, 159
pride, 125–26, 129
satisfaction with our level of realization, 82
of the self/belief in "I," 27, 144
six realms of, 125
wiping away all traces of, 98
See also deceptive phenomena;
stuckness...
denial of death, 5–6
depth of enlightenment, 55, 97–118
criteria for judging, 92–95, 100–1;
Ten Ox-Herding Pictures, 112–18.
*See also Five Modes of Endeavor
and Accomplishment*
"Kyūhō's Disapproval," 98–100
determination: great, 171–72
See also fervor
device-based koans, 74–76, 78–79
Dharma attachment, 131–32
Dharma body koans, 77–78
Dharma transmission lineage, 92
dhyana, 39–40
dhyana mudra, 180
Dialogues in a Dream (Musō Sōseki),
75–76
Diamond Sutra:
"All things...as if a dream...," 6
"Dwelling nowhere, the mind
emerges," 133
Tokusan and, 43–46
difficult-to-pass koans, 82–84
directed upward/downward koans,
74–75
discernment of the teacher, 92–93
*Discourse on Recommending Zazen to
All People* (Harada Sogaku), 71–72
distinctions in the phenomenal world,
110

Dōgen Zenji, 63
on the authenticity of the teacher, 91,
92–93; criteria for judging, 92–95
on benefitting (generosity), 158
on buddhas, 161
on cause and effect, 149, 151
China travel, 84, 139
enlightenment, 33, 53, 84–85, 139(2)
expressions/terminology for realization, 139–40
Extensive Record, 148
Guidelines for Studying the Way, 91,
134
and koans, 68
on life and death, 145–46, 148
and Nyojō Zenji, 84–85, 139(2),
150–51
Prayer for Arousing the Vow, 126
on seeing into our true nature,
137–38
"To study the Buddha Way...," 24
on zazen and realization, 53, 64, 86,
101, 120, 136–37, 137–38
on zazen practice, 181
*See also Principle of Practice and
Enlightenment; Recommending
Zazen to All People; Shōbōgenzō;
Talk on Wholehearted Practice of
the Way*
doubt, great, 169–71
dream, life as a, 6
dreaming of suffering story, 21–22
dreamlike hallucinations, 127–28,
128–29
dual and nondual perspectives, 23–26
dualistic opposition/consciousness, 125,
157, 159
duties: and rights, 8
"Dwelling nowhere, the mind
emerges," 133
dying at will, 99, 100
"Dying was...something other people
did," 5

E
ears in zazen, 185–86

Eastern psychology vs. Western psychology, 23–26
Echū, National Teacher, 48
eight great tenets of Mahayana Buddhism, 143–62
Eka Daishi: and Bodhidharma, 4, 29–30, 31, 45
Ekai Oshō, 170–71+q
"elevated dead people," 97
Emperor Yao, 102, 103
emptiness, 27–37
    of all things, 26, 31–33
    awakening to, 35
    form as/as form, 26–27, 70
    "hiding yourself high," 107, 108
    ideas of. *See* stuckness in ideas of emptiness
    life as, 13–14
    mind as, 31
    of the self, 26, 28–31, 34
    of subject, 31
    of subject and object, 26, 33–35, 157–58
    symbol for, 32
    See also the essential; true nature
Engo Zenji, 148q
enlightenment. *See* awakening
enlightenment sickness. *See* stuckness in ideas of emptiness
Enō Zenji: enlightenment, 133
entering the marketplace, 141
Enyadatta tale, 120–23
equality (of individuals): the basis of, 8–9
the essential (world of oneness), 13, 56, 63, 64, 69, 97
    experience of. *See* experience of the essential world/True Self
    heaven as, 174
    koans and, 70(2), 71, 72, 77
    vs. the phenomenal, 13, 35–36, 55, 69, 72
    symbol for, 70, 72, 146–47
    See also emptiness; true nature
essential nature. *See* true nature
Essentials of Zen (Arai Sekizen), 71

Essentials of Zen Practice (Harada), 133, 143, 150–51
"eternal subject," 25
eternalist views on life after death, 145–46
"Even a hairsbreadth of difference...," 42, 84
"Every day is a good day," 52, 108
everyday situations, 191–92
expectation of enlightenment: practicing with, 43, 60, 111–12
experience of the essential world/True Self, 13, 15–16, 21, 24, 70, 158, 186
    See also awakening; seeing into our true nature
experience-based spirituality vs. faith-based spirituality, 11–12
experiential understanding:
    vs. intellectual understanding, 14–15
    seeing into our true nature and, 147–48, 151, 157–58
Extensive Record (Dōgen), 148
external impediments to practice, 126
eyes in zazen, 181, 185–86

F
"...facing the sword of death...," 35
facing the wall, 187
faith, great, 169
faith-based spirituality: experience-based spirituality vs., 11–12
fanaticism, 134
fasting and zazen, 188
faults in a teacher/Zen master, 95
fervor (ardor) (in zazen), 186, 189–90, 196, 197
    great determination, 171–72
finding an authentic teacher, 91–96
"Finding the Tracks," 113–14
five aggregates, 26
five modes, koans of, 76, 77
Five Modes of Endeavor and Accomplishment (Tōzan), 101–12, 112
Five Modes of the Essential and the

Phenomenal (Tōzan), 69, 76, 101,
    110
five-way koan classification, 76–84
flow, 5, 32
following the breath, 184
following thoughts, 186
"To forget the self...," 24
"...forgetting the seed," 76–77
form:
    as emptiness/emptiness as, 26–27, 70
    life as, 13–14
four realms of enlightenment, 125
fox Zen, 130
freedom (of individuals): the basis of,
    8–9
freedom (from suffering):
    awakening and, 22, 23
    the key/way to, 4, 15–16, 16–17, 21,
        30, 40–41
*Fukan Zazengi. See Recommending
    Zazen to All People*
Fuketsu Oshō, 110q
full-lotus posture, 178–79
fundamental koans (initial koans),
    72–73, 77–78
fundamental particle theory, 32–33

G
Gateless Gate, 67, 72, 79, 91–92
    "Blow Out the Candle," 43–46
    "Bodhidharma Puts the Mind to
        Rest," 4, 29–31, 45
    "Hyakujō and the Fox," 129–30
    "A Non-Buddhist Questions the
        Buddha," 174–75
    "Tosotsu's Three Barriers," 28
    "Wash Your Bowls," 80
    See also "Mu"
Gateway to the Essentials... (Torei), 80
generosity (benefitting), 158
genjō koan, 71
    symbol for, 72
Gensha: awakening, 61
"the ghost that I saw," 11
"...grasses, sweeping, and inquiring...,"
    28–29

great death, 107
great determination, 171–72
    See also fervor
great doubt, 169–71
great enlightenment, 86–87, 106, 116,
    133, 139
    through breath counting/following,
        184
    experiences of, 61–62, 86, 122; the
        Buddha, 19, 61, 133; Dōgen, 33,
        53, 84–85, 139(2); Ekai, 170–71+q;
        Enō, 133; Hyakujō, 33; Jōshū, 111;
        Tokusan, 45–46; Yamada, viii, xiii,
        203
    through just sitting, 85–86, 88–89;
        Dōgen, 84–85
    perfect enlightenment, 55
    practice after, 66, 88, 106–12,
        116–18
great faith, 169
the Great Way. *See* the Supreme Way
Guidelines for Studying the Way
    (Dōgen), 91, 134
Guidelines for Zazen (Keizan), 127

H
"a hairsbreadth of difference..., not/
    Even," 25–26, 42, 84, 120, 158
Hakuin Zenji:
    awakening, 61–62
    difficult koans, 83+q
    koan system, 76–84
    "The Sound of One Hand," 72, 77,
        78
    Zen sickness, 129
    See also Song in Praise of Zazen
half-lotus posture, 178–79
hallucinations, dreamlike, 127–28,
    128–29
Hanamoto Kanzui Roshi, 202–3
hand position in zazen, 180
Harada Sogaku Roshi, 39, 105, 141,
    170q, 203
    *Discourse on Recommending Zazen
        to All People,* 71–72

Essentials of Zen Practice, 133, 143, 150–51
on finding an authentic teacher, 96
on Hakuin's koan system, 76–77
on just sitting, 88, 185
The Key to Zen Practice, 185
Matters of Immediate Importance, 177
and Shaku Sōen, 147–48
on *Song in Praise of Zazen*, 22–23
on zazen practice, 182
Heart Sutra, 26–27, 34, 70
heaven as the essential world, 174
hell, 34
"hiding yourself high," 107, 108
hokkū, 31
home areas for zazen, 187–88
"horns," 111
"a…horse that runs at the shadow of a whip," 175
"How will you free yourself…?," 28
Hui-neng. *See* Enō Zenji
Husserl, Edmund, 24–25
Hyakujō: realization, 33
"Hyakujō and the Fox," 129–30

I
"I". *See* the self
"I cut the water…," 5
ideas of emptiness. *See* stuckness in ideas of emptiness
identity, the question of, 20–21
ignoring mortality, 5–6
Iida Tōin Roshi, 60–62q, 139
Ikkyū, 30q, 31q
illusion. *See* delusion
immutability, 146
impediments to practice: external, 126
See also internal impediments to practice
independent operation, 157
initial koans (fundamental koans), 72–73, 77–78
"…inquiring, sweeping grasses and…," 28–29
intellectual understanding (concepts):

of the Buddha Way, 134–36
enlightenment as unattainable through, 43–53
experiential understanding vs., 14–15
See also philosophy
interaction between sentient beings and buddhas, 154–57
internal impediments to practice, 125–26
See also deceptive phenomena; delusion; *and under* intellectual understanding; philosophy
Isan Reiyū Zenji:
and Kyōgen, 47–49
and Rei'un, 61

J
Japanese warriors, 40
Japanese-style sitting posture, 179
jōriki, 39–41
Jōshū, 148q
"All things return to one…," 162
"Mu," 72, 77, 78
and Nansen, 111
"Zen of lips and tongue," 79–80+q
joy of awakening, 21, 33, 48
Jōzai Daishi, 34q
Jūetsu Zenji, 28q
just sitting, 84–89, 184–86
awakening through, 85–86, 88–89; Dōgen, 84–85
Harada Roshi on, 88, 185
and koan study, 87–88
vs. Zen of little consequence, 84, 87

K
kachi ichige, 48, 60
karma (power), 65, 69, 146–47, 151, 198
See also cause and effect
"Karma of the Three Times" *(Shōbō-genzō)*, 151
Keizan Jōkin:
Guidelines for Zazen, 127
Transmission of the Lamp, 86–87
"Warnings on Zen Practice," 71

on zazen, 34, 98
kenshō. *See* seeing into our true nature
The Key to Zen Practice (Harada), 185
kikan (device-based koans), 74–76,
   78–79
Kitarō, Nishida, 52+q
koan study (koan practice), 55, 67–84,
   185
   concentration in, 52
   history, 67–68
   and just sitting, 87–88
   in Rinzai Zen, 72–73
koans:
   clarify-with-words koans, 79–82
   classifications, 73–84
   device-based, 74–76, 78–79
   Dharma body koans, 77–78
   directed upward/downward, 74–75
   and the essential world, 70(2), 71,
     72, 77
   of the five modes, 76, 77
   genjō koan, 71, 72
   initial/fundamental koans, 72–73,
     77–78
   irrationality, 68–70
   practice with. *See* koan study
   of the precepts, 76–77
   principle-based, 74–76, 77–78
   in Rinzai Zen, 72–73
   significance/use, 68, 72, 87
   in Sōtō Zen, 71–72
   See also under Blue Cliff Record;
     Book of Equanimity; Gateless Gate
Koizumi Shinzō, 6–7+q
kōjō/kōge (directed koans), 74–75
Kōno Sōkan Roshi, 202
Kōsankoku: awakening, 61
kū, 27
Kyōgen Oshō: and Isan, 47–49
"Kyōgen Strikes the Bamboo," 47–49
"Kyūhō's Disapproval," 98–100

L
Lao-tse, 150
Lassalle, Father Enomiya, 174
law of cause and effect, 129–31

Li Po: "I cut the water...," 5
life:
   as a dream, 6
   everyday situations, 191–92
   as form and emptiness, 13–14
   continues, 144–49
   religious life phases, 11–12
   suffering in. *See* suffering
   the unity of, 24
life and death, 16–17, 145–46, 148
"Life and Death" *(Shōbōgenzō)*, 148
lighting for zazen, 188
lineage, Dharma transmission, 92
Lotus Sutra, 171
love (compassion), 159–60
"...love at first sight," 31

M
Mahayana Buddhism: eight great
   tenets, 143–62
Mahayana Zen, 55, 60–62, 161, 195
   vs. Supreme Vehicle Zen, 63–64, 67
   vs. Zen with the expectation of
     enlightenment, 43
the marketplace, entering, 141
"master of any situation," 191
materialism, 12
"the matter of one color," 99–100
Matters of Immediate Importance
   (Harada), 177
meal times and zazen, 188
meal verses, 161
meditation: true way of, 83
   See also zazen
meditation cushions, 177–78
Mencius, 149–50
mental habits: persistence, 98, 117
mind, 16–17, 29
   "body and mind fall away," 24, 33,
     60, 86, 87
   and brain, 30–31
   as emptiness, 31
   peace of mind, 55
   "What is mind?," 30
mind ground, 34
mind-related practices in zazen, 183–86

mondos, 68–69
"the moon is bright...," 107, 108
morality: decline of, 6–8
mortality. *See* death
"Mr. Original Face...," 31
"Mu," 72, 77, 78
  Ekai's commentary on, 170–71
  practicing, 104, 106, 169–70
Musō Sōseki: *Dialogues in a Dream,*
  75–76
"...my life's search has come to an
  end," 53
Myōzen Oshō, 84

N
Nakagawa Sōen Roshi, 50, 106, 201,
  202
Nansen, 148q
  and Jōshū, 111
nihilistic views on life after death,
  144–45
nirvana: life and death as, 146, 148
"No trace of realization remains...," 24
noema and *noesis,* 24–25
"A Non-Buddhist Questions the Buddha," 174–75
nondual perspective: dual perspective
  and, 23–26
"...not a hairsbreadth of difference...,"
  25–26, 120, 158
not knowing, 30, 83–84
"not two, self and other are," 157–60
"Not yet! Not yet!," 106
note taking during zazen, 194
Nyojō Zenji: and Dōgen Zenji, 84–85,
  139(2), 150–51

O
object. *See* subject and object
objectification of the subject, 27
the objective world. *See* the
  phenomenal
"old case" koans, 72
the old woman: Tokusan and, 44–45
"one..., All things return to," 162
"One knock!...," 48–49

one-hundred-foot pole, stepping off the
  top of, 110
one-sided enlightenment. *See* stuckness
  in ideas of emptiness
ordinary Zen, 59–60, 87
original nature. *See* true nature
original sin, 159
others:
  benefitting, 158
  "treating...with propriety," 102, 103
Ox-Herding Pictures, Ten, 112–18

P
paying attention, 186
peace:
  of mind, 55
  in the world, 14, 16
perfect enlightenment, 55
  See also great enlightenment
perfection of character, 54–57, 66
  See also personalization of the
  Supreme Way
perfection of wisdom, 26–27
  practicing, 26–27, 34
period-of-time goals for Zen practice,
  195–96
periods of time for zazen. *See* sitting
  periods
persistence of mental habits/views, 98,
  117
personality: zazen and, 198–99
personalization of the Supreme Way,
  12, 54–57, 62–66, 97, 98, 141
the phenomenal (objective world), 13,
  31–32, 69
  distinctions in, 110
  vs. the essential, 13, 35–36, 55, 69,
  72
  symbol for, 70, 72, 146–47
  See also all things; the world
philosophy:
  dual and nondual perspectives, 23–26
  limitations, 7, 13, 42–43, 52
  materialism, 12
  Zen vs., 13, 42–43, 60
  See also intellectual understanding

physics: fundamental particle theory,
32–33
places for zazen, 187–88
"plowing a field...," 76–77
poor son of a rich man story, 22–23
popular books on Zen, 135
posture in zazen, 178–79, 180–81
practice. *See* Zen practice
practicing "Mu," 104, 106, 169–70
practicing the perfection of wisdom,
26–27, 34
practicing with expectation of enlightenment, 43, 60, 111–12
Prayer for Arousing the Vow (Dōgen),
126
the precepts (Buddhist precepts), 57
koans of, 76–77
"Precious Mirror Samadhi" (Tōzan),
132
pride, 125–26, 129
Principle of Practice and Enlightenment
(Dōgen), 141, 149, 155
principle-based koans, 74–76, 77–78
privacy of practice (keeping to oneself),
132, 164
private interviews, 163–67
with the Buddha, 163, 175
form/process, 165, 166–67
need for, 163–64
progress in Zen practice, 195, 196–99
checking, 194–95
"propriety, treating others with," 102,
103
psychology: Eastern vs. Western, 23–26

R
realization. *See* awakening
realms, ten/six/four, 125
Recommending Zazen to All People
(Dōgen), 42, 71, 84, 181
Record of Rinzai, 79
refuge precepts, 57
koans of, 76–77
Rei'un: awakening, 61
religion:
renunciation of, 12

Zen as/as not, 12, 19–20
Zen practice for people of other religions, xi, 173–75
See also religious experience;
spirituality
religious experience, 173
See also experience of the essential world/True Self; experiential
understanding
religious life phases, 11–12
renunciation of religion, 12
response of buddhas: sensitivity of
sentient beings to, 154–57
responsibility of the Zen master, 55,
115–16
revelation of buddha nature/the essential, 57, 72, 122
richi (principle-based koans), 74–76,
77–78
ridding yourself of what you've realized, 123
"riding backward," 107–8
rights: and duties, 8
Rinzai Zen, 63–64, 66, 67
koans/koan study in, 72–73
Rinzai Zenji, 24q, 43, 70, 191q
Record of Rinzai, 79
rocking sideways before/after sitting,
181, 182, 189
Ryūtan Oshō: Tokusan and, 43–46

S
this *saha* world, 3
salvation, 12
in Christianity, 20
in Zen, 20–23, 25–26, 37
satisfaction with our level of realization, 82
saving all beings, 109–10
the scientific approach, 31–32
the contemplative approach vs.,
23–26
fundamental particle theory, 32–33
limitation, 25
secrecy. *See* privacy of practice
seeing into our true nature (kenshō),

12, 14–15, 15–16, 16–17, 21,
    33–34, 54–55, 60–61, 70, 114–16,
    137–39, 171–72
deceptive phenomena after, 128–32
deceptive phenomena before, 126–28
Dōgen on, 137–38
and experiential understanding,
    147–48, 151, 157–58
practice after, 54, 73, 98, 104–5, 129
young American woman, 50–51,
    51–52
See also awakening
"Seeing the Ox," 114–16
See also seeing into our true nature
"Seek and you shall find," 121–22
"Seeking the Ox," 113, 154–55
"seeking the Way, the spirit of,"
    154–55
Sekisō, 99–100
the self:
    delusion of/belief in "I," 27, 144
    emptiness, 26, 28–31, 34
    symbol for, 146–47
    "To study..." and "To forget...," 24
    See also subject
"self and other are not two," 157–60
self-nature. See true nature
sensitivity of sentient beings to response
    of buddhas, 154–57
sentient beings: sensitivity to response
    of buddhas, 154–57
"Seppō's Grain of Rice," 19
Serving mode (Tōzan), 104–6, 116
Shaku Sōen Roshi: and Harada Roshi,
    147–48
Shakyamuni. See the Buddha
Sharing Accomplishment mode (Tōzan),
    109–10, 141
Shibayama Zenkei Roshi, 112–13
Shōbōgenzō (Dōgen), 42
    "Believing Deeply in Cause and
        Effect," 149
    "Bendōwa," 46–47, 64–66, 115–16
    "Karma of the Three Times," 151
    "Life and Death," 148

Shōdōka. See Song of Realizing the
    Way
Shōichi Goroku, 73, 74q
shūkyō, 19, 20
Shūmitsu Zenji: Collected Discourses...,
    59, 60, 62
sickness, Zen. See stuckness in ideas of
    emptiness
Silent Illumination Zen, 88
sin, original, 159
sitting cushions, 177–78
sitting meditation. See zazen
sitting periods:
    length, 189–91
    number per day, 193–94
sitting postures, 178–79
six realms of delusion, 125
sleepiness in zazen, 188, 189
Sōkei, 71
Song in Praise of Zazen (Hakuin),
    22–23, 112, 119, 120
Song of Realizing the Way (Yōka
    Daishi), 24, 34, 37, 45, 108, 131,
    151, 201
Sorori Shinzaemon, 5–6+q
Sōtō Zen, 52–53, 63–64, 66, 67
    koans in, 71–72
"The Sound of One Hand," 72, 77, 78
"the spirit of seeking the Way," 154–55
spirituality: experience-based vs. faith-
    based, 11–12
    See also religion; religious experience
"spring outside of time," 107
"stages with no stages...," 119–20,
    140–41
"...stain on the pure ground...," 111,
    117
stepping off the top of a one-hundred-
    foot pole, 110
stuckness in ideas of emptiness (Zen
    sickness), 35, 36–37, 97, 100,
    129–31
stuckness in ordinary seeing, 33
"To study the Buddha Way..." and "...
    the self...," 24
studying the teachings, 134–36

subject, 27
  emptiness, 31
  "eternal subject," 25
  objectification of, 27
subject and object, 24–25, 133
  emptiness, 26, 33–35, 157–58
  views of, 131
Sudhana story, 112
suffering (anxiety/distress), 3–5, 40
  awakening as release from, 21, 26,
    31, 34
  dreaming of suffering story, 21–22
  escape attempts, 5
  freedom from. See freedom (from
    suffering)
  source, 21
suicide note, 4
superstition, 134
Supreme Vehicle Zen, 57, 62–66
  vs. Mahayana Zen, 63–64, 67
the Supreme Way (Great Way), 57
  attaining, 93
  authentication of, 139–40
  personalization of, 12, 54–57, 62–66,
    97, 98, 141
  See also the Buddha Way
"...sweeping grasses and inquiring...,"
    28–29
symbols:
  for emptiness/the essential/true
    nature, 32, 70, 72, 146–47
  for the phenomenal/the self, 70, 72,
    146–47
  for the true fact/genjō koan, 70, 72,
    146–47

T
taigo Zen, 43
Talk on Wholehearted Practice of the
  Way (Dōgen), 136–37, 197–98, 199
"Taming the Ox," 117–18
the teacher (Zen master):
  authenticity, 91, 92–93; criteria for
    judging, 92–95. See also under
    depth of enlightenment
  authority, 164–65

changing to another, 165–66
  discernment, 92–93
  faults, 95
  finding an authentic teacher, 91–96
  importance, 91, 177
  practice with, 95–96, 101, 105–6,
    134, 135
  responsibility, 55, 115–16
  trust in, 126, 164–65, 177
  words, 91–92
teachers, unqualified, 94, 97, 137
the teachings: studying, 134–36
temperature for zazen, 188
ten grave precepts, 57
  koans of, 76
Ten Ox-Herding Pictures, 112–18
ten realms, 125
"...this very body the Buddha," 112
thoughts: following, 186
  See also intellectual understanding
"Three Barriers, Tosotsu's," 28
three phrases (Unmon), 81–82
three pure precepts, 57
  koans of, 76–77
three-way koan classification, 73–76
time keeping during zazen, 192–93
"To study the Buddha Way...," 24
Tōin Roshi, 60–62q
Tokusan, the old woman, and Ryūtan,
  43–46
Torei Zenji: Gateway to the Essentials..., 80
"Tosotsu's Three Barriers," 28
"totally covering the universe," 81
Toyoda Dokutan Roshi, 66
Tōzan Gohon Daishi, 77q
  Five Modes of Endeavor and Accom-
    plishment, 101–12, 112
  Five Modes of the Essential and the
    Phenomenal, 69, 76, 101, 110
  "Precious Mirror Samadhi," 132
Transmission of the Lamp (Keizan),
  86–87
trap of emptiness. See stuckness in ideas
  of emptiness

"treating others with propriety," 102, 103
Treatise of Seng Chao, 158
the true fact, 29, 36, 70, 110, 133
  See also True Self
true nature (buddha/essential/original/ self-nature), 16–17, 33, 56, 66, 120, 133, 198
  of all beings, 120–21, 143–44
  experience of. *See* experience of the essential world/True Self
  revelation of, 57, 72, 122
  symbol for, 72
  "...where is your own nature...?," 28, 29
  See also emptiness; the essential; True Self
True Self, 12, 15, 29, 33, 34, 36, 77, 101, 133, 186, 198
  experience of. *See* experience of the essential world/True Self
  See also the true fact
trust in the teacher, 126, 164–65, 177
Turning mode (Tōzan), 102–4
"turning toward it":
  in beginning practice, 102–4
  after enlightenment, 111–12
two wheels of Zen practice, 134

U
understanding: not knowing, 83–84
  See also experiential understanding; intellectual understanding
the unity of life, 24
Unmon, 52q, 79q, 80–81+q
  three phrases, 81–82
unqualified teachers, 94, 97, 137
upward-directed koans, 74–75

W
walking meditation: and zazen, 190, 191–92
"Warnings on Zen Practice" (Keizan), 71
warriors, Japanese, 40
"Wash Your Bowls," 80

"wave following upon wave," 81
the Way. *See* the Buddha Way; the Supreme Way
Western psychology: Eastern psychology vs., 23–26
"What bliss to know...," 35
"What is Buddha?," 77–78
"What is mind?," 30
"When we witness reality...," 24, 34
"...where is your own nature/True Self...?," 28, 29
"...where will you go?," 28
wiping away all traces of enlightenment/delusion, 97, 98
"Wither'd pampas grass...," 11
words of a teacher/Zen master, 91–92
the world:
  the actual. *See* the true fact
  peace in, 14, 16
  this *saha* world, 3
  See also the essential; the phenomenal

Y
Yamada Roshi, viii–ix, 201–3
  enlightenment, viii, xiii, 203
  presence, vii, xi
Yao, Emperor, 102, 103
Yasutani Haku'un Roshi, 39, 53, 107+q, 108q, 141, 203
  Commentary on Transmission of the Lamp, 85–86
  on Sekisō, 100
Yōka Daishi. *See Song of Realizing the Way*
young American couple practicing Zen, 49–52

Z
zabuton, 177
zafu, 178
zazen:
  benefits/merits, 193–94, 194–95, 197–99
  body-related practices, 177–83
  breaks from (rest periods), 190
  busyness complaint re, 193

cause and effect as one in, 119–23
conditions for, 187–88, 189–94
content of as the same, 119–20
daily practice, 120, 122, 193–94
facing the wall, 187
fervor in, 186, 189–90, 196, 197
by Japanese warriors, 40
meal times and, 188
mind-related practices, 183–86
note taking during, 194
periods of time for: length, 189–91;
    number per day, 193–94
places for, 187–88
and realization, 21; Dōgen on, 53,
    64, 86, 101, 120, 136–37, 137–38;
    Keizan on, 34, 98
sleepiness in, 188, 189
time keeping, 192–93
true way of meditation, 83
and walking meditation, 190, 191–92
See also just sitting; Zen practice
zazen mudra, 180
Zen, xiv, 12, 12–13
    academic approach to, 42–43
    aims/goals, 26, 39, 59, 60, 63
    books on, 135–36
    degeneration of, 96
    as for everyone, 175
    fox Zen, 130
    of little consequence vs. just sitting,
        84, 87
    ordinary Zen, 59–60, 87
    vs. philosophy, 13, 42–43, 60
    practice. See Zen practice
    as a religion or not, 12, 19–20
    salvation in, 20–23, 25–26, 37
    Silent Illumination Zen, 88

word origin, 39–40
    See also Mahayana Zen; Rinzai Zen;
        Sōtō Zen; Supreme Vehicle Zen
Zen master. See the teacher
Zen mondos, 68–69
"Zen of lips and tongue" (Jōshū),
    79–80+q
Zen practice, 12, 136–37
    and authentication, 140
    belief in, 133–34
    bodhisattva practice, 98
    conditions for, 15, 169–72, 174
    continuity, 196–99
    after enlightenment, 54, 73, 98,
        104–5, 129; great enlightenment,
        66, 88, 106–12, 116–18. See also
        personalization of the Supreme Way
    with the expectation of enlighten-
        ment, 43, 60, 111–12
    in motion, 191–92
    for people of other religions, xi,
        173–75
    period-of-time goals, 195–96
    privacy/keeping to oneself, 132, 164
    progress in, 195, 196–99; checking,
        194–95
    with the teacher, 95–96, 101, 105–6,
        134, 135
    two wheels of, 134
    types, 59–66
    "Warnings on..." (Keizan), 71
    See also just sitting; koan study; prac-
        ticing...; zazen
Zen sickness. See stuckness in ideas of
    emptiness
Zengen Shosenshū (Shūmitsu), 59, 60,
    62

About the Author

Kōun Yamada became a Dharma successor to the renowned Zen master Haku'un Yasutani while maintaining a prominent career in business and public health. He guided the Zen practice of many students, including a large number of Christian priests, monks, and nuns. He is also the author of *The Gateless Gate: The Classic Book of Zen Koans*.

About Wisdom Publications

Wisdom Publications is the leading publisher of classic and contemporary Buddhist books and practical works on mindfulness. Publishing books from all major Buddhist traditions, Wisdom is a nonprofit charitable organization dedicated to cultivating Buddhist voices the world over, advancing critical scholarship, and preserving and sharing Buddhist literary culture.

To learn more about us or to explore our other books, please visit our website at www.wisdompubs.org. You can subscribe to our eNewsletter, request a print catalog, and find out how you can help support Wisdom's mission either online or by writing to:

Wisdom Publications
199 Elm Street
Somerville, Massachusetts 02144 USA

You can also contact us at 617-776-7416 or info@wisdompubs.org.

Wisdom is a 501(c)(3) organization, and donations in support of our mission are tax deductible.

Wisdom Publications is affiliated with the Foundation for the Preservation of the Mahayana Tradition (FPMT).

More Books from Wisdom Publications

The Gateless Gate
The Classic Book of Zen Koans
Kōun Yamada
Foreword by Ruben L. F. Habito

"Yamada Roshi's straightforward commentary
on the Wu-men kuan (Mumonkan) is again available
in this new edition, and I'm delighted."
—Robert Aitken, author of *Taking the Path of Zen*

The Book of Mu
Essential Writings on Zen's Most Important Koan
James Ishmael Ford and Melissa Myozen Blacker
Foreword by John Tarrant

"The most important of all koans finally gets the attention it
deserves. For those considering koan study, or just curious about
this unique spiritual practice, this is a very valuable book."
—David R. Loy, author of *Money, Sex, War, Karma*

On Zen Practice
Body, Breath, and Mind
Taizan Maezumi Roshi and Bernard Tetsugen Glassman
Foreword by Robert Aitken

"I recommend *On Zen Practice* to beginners and advanced Zen
practitioners. It is challenging, wise, and encouraging."
—Roshi Pat Enkyo O'Hara, Village Zendo

The Book of Equanimity
Illuminating Classic Zen Koans
Gerry Shishin Wick
Foreword by Bernie Glassman

"Every student of Zen would do well to read this fine book."
—Robert Jinsen Kennedy, author of *Zen Spirit, Christian Spirit*

A New Buddhist Path
Enlightenment, Evolution, and Ethics in the Modern World
David R. Loy

"This is a manifesto of genuine spiritual freedom."
—James Ishmael Ford, author of *If You're Lucky, Your Heart Will Break*

Dongshan's Five Ranks
Keys to Enlightenment
Ross Bolleter

"Very well done."
—Robert Aitken, author of *Taking the Path of Zen*

Living Zen, Loving God
Ruben L. F. Habito
Foreword by John Keenan

"A brilliant meditation that brings new depth
and scope to the study of religion."
—*New York Resident*